Marketing Financial Services

The Marketing Series is one of the most comprehensive collections of textbooks in marketing and sales available from the UK today. Published by Heinemann Professional Publishing on behalf of the Chartered Institute of Marketing, the series has been specifically designed, developed and progressively updated over a number of years to support students studying for the Institute's certificate and diploma qualifications. The scope of the subjects covered by the series, however, means that it is of equal value to anyone studying other further or higher business and/or marketing related qualifications.

Formed in 1911, the Chartered Institute of Marketing is now the largest professional marketing management body in Europe with over 22,000 members and 25,000 students located worldwide. Its primary objectives are focused on the development of awareness and understanding of marketing throughout UK industry and commerce and in the raising of standards of professionalism in the education, training and practice of this key business discipline.

OTHER TITLES IN THE SERIES

Marketing Financial Services

Edited by Christine Ennew, Trevor Watkins and Mike Wright

Published on behalf of the Chartered Institute of Marketing

Heinemann Professional Publishing

Heinemann Professional Publishing Ltd
Halley Court, Jordan Hill, Oxford OX2 8EJ

OXFORD LONDON MELBOURNE AUCKLAND SINGAPORE
IBADAN NAIROBI GABORONE KINGSTON

First published 1990

British Library Cataloguing in Publication Data
Marketing financial services – (The marketing series).
  1. Finacial services. Marketing
  I. Ennew, Christine   II. Watkins, Trevor   III. Wright,
  Michael *1952*–   IV. Chartered Institute of Marketing   V.
  Series
  332.10688

ISBN 0 434 92202 1

Printed in Great Britain by
Redwood Press Limited, Melksham, Wiltshire

Contents

Contents

Figures

About the editors

Christine Ennew, BA, PhD, is Lecturer in Marketing in the Department of Industrial Economics at Nottingham University. Her research interest concern the nature and development of marketing strategies, particularly in the context of the financial services sector. She has published a number of articles on these topics and has also been involved in consultancy in related areas.

Trevor Watkins, BA, MSc, PhD, FRSA, FCIM, is ASDA Professor and Head of the School of Business at Oxford Polytechnic and an Associate Member of the Nottingham Institute of Financial Studies at the University of Nottingham. He has published a number of articles on the marketing of financial services in both trade and academic journals including *International Journal of Bank Marketing*, *Service Industries Journal*, *Banking World*, *Insurance Week*, *Euromonitor*, *Quarterly Review of Marketing*, *Economist Intelligence Unit*, and *Insurance Monitor*. He is editor of the *International Journal of Bank Marketing* and is senior examiner for the new marketing financial services diploma for the Chartered Institute of Marketing.

Mike Wright is Professor of Financial Studies in the Department of Industrial Economics at Nottingham University, and Director of the Centre for Management Buy-Out Research. He has published extensively in professional and academic journals on a wide range of topics relating to finance and the financial services sector. His books include *The Future of the Building Societies*, *The Logic of Mergers Marketing Financial Services* and *Internal Organisations, Efficiency and Profit*. He was formerly employed in Market Research for British Gas and has acted as consultant for a variety of organizations.

Contributors

Professor Donald Cowell is the Barker's Dean of Birmingham Polytechnic Business School. He has published widely on management and marketing topics. His current research interests include the marketing of services and he is the author of a major text on the subject. Recent research on building societies which he has directed has explored the relationship between building society marketing strategies and marketplace image.

Following graduation and work in industry with the Chloride Group, Professor Cowell held previous academic posts at the University of Bradford Management Centre, the University of Loughborough and Plymouth Business School at Polytechnic South West.

Paul Draper is Professor of Finance at the University of Strathclyde. He taught previously at the Universities of St Andrew's, Edinburgh and Indiana. His current research is in accounting for new financial instruments and pension fund performance measurement. He has published *The Investment Trust Industry in the UK* (Avebury, 1989) and *The Scottish Financial Sector*, with I. Smith, W. Stewart and N. Hood (Edinburgh, 1988), as well as articles in a number of journals including *Applied Economics, Journal of Business Finance and Accounting* and *The Investment Analyst*.

Dr Barbara R. Lewis is Senior Lecturer at the Manchester School of Management. Her main interests are in services marketing, in particular financial services; professional services; leisure and tourism; and health care. Her present research is focused on service quality to include investigation of organizations' customer care programmes, and their impact on both employees and customers. She was the founder of the *International Journal of Bank Marketing*, and has published articles in a variety of marketing journals.

Malcolm Hughes is Director of Marketing of TSB Bank plc. Previously he was General Manager, Marketing of the UK Individual Division of Prudential Corporation and a Director of Prudential Property Services Estate Agents Ltd. Since graduating in Natural Science from Manchester University, he had held senior sales and marketing positions at Colgate-Palmolive, J Lyons and Fine Fare Supermarkets.

He also spent a period in advertising as an Account Supervisor at Wasey Quadrant Advertising. Prior to his appointment to Prudential Assurance Company he was for nine years at Nationwide Building Society as General Manager, Marketing. At TSB Bank plc he is responsible for overall marketing policy for the Bank.

Barry Howcroft was previously employed by Donald MacPherson & Co. Ltd and the National Westminster Bank plc before joining Loughborough University where he is currently a Senior Lecturer in the law and practice of banking. He is the Course Director of the banking and finance degree and the Deputy Director of the banking centre at Loughborough University. To date he has written four books on banking law, syndicated lending, retail banking and currency and interest rate risk management. In addition, he has written numerous articles and papers on a wide range of topics relating to banking. Over the past few years he has acted as a consultant to several major domestic and foreign banks. Currently his main research interests lie in the area of retail banking.

Julia Kiely was employed in personnel by Delta Metal Company after obtaining a degree in social administration. In 1980 she was awarded a PhD by the University of Aston in organizational behaviour. Her main research interests are in work motivation and job stress and she has published in numerous British and American journals in these areas. She was a Principal Lecturer in the Department of Business Management, Dorset Institute, before taking up her current post as Lecturer at the University of Loughborough.

Preface

Readers of this book are probably most familiar with the marketing efforts of financial services firms as a result of the avalanche of letters they have received in the last few years, exhorting them to purchase life insurance products or borrow to fund the purchase of a car or holiday. Such 'junk mail' is merely one manifestation of a major revolution in marketing financial services provoked by deregulation and increasing competition.

For the first time, financial services firms needed to be proactive in their marketing efforts. Many had to establish marketing departments and computerized marketing information systems and move rapidly along very steep learning curves. Such major shifts in the focus of financial services firms were not without their problems. Databases were often inappropriate for direct mail marketing shots. As a very minor illustration, one of the editors of this book was both perturbed and delighted to receive a direct mail shot from a well-known motoring organization with interests in financial services advertising a special birthday offer on life insurance purchase. He was delighted as the organization thought he was somewhat younger than he really was, but rather perturbed that his birth date had become confused with that for his car insurance!

The motivation for writing this book has been to help those interested in the financial services sector to address these and other related issues in a systematic way through the provision of a conceptual framework closely linked to applications.

Given the nature of the sector and the location of the human capital available to tackle the issues involved in marketing financial services we deliberately chose to obtain contributions from a number of specialists in the area. We would particularly like to thank our contributors for the quality of their submissions and for writing to remit and on time. We have also adopted a different approach to each of the four main sectoral chapters in order that the application of the conceptual material in the early chapters can be demonstrated most clearly.

Additional thanks are due to Kathryn Grant of Heinemann Professional Publishing for her interest and support for the book from its inception. Grateful thanks are also extended to the various secretaries who typed individual authors' chapters, and especially to Rosemary Hoole whose assistance and efforts were invaluable in producing the final version of the manuscript.

Chris Ennew, Trevor Watkins, Mike Wright

Introduction

The financial services sector has, in recent years, been among the fastest-growing areas in the UK economy. Progressive deregulation, starting with competition and credit control in 1971 and culminating in the EC's 1992 programme, has dramatically altered the operating environment facing suppliers of financial services. These changes, in conjunction with increases in personal income and wealth, expansion in other sectors of the economy, trends towards globalization and developments in information technology, have created an increasingly competitive and demand-driven financial services sector. As a consequence of these changes, the sector has witnessed considerable innovation not only in terms of products but perhaps more importantly in terms of processes and market arrangements (Carter *et al.*, 1986).

Initially, the pattern of deregulation probably had its greatest impact in the corporate banking sector and was fuelled by the expanding role of multi-national firms. Many banks, particularly the American and Japanese ones, tended to follow their corporate customers into non-domestic markets. Once a position had been established, the maintenance of that position required strategies to extend their customer base to include national corporate and even, in some cases, personal customers. Although these developments were perhaps most noticeable during the 1970s, the EC's 1992 programme has resulted in a further wave of international expansion among financial services organizations (Wright and Ennew, 1990).

The pattern of change was more rapid in the 1980s and the impact on retail markets was much greater. The sequence of the 'Big Bang', the Building Societies Act and the Financial Services Act increased competition, particularly in retail markets, and forced many suppliers to move away from the supply-orientated approach which they had traditionally adopted in those markets. The barriers which had delineated retail and corporate markets and which had separated large- and small-scale investors were slowly being eroded. Similarly, the distinctions between institutions such as banks and building societies were breaking down as organizations sought to supply an increasingly broad range of products. Despite the expansion in demand for financial products, the battle for market share has increased in importance, and with many organizations offering a much broader range of products, the strategy of cross-selling to an existing consumer base has become a key component of marketing.

Within organizations the marketing concept has grown in significance as a consequence of these changes in the operating environment. The traditional sales-orientated view of business in the financial sector was based on the notion of the 'hard sell' in insurance or the belief that customers would make the first approach if they required a particular service in the case of banks and building societies. This has been replaced by a market orientation in which financial services suppliers are increasingly looking to respond to the particular financial needs of their customers. A recent survey of financial institutions (Hooley and Mann, 1988) reported that some 53 per cent of organizations surveyed currently considered themselves to be market-orientated, compared with 5 years previously when the figure was only 2 per cent and the majority saw themselves as being either operations- or finance-driven. Furthermore, when the organizations were asked to describe their approach to marketing, the majority response was that 5 years ago the attitude had been one of supplying a traditional range of products to anyone interested in buying. The current attitude, by contrast, was to emphasize some prior analysis of customer needs and attempt to tailor products to meet those requirements. There is also evidence that the marketing function itself is not so well established in financial services as it is in other sectors of the economy, although the increasingly competitive environment has induced a 'catching-up' process (Davison *et al.*, 1989). The increasing use of market research for the development of products and monitoring the marketing environment is also an indication of the growing sophistication in the marketing activities of financial service organizations.

Although the role of marketing has increased in importance in the financial services sector, it has tended to play a primarily tactical, rather than strategic, role in business development. Hooley and Mann (1988) cite the comparatively low status accorded to marketing and the tendency for the most senior levels of management to remain the provinces of executives with a background in finance. However, Clarke *et al.* (1988) suggest that financial services organizations and particularly banks are moving towards a strategic-marketing orientation, which requires that marketing takes a more active role in the determination and development of corporate strategy. Recent surveys conducted by the authors of this volume (Watkins and Wright, 1986; Ennew, Watkins and Wright, 1989) show that the most important factors in the growth strategies of financial services organizations are advertising, direct marketing, information technology and internal organizational factors. This reflects a growing realization that marketing, almost by definition, is a strategic activity, and that in a period of rapid environmental change organizational efficiency is not sufficient to ensure business success. The successful organization needs to be effective, i.e. it needs to be in the right markets with the right products and at the right time. This requires that organizations adopt a more pro-active stance and that, in this context, marketing has a key role to play in identifying the most appropriate markets and products.

The growing importance of marketing and its strategic function in the financial services sector provides part of the rationale for the present book. However, we should consider whether this need for a greater understanding of marketing issues in the financial services sector warrants separate treatment. A variety of texts deal with general marketing issues and a separate treatment for service products in the literature is justified on the basis of certain distinctive characteristics (Cowell, 1984). These include, first, the fact that services are intangible: the consumer has nothing physical to show for the purchase, the service cannot be displayed or tested prior to use. Second, services are usually inseparable, which means that they are produced and consumed simultaneously and production requires the presence of the consumer. Accordingly, services are also perishable and cannot be stored for future sale. Third, as a consequence of inseparability, services are heterogeneous; quality control is difficult and the quality of the service itself is often highly dependent on the quality of the service provider. These particular characteristics of services mean that the application of marketing principles and the emphasis placed on specific areas can be quite different from the case of product marketing.

Furthermore in the case of financial services, the complexity of many products, particularly on the investment side, creates problems for the presentation of such products to the consumer. This adds to the dimension of intangibility in that not only are financial services impalpable, in the sense that they have no physical form, they are also intangible from a mental point of view, in that they are not easily defined and may be difficult to understand (Donnelly *et al.* 1985). A further, and related, complication from the marketing perspective is the implicit responsibility which financial services organizations have in relation to the management of funds and the financial advice they supply to their customers. This element has been incorporated into notions of 'best advice' as a component of the recent regulatory changes. Despite these formal requirements, any organization providing financial services must retain an awareness of the magnitude of the impact which their marketing and selling activities can have on the lifestyle of an individual or the prosperity of a company.

In this text we seek to provide a thorough coverage of the key issues which surround the marketing of financial services. It is anticipated that the reader will have some familiarity with basic marketing concepts and, accordingly, the authors concentrate on illustrating the application of these concepts in the financial services sector. The diversity of the financial services industry seemed to warrant an approach which brought together experts in the various sectors. Indeed, while the boundaries between the activities of the different financial institutions have become increasingly blurred, most organizations can identify a core business and, as a consequence, still face a number of distinct marketing issues. Indeed, although it is common to talk about financial services products and institutions, it would be rare to encounter a financial services marketing manager.

The book itself comprises three integrated parts. In view of the importance of changes in environmental factors in the development of an organization's strategic and tactical marketing, which have been briefly mentioned above, the first two chapters review these developments and consider their marketing implications. The first chapter, by Mike Wright considers supply-side factors, which include regulatory changes in both the UK and the EC, the effects of globalization and the impact of developments in information technology. In Chapter 2 Trevor Watkins deals with aspects of the demand for financial services, considering both buyer-behaviour at the level of the individual and broader trends in the aggregate market.

The second section of the book deals with the strategic and tactical aspects of marketing. In Chapters 3 to 5 Christine Ennew examines, first, aspects of the development of marketing strategies for the suppliers of financial services in broad terms and sets the framework for the examination of the individual elements of the marketing mix. Second, the nature of product strategy and new product development are considered, with particular attention to some of the specific marketing issues which occur in the context of services marketing. Third, in Chapter 5 the nature of advertising and promotion are analysed, with the focus on issues surrounding the development of an appropriate promotional mix. Chapter 6, by Malcolm Hughes, deals with the complex issue of pricing in relation to financial services and highlights the problems associated with developing trade-offs between risk, return and liquidity. Chapters 7 and 8 deal with aspects of distribution. In Chapter 7 Julia Kiely deals explicitly with direct distribution and the problems surrounding the management and motivation of an effective sales force in the financial services sector. Strategies for the development of indirect distribution methods are examined in Chapter 8 by Barry Howcroft, with particular attention being paid to the development and management of branch networks.

The third part of the book consists of sector-specific case studies which seek to highlight the particular marketing problems confronting different organizations. Rather than conforming to a standard approach, each of these chapters employs different analytical frameworks in order to reinforce the practical application of concepts discussed in earlier chapters. In Chapter 9 Barbara Lewis examines the development of strategies in the banking sector in the context of Ansoff's product/market matrix. Chapter 10, by Don Cowell, focuses on the building societies and examines their marketing approach in the context of three generic strategies, namely cost/differentiation, leadership and focus strategies. In Chapter 11 Trevor Watkins examines the development of marketing in insurance companies and deals with the development of a marketing mix in the context of a product life-cycle. Finally, in chapter 12, Paul Draper analyses the marketing of unit and investment trusts, paying particular attention to the impact of regulatory changes on the marketing activites of organizations in this sector.

CHAPTER 1
The changing environment of financial services
Mike Wright

Introduction

In 1968, at the time of its creation by the merger of three smaller banks, the National Westminster, the UK's largest clearing bank, provided few services beyond traditional retail banking. Two decades later its interests have spread worldwide and include venture capital, a substantial network of automatic teller machines and a wide range of corporate financial services. In the late 1980s the bank's strategy continued to evolve with the divestment of certain activities, most notably its unit trust management company, following the decision to register as an independent intermediary under the Financial Services Act.

Up to 1986 the Abbey National, as the UK's second largest building society, was restricted to the provision of housing finance, various retail savings products and the introduction of insurance policies associated with house purchase. In 1989 the Abbey National, which became the first building society to convert to a public quoted company, had developed an extensive range of new products, including a substantial estate agency network and an office in Spain.

These two illustrations of developments in products and markets reflect major environmental changes which began in the late 1960s and which continue to influence the behaviour of financial services firms. In any market economy change is a continuous, dynamic process. Competition between firms is an important factor in effecting change but is itself influenced by the degree to which profitable opportunities are perceived to be available, the regulatory framework which places constraints on what firms may legally undertake, and changes in information technology which may reduce costs and introduce new methods of distribution. Changes in these environmental factors may require changes in both the external and internal boundaries of financial services firms. By redrawing their internal boundaries, through emphasizing product categories and changing external boundaries by acquisitions and joint ventures, firms may be better placed to formulate new strategies in a pro-active or reactive manner, and to achieve efficient delivery of their range of products. All these factors provide the context in which the marketing effort of financial services firms will be developed.

The changing environment for financial services is examined in this chapter under the following headings: changes in the nature of personal assets and liabilities, changes in the regulatory framework, the trend towards globalization, the effects of fundamental changes in information technology, and the redrawing of the boundaries of financial services firms. Competitive action has been influential in exerting pressure for regulatory change at a time when several governments have been predisposed towards market forces. The regulatory changes which have been introduced both reflect new market conditions and permit further developments. In view of their fundamental importance, they are treated in some depth in what follows.

Personal assets and liabilities in the UK

Financial assets of the personal sector in the UK increased more than fourfold in current price terms from 1978 (Table 1.1). Financial liabilities, such as loans and consumer credit, rose more than fivefold in the same period (Table 1.2). The last decade has also witnessed considerable shifts in the composition of personal sector assets and liabilities in the UK. These changes have been closely associated with a continuing emphasis on individual home ownership, reinforced by a fundamental change in attitudes towards share ownership, ushered in by the election of the first Thatcher government in 1979.

In broad terms, there has been a shift towards investment in equities, either directly or indirectly (Table 1.1). The importance of

Table 1.1 *Financial assets of the UK personal sector (percentages)*

	1978	1984	1987 Q3	1988 Q3
Notes and coin	15.0	12.3	9.3	11.6
Building society deposits	17.3	16.3	12.9	15.6
UK shares and loan stocks	14.2	10.9	17.7	14.9
Unit trusts	1.2	1.4	2.4	2.0
Equity in insurance & pension funds	31.7	42.1	45.0	41.9
Other	20.6	17.0	12.7	14.0
Total (%)	100.0	100.0	100.0	100.0
Total (£m)	211,508	555,857	962,239	921,463

Source: Financial Statistics

Table 1.2   *Financial liabilities of the UK personal sector (percentages)*

	1978	1984	1987 Q3	1988 Q3
Bank loans	13.6	19.4	18.8	19.2
Loans by credit Co.s and Retailers	4.8	2.4	2.4	2.2
Housing: Banks	2.8	9.7	12.1	13.5
Housing: Building Socs and Ins Co.s	51.5	49.2	50.7	50.8
Other	27.3	19.3	16.0	14.3
Total (%)	100.0	100.0	100.0	100.0
Total (£m)	64,659	174,498	271,290	327,668

Source: Financial Statistics

equity in insurance and pension funds has become particularly dominant over this period. This shift reached a peak immediately before the stock market crash of October 1987, with a subsequent fall thereafter. Direct investment in equities forms a higher proportion than in 1984, but there has been a shift in the balance back towards building-society deposits. The proportion of personal sector assets held in unit trusts doubled in the decade from 1978, but still accounted for little more than 2 per cent of the total. Even so, unit trusts form an important part of the product range of banks and life-insurance companies. Moreover, the changes in the regulatory framework discussed below and in Chapter 12 have paid considerable attention to dealing with the satisfactory marketing of, among other things, unit trusts.

On the liabilities side the past decade has witnessed the maintenance of the building societies as the main source of borrowing for housing finance, but with the banks and other forms of institution substantially increasing their market share (Table 1.2). While the total value of assets declined in the year following the October 1987 stock market crash, personal sector borrowing increased by a fifth, partly associated with a very buoyant housing market, but partly to finance retail spending.

Against this background of increasing personal wealth, further details of which are analysed in Chapter 2, financial services firms have sought to introduce a myriad of new products. Moreover, non-traditional suppliers have also entered the market. For example, a securitized mortgage product aimed particularly at the higher income end of the market has been introduced by new institutions and the traditional credit-card companies face increasing competition from several high-street retailers, such as Marks and Spencer, Burtons and Debenhams, who have introduced their own store cards (Robbie and Wright, 1988; Worthington, 1988).

Regulatory changes

The history of the regulation of financial services up to the beginning of the 1980s was one of restrictions upon both the range of products that a particular firm might offer and constraints upon the geographical area in which services could be sold. This relatively tight control in comparison with manufacturing industries was to be found throughout liberal democracies. In the US, for example, banks were prevented from participating in securities markets, savings and loan institutions were unable to offer checking services, and insurance institutions were precluded from offering banking business (Channon, 1986). In addition, US banks were severely restricted in the extent of their branch networks and their ability to undertake interstate activities (Lewis, 1986). In the UK, branching was not so restricted, but the Building Societies Act, 1962, tightly restricted the activities of societies. In addition, Stock Exchange rules placed limits on the investment of outside capital in member firms and maintained the single-capacity dealing system, whereby brokers conducted all their business through jobbers who did not deal directly with market customers.

Many of these restrictions had developed in order to offer some degree of protection to consumers, but were not always consistent with market efficiency. Competition could be limited by the exclusion of firms from one product market from providing services allocated to institutions in another sector. In addition, such restrictions may also have hindered innovation in new product development and in distribution systems. Moreover, differences also existed in the regulations applying to different types of services and products, with further potentially adverse implications for competition. Hence, for example, in the US non-bank institutions had been able to enter markets that banks were precluded from.

In the 1980s, there were widespread changes in regulatory regimes. These developments arose from technological innovations which radically changed the pattern of operation of financial services' firms, and increasingly competitive pressures from similarity of service provision in those areas of overlap between traditionally separate institutions. The election of governments in western democracies with a much stronger free market perspective than had been seen for some time also provided the political will to enact legislation which would reduce regulatory barriers inhibiting competition.

The first part of this section examines the changes in the UK framework for the regulation of financial services. The second part addresses the changes brought about by the attempts of the European Community (EC) to create and regulate a single market in financial services, and the next section examines the implications of regulatory constraints, together with other factors, for globalization of financial services markets. As will be seen, these developments have implications both for the types of products that financial services firms may offer and for the manner in which business is conducted, with particular emphasis on marketing.

The UK regulatory framework and relevant legislation

An important move from institution-based regulation towards market-based regulation for all types of investment business was introduced by the Financial Services Act, 1986. Other types of financial services continue to be regulated by separate legislation, which itself has changed recently to enhance consumer protection and competition.

The structure of the new system of investment business regulation introduced by the Financial Services act (FSA), 1986, is shown in Figure 1.1. The Building Societies Act, 1986, which replaced the Building Societies Act 1962, widened the scope of products that societies could offer. These two pieces of legislation are examined in detail below. However, it is also important to note, as may be seen from Figure 1.1, that the framework established in these Acts is linked to other supervisory agents.

The ability of banks to diversify stems from the late 1960s and early 1970s when the Bank of England dissolved the interest rate cartel and actively encouraged competition between institutions. In 1968 diversification was essentially limited to merchant banking, eurocurrency lending, unit-trust management, leasing, credit finance, trade finance and trustee services, with credit cards just beginning. Over the next 20 years the range of activities of the four main UK clearing banks developed to include securities dealing, insurance broking, mortgage lending, insurance underwriting, venture capital, computer bureau, personal financial planning, estate agency, cash management and services for high net worth individuals (Lewis and Wright, 1986). However, there was concern following the secondary banking crisis of the mid-1970s to strengthen supervision, and the Banking Act, 1979, was introduced principally for this reason. The Banking Act, 1987, which replaced the Banking Act, 1979, sought to strengthen the control of banks so as to avoid the risk of over-exposure and failure (Hall, 1989). As part of this new control mechanism, the Bank of England is now responsible for supervising all activities of a banking group.

Following an agreement between the Secretary of State for Trade and Industry and the Chairman of the Stock Exchange, in July 1983, the system of trading on the Stock Exchange was changed in October 1986 ('Big Bang') to allow greater competition and avoid a referral to the Restrictive Trade Practices Court.

5

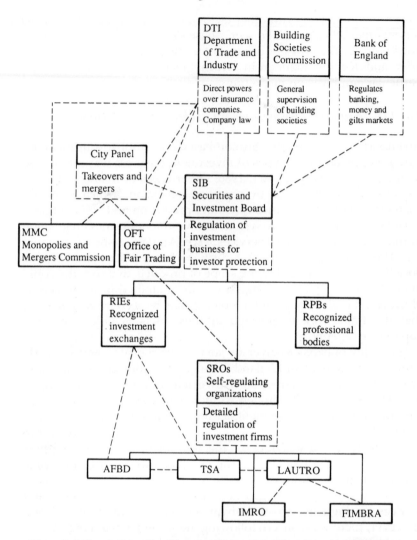

Note: Solid lines indicate direct hierarchical links. Dotted lines show overlapping of
responsibilities. Not all links shown.

Figure 1.1 *Personal financial services – the regulatory framework*

As it is the FSA and the Building Societies Act which have
introduced the most fundamental changes, this section focuses
greatest attention in these areas. Links and overlaps with other areas of
regulation are referred to where appropriate.

The Financial Services Act, 1986

The Financial Services Act (FSA), 1986, embraces all types of financial securities and collective investments, and all types of investment activity, including the management of, giving advice regarding, and arranging deals in, investments. The twofold purpose of the FSA is to define and regulate so-called 'investment' business (thus affording greater protection to investors) and to promote competition in the saving industry. Two key features are the consistency of treatment between competing types of financial service, and the degree of reliance to be placed on self-regulation within a statutory framework. The FSA only applies to 'investment' business, and so excludes general insurance, short-term deposits, mortgages and loans, deposit-based pensions and Personal Equity Plans, all of which are covered by other legislation. Hence, the Banking Act, 1987, provides for the Bank of England to supervise the deposit-taking functions of banks and to monitor their capital adequacy. Capital-adequacy rules have important implications for the ability of banks to effect growth strategies, and, as will be seen below, recur in other contexts with the same goal of ensuring prudent behaviour. Where banks conduct investment as well as other types of business and there is thus supervisory overlap, the Bank of England under the 'lead regulator' approach, coordinates the supervision exercised by itself and other supervisory bodies. According to the Memorandum of Understanding between the Bank of England and the Securities and Investments Board (SIB) Limited, the former will monitor capital adequacy, and the SIB, together with the relevant Self Regulatory Organization (SRO, see below), will monitor compliance with conduct of business rules (Hall, 1989).

Under the FSA, an individual or company transacting investment business will have to be authorized by an appropriate Self-Regulating Organization (SRO), a Recognised Professional Body (RPB), or directly by the SIB, it being a criminal offence not to do so. The emphasis on self-regulation arises from a belief that regulation is best undertaken by people with practical experience of the business in question; the costs of the SROs will also then fall directly on the investors whose interests they are designed to protect. The Act establishes the SIB as a 'designated agency' responsible for overseeing the working of the legislation and the operation of the SROs. In order to promote competition in investment business, self-regulating organizations are required to submit their rules and regulations to the Director General of Fair Trading. The Director General is then required to report to the Secretary of State if, in his opinion, such rules have, or are intended or likely to have, the effect of restricting, distorting, or preventing competition to any significant

7

extent. The Secretary of State may then require such rules to be modified if the distortion of competition is greater than is necessary for the protection of investors (see Wright and Diacon, 1988, for further details).

The self-regulating organizations

The place of the self-regulating organizations in the regulatory framework is shown in Figure 1.1. There are five main self-regulating organizations: The Securities Association (TSA) covering stockbroking and market-making, the Investment Management Regulatory Organisation (IMRO) covering fund management operations, the Life Assurance and Unit Trust Regulatory Organisation (LAUTRO), FIMBRA – the Financial Intermediaries, Managers and Brokers Regulatory Association, and the Association of Futures Brokers and Dealers (AFBD).

LAUTRO

LAUTRO's main function is to deal with the process of marketing investment-related life-insurance and unit-trust units. The authorization and prudential supervision of life-insurance companies will continue to be undertaken by the Department of Trade and Industry and the provisions of the Insurance Companies Act, 1982. However, authorization can be withdrawn by the DTI for serious infringement of the SIB/LAUTRO rules. The authorization and regulation of unit trusts was formerly undertaken by the DTI, but since July 1988 unit-trust management companies have been regulated by the Securities and Investments Board.

The LAUTRO rules cover the registration of salesmen and the behaviour to be expected of the employees of life offices and unit-trust management companies. Salesmen are expected to offer 'best advice' in the light of their customers' circumstances, and should sell the type of product most suitable for the client (rather than the one which might produce greater remuneration for themselves). In the absence of any suitable product from within their company's range, the salesmen must refrain from recommending any.

The LAUTRO rules require very detailed information (on benefits, premiums payable, surrender value for the first 5 years, expenses, and commissions paid to independent intermediaries) to be provided to the client at the point of sale or as soon as possible thereafter. Companies must issue a cancellation notice (which will apply to almost all types of long-term insurance, personal pensions, and unit trusts) to give clients time to change their minds about affecting the contract. LAUTRO also controls the projections of future benefits from investment products. The projections of benefits under personal pensions contracts must be given in real as well as monetary terms in order to demonstrate the likely effects of inflation.

The most contentious issues relating to marketing undoubtedly concern the fixing of maximum commission rates paid to independent intermediaries, and the disclosure to the client of such commissions and of the expenses levied by the life office. These important issues are returned to below.

FIMBRA

FIMBRA's role is in regulating the provision of services by the 10,000 or so independent investment intermediaries to their retail customers. In order to qualify for membership, an applicant has to demonstrate that he is a fit and proper person to carry on investment business of the specified category, and must conduct that business in a prudent manner. FIMBRA members are required to observe high standards of commercial honour and just and equitable principles of trade, and to give paramount importance to the client's interest where conflicts of interest arise.

In their dealings with clients, FIMBRA members are required to maintain an independent status, take steps to discover the relevant personal and financial circumstances of their clients ('know your client'), use reasonable care in arranging and effecting investment transactions which are most suitable for their clients (i.e. 'best advice'), and effect the transaction upon terms which are no less advantageous than the best currently available in the market, paying regard to the performance, charges, and reputation of the institution concerned ('best execution'). In addition, members must give clients written details of their professional standing and the service to be provided. The conduct of business rules also regulate the advertising standards to be observed by members, the records that they should keep, the standards of staff supervision, and the way in which complaints should be dealt with.

IMRO

IMRO is concerned with the authorization of managers in respect of the conduct of business and financial requirements and the authorization of trustees. Managers must continually know and demonstrate that they have adequate financial resources. Regular financial statements have to be filed, together with statements on compliance and representation. IMRO has to be notified if rules are breached at any time. Managers also have to keep records where they deal for their own account. Separate accounting records for each product line (e.g. each trust) have to be maintained. Similar financial regulation applies to trustees.

TSA

The TSA replaces the Stock Exchange as the monitor of several hundred firms ranging from provincial stockbrokers and licensed securities dealers to large international investment banks. Monitoring activities of the TSA extend beyond the stockbroking and jobbing firms covered by the former Stock Exchange. The change in the means of operation of firms on the Stock Exchange has itself contributed to the need to make a more detailed set of rules which give investors legal rights. The SIB has laid down that functions should be separated as between SRO functions and those which come under the Act's Recognised Investment Exchange (RIE) provisions. Concern also arose in respect of TSA's proposal to deal with the investment management and futures dealing activities of its members, which would have obviated the need to join SROs such as IMRO and AFBD, in addition to TSA.

AFBD

Any firm that wishes to carry out futures and options dealing, or management of portfolios in options and futures as a primary business, has to be a member of the AFBD, whether or not it is a member of an exchange. TSA, however, will authorize firms for futures and options trading where this is ancillary to their main activities.

Decisions as to membership of the exchanges will continue to be made by individual exchanges, such as the London International Financial Futures Exchange (LIFFE). Since futures and options markets operate with only a small portion of underlying contract values being paid as a security deposit, there may be scope for abuse and for significant losses to occur, hence provoking a need for satisfactory monitoring. AFBD is mainly responsible for conducting spot checks of members and for checking computer data on trading activity to identify possible abuses or trading with insufficient funds.

The recognized professional bodies

Under Sections 15 to 21 of the Financial Services Act, 1986, members of professions whose business does not consist wholly or mainly of investment business may become authorized to undertake investment business, provided they hold a certificate issued for that purpose by a recognized professional body (RPB) reporting directly to the Securities and Investment Board. Included amongst the professional bodies accepted by the Secretary of State for Trade and Industry as 'recognized professional bodies' are the three main Institutes of Chartered Accountants, the Insurance Brokers' Registration Council, and the

Law Society. In registering with a RPB, members will have to comply with regulations which are approved by the Securities and Investment Board, and which are broadly similar to those of such self-regulating organizations as FIMBRA.

Issues arising on the implementation of the FSA

The new regulatory framework is complex and its implementation has been the subject of considerable debate. There are a number of issues concerning the implementation of the FSA which have important implications for the behaviour of firms and, in particular, the marketing of financial services. Each issue is addressed in what follows.

Polarization

A key feature of the FSA is polarization. Intermediaries who advise on investments will have to conform to one of two categories: fully independent intermediary ('independent') or representative of just one company ('tied'). The polarization rule is to apply to financial conglomerates (such as banks), although separately incorporated parts of a group can polarize in different ways. Independent intermediaries will be required to conform to the rules of FIMBRA or to those of the appropriate recognized professional body. Tied representatives are restricted to selling the investment products of one company only, and will have to so inform their clients. They will not have to reveal any commission payment received from their 'employers', but are still required to offer 'best advice' by recommending investments which are appropriate to the circumstances of their clients. The employer, rather than a SRO, will be responsible for the behaviour of its salesmen. Companies operating a tied sales force will now have to take considerably more care in the training and licensing of their employees. The remuneration of company representatives must not be structured so that it influences the representatives unduly to recommend particular trusts or, say, life policies in preference to trusts.

Much attention in the polarization debate has been focused on the decisions of the various banks and building societies. Of the major clearing banks, Barclays, Lloyds, Midland and TSB have opted for 'tied' status for their branches, so that these will only be able to sell the investment products of one company. Originally the Midland did not have a life-office subsidiary, and in late 1987 it formed a new company jointly with the Commercial Union. These banks also own insurance-broking subsidiaries, which will operate independently of the branches. The other clearing banks – National Westminster and the three Scottish banks – initially chose to polarize the other way by pledging to offer independent advice through their branches (and hence committing themselves to massive staff-training programmes). Consequently NatWest sold County Unit Trust, its unit-trust management company. However, the Bank of Scotland has now decided to adopt tied status.

According to information provided by the Building Societies Association, a minority of societies (23 per cent) adopted independent intermediary status under the polarization rules. Most of these societies were the larger ones, which had the resources to provide independent advice. Initially, the main exceptions amongst the larger societies were the Abbey National, which has a tied relationship with Friends' Provident, and the Cheltenham and Gloucester which has changed from independent to tied status. Subsequently, however, many other societies altered their plans in this respect and opted for tied status, including the Halifax, the Woolwich, the Alliance and Leicester, and the Leeds Permanent. The impetus for this change came, first, from the realization that many customers did not appreciate the significance of 'independent financial advice' and, second, that there were considerable efficiency gains to be made from dealing with only a single supplier, together with high commission rates being offered to encourage societies to switch to tied status (Ennew and Wright, 1990b). It is also important to note that societies may adopt a dual approach, with the society itself being 'tied' and a separate subsidiary offering 'independent' advice (e.g. Halifax, Northern Rock, Lancastrian, Principality and Skipton).

The trend away from independent intermediaries to tied status is further illustrated by the decision of a majority of the CAMIFA (Campaign for Independent Financial Advice) life-insurance firms to accept tied agents, a reversal of the rationale for establishing CAMIFA in the first place. Industry estimates suggest that up to mid-1989 about 3,000 independent brokers also adopted tied status in some form (Shelton, 1989) because of compliance costs, expected falls in income and attractive offers by some insurance companies wishing to develop direct sales forces. The largest twenty tied chains of bank and building-society branches now account for about 46 per cent of all outlets. Moreover, whereas before the Act banks and societies may have chosen from a panel of, say, half a dozen insurance providers, they are now forced to single source. Hence, polarization has produced increased concentration at the retailing stage.

Best advice and best execution

All salesmen of investment products, be they tied employees or independent intermediaries, are required to give the client 'best advice' on the type of investment which is suited to his/her needs and circumstances. Independent intermediaries may have regard to non-financial considerations such as the quality and assurance of performance. Where precise comparisons between products are impossible, independent intermediaries will be expected to survey the market regularly and make a judgement on which of the top group of products it would be reasonable to recommend. Differential pricing or price discrimination, that is the practice of offering products at different prices to different sellers, has implications for the giving of best advice. The LAUTRO rulebook initially prevented differential pricing, but in November 1987 SIB announced relaxations to this rule. The requirement to offer best advice on the type of investment may force intermediaries to expand the range of their advice beyond unit trusts and investment products.

Commission payments and expenses charges

The original LAUTRO proposals set maximum commission rates, along with a 'soft disclosure' rule that clients need not be told what commission the independent intermediary earned on a transaction so long as the client did not ask directly and the commission did not exceed the maximum payable under the maximum commissions agreement. The commission agreement was justified on the grounds that it protected the consumer from the possibility of receiving biased advice (even though it is contrary to the FIMBRA rules for an intermediary to be influenced by commission) and that it prevented a commission war which would be detrimental to the interests of clients. However, the Office of Fair Trading objected that the agreement was an illegal price/commission-fixing cartel (since the maximum level for commission would probably also act as a minimum), that it limited an independent intermediary's ability to compete with direct sales forces (since the payments these salesmen receives were not to be controlled and there was no obligation for them to reveal their commission earnings), that it kept clients in the dark on the amounts that their advisers earned from dealing with the client's business, and that, in any case, clients were entitled to negotiate with their advisers for a share in the commission.

Furthermore, the Office of Fair Trading recognized that insisting on 'hard disclosure' (that is the compulsory full disclosure by inter-mediaries of their commission earnings) would not by itself help the cause of the independent intermediary. Consequently, the Office of Fair Trading recommended that the commission agreement be erased from the LAUTRO rulebook, and that intermediaries be obliged to make a 'hard disclosure' as a first step towards a fully fee-based system; competition between intermediaries should then ensure that commission rates were maintained at a low level. In addition, following the recommendations of a report commissioned by the SIB, the OFT also requested that all life offices be required to reveal the expenses to be charged under their contracts. However, commission and expense disclosure is not required in monetary terms, but may be expressed as a percentage of the appropriate base. The ending of the Maximum Commissions Agreement in May 1989 led to commission rates being increased by some 30 per cent above the LAUTRO rules.

The disclosure and basis for charges is a vexed issue in relation to competition between various types of investment product. The unit-trust industry, for example, has fully disclosed charges for many years, while the extent to which life-assurance charges are disclosed has been the subject of considerable discussion. The investment-trust sector has argued strongly against the remuneration of intermediaries by the investment product producer, expressing a preference for charges to be divided into a fixed management advisory fee plus a commission on dealing. Traditionally, a drawback of recommending investment trust shares has been considered to be the lack of remuneration available to intermediaries. Being limited companies, investment trusts are not permitted to pay commissions to purchasers of their shares.

Advertising

The Securities and Investments Board rules on advertising cover all media and extend to direct mail. Three types of advertisement are identified: image advertisements, to promote awareness of a company and its products; short form advertisements, which include listings of fund prices in publications and computer networks; and advertisements relating to a particular product. Advertisements are required to be legal, decent, honest and truthful, clear and precise, in no way false or tendentious and compatible with the principles of fair competition. Section 57 of the Financial Services Act, 1986, stipulates that no person other than one authorized under the Act shall issue an investment advertisement.

The SIB rules governing the above types of advertising cover a wide range of issues. Clearer guidelines for practitioners are provided in the LAUTRO and FIMBRA rulebooks, and there are specific regulations for 'off-the-page' advertisements. For savings and investment products, LAUTRO distinguishes between three categories of advertisement. Those in category A simply announce the product or company (essentially 'image' based advertisements), those in category B invite a response for further information and those in category C actually try to sell the product. The tightest restrictions operate with respect to category C advertisements which are required to include as part of the copy the precise details of the product.

Each investment firm must appoint a registered individual to approve advertisements. Apart from spot checks, LAUTRO will not vet advertisements, although the Independent Television Companies Association will continue to do so. LAUTRO requires copies of advertisements to be kept for 3 years from the date of issue. Advertisements found to be in breach of the rules will be withdrawn.

Both the LAUTRO and FIMBRA rules specify in detail the information to be disclosed in investment advertisements, particularly the basis of forecast performance and the level of future benefits, the risks concomitant on acquiring or holding the investment, and the penalties which may be incurred from liquidating the investment. The LAUTRO rules make specific provision for information disclosure about the performance of investments, especially for unit trusts and linked life insurance. Firstly, all comparisons must be fair and must compare like with like. Secondly, investments which refer to an actual investment return must do so on an offer to bid price basis. Thirdly, performance statistics must be shown over a 5-year period or date since launch, whichever is the lower. Efforts are under way to seek a simplification of the rules.

However, the need to assess comparative performance may be problematical across different types of product. Hence, for example, the comparison of investment-trust and unit-trust performance has been the subject of considerable debate.

Costs

The new regulatory framework has been criticized as too expensive and too cumbersome. The regulatory environment imposes increased costs because of the need for compliance in marketing and administration, often requiring the introduction of new systems; an increased emphasis on investment performance in order to win business on best advice recommendations from independent advisers; effects on commissions; and a pressure on profits. The direct costs of the SIB and SROs may well be in excess of identified losses suffered by investors in public scandals. To these more obvious costs may be added the potential costs of financing compensation funds, the diversion of business overseas, the restriction of competition and the possible stifling of financial innovation.

A survey by the OFT of financial intermediaries identified possible significant falls in income as a result of the costs of compliance with the new regime, and if maximum commission rates continued to be enforced (OFT, 1987). A survey of Unit Trust Managers carried out by

15

Touche Ross (Davies, 1989) of the effects of the new regulatory regime on costs and attempts being made to deal with the problem found that the median unit-trust group had total expenses of 1.45 per cent of funds under management, which are high in relation to annual management charges. Larger firms appeared better able to control costs. Average sales and marketing costs were 1.3 per cent of sales, with a substantial variation depending upon the balance of distribution between direct sales forces and direct sales advertising and whether service providers were subsidiaries of larger groups or independent. Compliance was estimated to be costing the unit-trust industry £8 million per annum.

Compensation funds could encourage the taking of excessive risks as firms know that losses will be borne by the funds. This problem may be reduced by the introduction of a generous depositor insurance scheme plus strong capital adequacy requirements. Tougher penalties for transgressions and greater requirements for public disclosure of information may also have important roles to play. The possibility of regulatory capture is a remaining, well-known possibility.

As the above aspects of the implementation of the Financial Services Act demonstrate, the new system of regulation is complex and contentious. Hence, new proposals to simplify the procedures are being discussed at the time of writing. The proposed new guiding principles of conduct emphasize the need on the part of the providers of financial services to pay attention to integrity, skill, observation of standards, fairness, provision of information about the customer, provision of information for the customer, avoidance of conflicts of interest, customer assets, financial resources and internal organization.

The Building Societies Act, 1986

The Building Societies Act, 1962, closely constrained the activities of societies. Competition between societies was also restricted by the interest-rate cartel, which ensured that prices moved closely in the same direction. The formal ending of the cartel in the early 1980s reflected growing competitive pressures, but societies' abilities to compete with banks and other financial institutions, many of which were increasingly encroaching on societies' traditional markets, remained tightly controlled (Wright *et al.*, 1986). Concerted effort to establish a strong presence in the mortgage market by the banks, together with the introduction of securitization of mortgages by new market entrants (Robbie and Wright, 1988) contributed to the fall in societies' share of new advances to its lowest level of 50.3 per cent in 1987. In addition, the introduction of interest-bearing cheque accounts by the banks put pressure on societies' traditional retail sources of funds and correspondingly on their profit margins. The existing regime placed tight controls on societies' access to the lower cost wholesale markets.

Changes to the legislative framework contained in The Building Societies Act, 1986, allowed societies, particularly the larger ones, to provide a much wider range of services than hitherto, under the supervision of a newly created body, the Building Societies Commission. The main new powers concerned the ability to extend unsecured lending, the provision of housing, the provision of an integrated house-buying package (including the provision of estate agency services), the provision of agency services, enhancements to the provision of insurance-broking services, the provision of full personal banking and money transmission services, and an extension of the range of financial services able to be provided. Organizationally, societies were permitted to create subsidiaries to carry out certain of the riskier new activities as a means of protecting the central function of housing-finance provision. Certain other services were permitted through joint ventures. Societies' abilities to raise funds from sources other than individual members were to be increased to a level of 20 per cent of all funds.

Although the Act essentially embodied the Green Paper's proposals, certain important caveats were imposed. First, unsecured lending was to be limited to £5,000 per individual. Three classes of societies' assets were created. Class 1 assets, comprising advances secured on a mortgage of residential property, were to remain the main form of activity. At least 90 per cent of commercial advances would need to be of this kind. Class 2 assets comprised other forms of secured lending, but might amount to no more than 10 per cent of commercial assets. Class 3 assets related to unsecured lending and housing provision and were limited to 5 per cent of commercial assets within the 10 per cent Class 2 limit. It is clear that the ability to introduce new forms of lending was heavily restricted, being allowable only for about sixty societies, which at the time of the passing of the Act had total assets in excess of £100 million. However, smaller societies were to some extent able to deal with the problem of restrictions imposed by the new regulations by engaging in a variety of joint arrangements (Wrigglesworth, 1989).

The recent changes to the regulatory framework include powers for societies to convert from mutual to public limited company status. Any society so doing would become subject to banking regulation and cease to be subject to the Building Societies Act. In order to protect members' interests, high levels of participation in a vote to become a public limited company have been set by the legislation. Protection from a hostile takeover following conversion is also built into the legislation in the form of super-majority requirements for shareholders to vote in favour of such an acquisition. Societies may wish to convert to the status of a bank to reduce the restrictions on obtaining funds and on the product areas into which diversification may take place. In a survey carried out in 1986 as the legislation was passing through Parliament, 16.9 per cent of sixty-five respondents said they were seriously considering conversion (Wright *et al.*, 1986). To late 1989, only the Abbey National had converted to public limited company status.

The speed of increased competition taking place in the UK personal financial services sector in the late 1980s meant that, despite the regulatory relaxation contained in the Building Societies Act, societies still considered themselves to be at a competitive disadvantage in relation to banks. In late 1987 a major review of the 1986 Act was completed. The recommendations resulting from the review were to allow societies to increase their unsecured lending limits from £5,000 to £10,000 per individual and to offer a wider range of banking and housing-related services.

Societies were also permitted to undertake unit trust fund management and allowed to hold a minority stake in stockbrokers. Most crucially, societies are now allowed to become directly involved in the operation of life and general insurance companies, although the degree of involvement in non-life insurance will be limited to an equity stake of no more than 15 per cent of an existing or new insurer.

The relaxation of powers to provide insurance-broking services has been seen as of particular importance by societies. The survey carried out in 1986 by Wright *et al.* (1986) showed that fifty-two out of sixty-five respondents expected to be offering insurance-broking services by the year 2000. Schedule 8 of the Act also permitted societies to offer estate-agency services, and to the end of 1988 twenty-three societies had established estate-agency subsidiaries. Estate agents occupy a key place at the front of the house-purchase process. The manner in which entry into estate agency has been effected and the problems it brings are examined in detail in Chapter 8.

Societies' provision of unit trusts, Personal Equity Plans and sharedealing services was, up to late 1989, limited. A survey by Spicers Corporate Finance (1989) found that only a dozen out of 107 respondents were currently providing these kinds of services. The continuing impact of the events of October 1987 on customers' perspectives of equity-market investments has not helped new entrants to this sector.

Competition legislation

Whilst mergers have come within the powers of the Office of Fair Trading and the Monopolies and Mergers Commission, there has traditionally been less attention addressed to other anti-competitive practices (Chiplin and Wright, 1989). For example, the building societies' interest-rate cartel, which existed formally until 1983, was exempt from the restrictive trade practices legislation. Recent changes have attempted to strengthen the role of the Office of Fair Trading. Reference has already been made to the role of the competition authorities in ensuring that the Financial Services Act's provisions have the desired effect of protecting consumers and enhancing competition. The Building Societies Act prohibits societies from offering mortgages conditional upon customers taking a range of other products offered by the society. The threat of a reference of the Stock Exchange dealing arrangements to the Restrictive Trade Practices Court was also seen to have been a crucial factor in changing longstanding practices.

A further issue to have received the attention of the Monopolies Commission was the behaviour of credit-card companies and, in particular, the rate of interest charged to customers and the restrictions placed on retailers in respect of charging credit-card customers different prices from those wishing to pay in cash. The initial Monopolies Commission investigation in 1980 was critical of credit-card companies' actions, and the subsequent report published in 1989 had further grounds for taking an adverse view (Monopolies Commission, 1989). The Commission found that a monopoly situation existed in credit-card services and that agreements between Visa International and MasterCard/Eurocard and their UK members should not prevent their acting as merchant-acquirers as well as card-issuers. In respect of the first finding, the Commission considered that recent increased competition would reduce credit-card profitability and charges paid by retailers. The result of the second finding has been to quicken the pace of duality, the process which card issuers can be members of both Access and Visa and can issue both these cards under the brand name of their institution. Competition, which includes the growing availability of in-house credit cards offered by retailers (Worthington, 1988), should decide whether fees for credit cards, discounts for cash payments or shorter interest free periods should be introduced. However, the Commission did take the view that retailers' ability to set their own prices was adversely affected by the rule that goods and services had to be offered at the same price irrespective of the method of payment. At the end of 1989, in an effort to enhance competition, this no-discrimination rule was brought to an end, and credit-card companies were required to provide the Director General of Fair Trading with information on their charges to retailers.

Other legislation

While not directly influencing the regulatory framework, other legislation may be relevant to the behaviour of financial services firms. In particular, legislation may introduce new products. The conditions attached to these products, for example in terms of the tax benefits to be gained and the scope of their applicability, will influence the manner in which financial services firms market the products to consumers. In the UK important legislative changes which have given rise to new products have been associated with a government philosophy in the 1980s emphasizing individual share-ownership and personal provision for the future.

The annual Finance Acts may be particularly important in introducing new investment products. One of the most important developments in recent years has been the establishment in the 1986 Finance Act of a scheme for Personal Equity Plans (PEPs) aimed at direct investment in UK companies by individuals and specifically targeted at the first-time investor. PEPs have established themselves in a relatively short time as an element in the marketing strategy of most financial services groups. PEPs are run by approved plan managers who are professional investment advisers, authorized to deal in stocks and shares. The managers design individual plan contracts for the investor subject to the statutory limitations. Under the scheme, shares in UK companies can be bought without liability to income tax or capital gains tax. Shares must be ordinary shares of UK companies listed on the Stock Exchange, shares of USM companies, unit trusts or investment trusts.

Tax relief is available on three aspects of the scheme: dividends are free from income tax if reinvested in the plan, gains from selling shares within a PEP and withdrawals of capital are free of capital gains tax, and interest from cash held in a PEP is free of income tax if reinvested in the plan. For tax reliefs to be valid, PEPs have to be held for a relevant qualifying period.

While PEPs are now an established part of a financial service company's range of products, take-up rates following their introduction were low. A survey in early 1987 commissioned jointly by the Stock Exchange and the Treasury found that only 1 per cent of a sample of 7,008 persons had backed the scheme, while a further 2 per cent said that they intended to do so. Initially, clearing banks took a leading role in the introduction of PEPs, ahead of insurance groups.

The Finance Act, 1989, increased the limits on the amounts of money that individuals could invest in a PEP linked to an investment trust or unit trust, which may mean an increase in the number of unit trusts providing a PEP route to investing in their UK equity-oriented range of unit trusts. Under the new rules, investments in PEPs in unit or investment trusts are no longer restricted to 50 per cent of the total. PEPs may also be used as a means of repaying a mortgage, and as such may provide competition for the more traditional endowment mortgage.

A second influential piece of legislation was The Social Security Act, 1986, which set out wide-ranging changes to the operation of the State Earnings Related Pension Scheme (SERPS) and to the individual pensions market. The income of occupational pension schemes rose from £16.5 billion in 1981 to £19.1 billion in 1987. The personal pension market had hitherto been much smaller, but experienced greater growth in the 1980s. Between 1981 and 1987, annual premium income almost trebled from £0.45 billion to £1.6 billion, and the number of policies in force increased from 2,195 to 5,697 in the same period (Table 1.3). Further significant growth is expected in the 1990s. Under the provision of the new legislation, members are to be encouraged to contract-out of SERPS, either by taking up their own 'portable' personal pensions or by forming new contracted-out occupational pension schemes under simplified rules. The Act also widened the choice of providers of pension arrangements. Banks, building societies and unit-trust management companies, as well as life offices, are now able to design and offer their own personal pension plans and occupational pension schemes. Many of the large building societies have already indicated their intention to provide deposit-based pensions.

The draft regulations controlling the selling of deposit-based personal pensions, issued by the Department of Health and Social

Table 1.3 *Personal (self-employed) pensions in the UK, 1981–7*

	No. of policies in force (000s)	Increase (%)	Yearly premiums (£m)	Increase (%)
1981	2,195	–	450.2	–
1982	2,571	17.1	555.3	23.3
1983	2,971	15.6	668.9	20.5
1984	3,560	19.8	888.8	32.9
1985	4,460	25.3	1,228.4	38.2
1986	4,936	10.7	1,370.3	11.6
1987	5,697	15.4	1,614.2	17.8

Source: ABI

Security, are designed to be complementary to those rules governing the investment-based personal pensions of life offices and unit trusts. However, they are more relaxed on several counts. The major differences between the DHSS rules and those resulting from the FSA include no obligation on building societies to reveal charges, no requirement to make illustrations in 'real terms', and no cancellation period.

European Community regulation of financial services

The European Community's aim to create a single internal market by 1992 includes financial services. Significant differences exist in the prices of financial products between member states. The price reductions from establishment of an integrated market are difficult to determine precisely, partly because of the simultaneous effects of other restructuring, but are expected to be substantial. Estimates by Price Waterhouse (1989) suggest a central indicative price reduction for the eight main Community economies of 10 per cent. However, the price reductions are expected to vary substantially from country to country and from sector to sector. Spain is expected to experience the largest price falls, with Luxembourg, the UK and the Netherlands providing the lowest decreases. France, Germany and the UK were found to have relatively high prices in respect of consumer credit. Existing prices in respect of commercial banking products were found to be highest in Spain and Italy and lowest in Germany. The traditionally more competitive insurance markets in the UK and the Netherlands were found to have a significantly lower price than in Belgium, Luxembourg, France, Spain and Italy. In Belgium the insurance markets have traditionally been protected from competition, and are highly concentrated, with associated high overhead cost and profit levels. In France, regulatory costs are seen as being high coupled with an under developed retail distribution system. In Italy, the insurance markets are generally less well developed.

The creation of a free flow of capital and free trade in financial service and financial service firms are keys to the establishment of the Single Market. In respect of the first, exchange controls have been abolished for some time by the UK, West Germany and Denmark. Other EC member states are required by the Capital Movements Directive (88/361/EEC) to allow the free flow of capital by July 1990, except Greece, Ireland, Portugal and Spain, who have until the end of 1992 to comply.

The principle of free trade in financial services calls for neutrality between buying a service from a domestic institution, importing from another country or buying domestically from a local branch of a foreign institution. Once a provider of a financial service has been authorized in one country, it will be able to operate in other EC countries. If these moves become effective, benefits may be derived from economies of scale and scope, improvement of service provision by entry of the best providers into currently protected markets, and increased competition in markets currently tightly regulated or dominated by cartels.

In respect of banking services, the second Banking Directive (COM(87)715), the Own Funds Directive (COM(86)169) and the Solvency Ratio Directive (COM(88)184) are together concerned with requiring countries to recognize any financial institution authorized or licensed in another EC country on condition that it respects local regulations (the so-called 'passport principle'). Insurance companies already have freedom of establishment, although national regulations vary significantly from one country to another. However, in respect of cross-border trade in insurance services, it has been unusual for member states to permit foreign insurers to solicit business direct. Rather, insurance contracts have been required to be provided by established or authorized insurers. The Non-life Insurance Services Directive, which takes effect in 1992, provides the basis for a wholesale market in 'large risk' insurance, where policy holders are companies with a turnover of 12.8 m ecu or other equivalent criteria.

Changes have also been introduced to the regulatory regime concerning open-ended mutual funds (unit trusts). From 1 October 1989, the introduction of the UCITS (Undertakings for Collective Investments in Transferable Securities) directive has meant that a unit trust operated in other EC countries will be allowed to be marketed in the UK. The UCITS directive aims to harmonize the structure of collective investment schemes throughout the EC. UCITS covers open-ended investment schemes in transferable securities, but will not cover new unit-trust types such as money market, property or futures and options funds. Investment trusts are also not covered by the directive. UCITS defines common procedures for the authorization of UCITS schemes, the supervision of schemes by EC governments and the investment and borrowing powers of UCITS schemes. As long as a scheme meets the requirements of UCITS, it can be marketed in other EC member states and be subject to whatever marketing rules and regulations apply to financial services in each country.

The effects of UCITS may vary from country to country, depending upon the relative restrictiveness of the marketing regime from one state to another. While the UK has a large number of independent intermediaries charged with giving best advice, in France and Germany, for example, UCITS products are predominantly distributed through bank branches, which seem unlikely to recommend foreign-based products unless forced to do so. Hence, UK firms may need to engage in recruiting high-cost direct sales forces if they want to enter the continental European market, while European firms may gain entry through recommendation by independent intermediaries.

A number of problems are raised by the developing regulatory framework for the establishment of a single EC market. First is the problem of harmonizing the standards required for the different types of financial intermediaries and the difficulties such moves pose for designing regulatory compromises which are politically acceptable to all EC members.

A second difficulty concerns the distinction between licensing rules and operating rules. Hence an institution may be licensed to enter other EC member states' markets outside its own but face difficulties in using the same technique as it does in its home market. For example, UK building societies lend money for house purchase at variable rates of interest. In Belgium, it has traditionally been illegal to offer housing loans on these terms. The Mortgage Credit Directive, which implicitly required mutual recognition of techniques between member states, was superseded by the Banking Directive. While covering mortgage lending, the Bank Directive does not implicitly allow for mutual recognition of technique; rather, institutions were to be allowed to undertake any activity within a list of recognized banking activities on condition that this was possible in their home markets. However, as Davis and Smales (1989) point out, the manner in which the list is presented does not appear to give clear guidance and protection for institutions wishing to use techniques which are acceptable in the home market in other member states' markets.

A third problem emerges in that, despite the intention of the directives, individual governments may still erect barriers to entry through various forms of bureaucratic procedures which firms have to follow if they are actually to operate in other countries.

Fourth, long-standing and rational differences in national preferences and circumstances may inhibit the extent of change and the acceptance of new entrants. Finally, the actual extent and method of entry may be problematical.

Nevertheless, in principle the approach to market integration has its attractions. The presence of deregulation and hence market entry ought to provide a significant threat to states which have hitherto had unnecessarily restrictive domestic regulations to remove them in order that domestic firms can meet foreign competition. In addition, the threat or actuality of entry may go a long way towards breaking down restrictive cartels which exist in certain financial sectors, as has happened elsewhere (O'Brien *et al.*, 1979). Similarly, the threat of takeover, the replacement of underperforming managers, and the erosion of market share in underperforming sectors exposed to the possibility of foreign competition, may also improve managerial performance. However, these points ought not to be overstated.

Globalization

The spread of financial services firms' interest into global markets has been influenced by two main factors – regulatory constraints and developments in information technology. Regulatory constraints in domestic markets may push firms to seek international markets as a means of achieving growth. For example, restrictions on interstate or even intercounty banking in the US meant that branch networks were limited to a small geographical area. Banks could achieve growth by focusing on the provision of a range of services for corporate clients. Development of these banks as cross-border institutions was in part to extend the range of services offered to the corporate sector but also to escape regulatory constraints. This development was particularly true of the more restricted New York banks and less so for those in California, where state-wide branching was permissible (Lewis, 1986).

However, the ability to extend into foreign markets was severely constrained by regulations in individual countries which limited cross-border activities, as the position before the development of the Single European Market discussed in the previous section illustrates. Similar barriers to entry existed elsewhere, e.g. in Japan, Canada and Australia. In Japan the brokerage market had been regulated so as to prevent entry by US firms, and in Canada and Australia entry by foreign banks was not permitted until the early 1980s (Channon, 1989).

The development of international and global markets was slowly made possible by the ability of firms to exploit differences between national regulations and the lack of coordination between regulatory regimes. The different rate at which deregulation occurred between countries gave a further impetus to this process.

Where regulatory barriers persisted, innovations in delivery systems provided an increasingly effective means of entering international markets and introducing new types of product, particularly by new types of competitor. The evolution of the global securities and capital markets has been facilitated by electronically based dealing systems.

Worldwide branch networks began to be developed in the 1970s, but by the 1980s many firms were experiencing problems in generating sufficient profitability and were seeking either to rationalize or add new services. By the late 1980s a number of retail services had been developed on a European or even global scale, e.g. travel and entertainment cards, automatic teller machine (ATM) networks, travellers' cheques and private banking. For corporate clients, global cash management, foreign exchange and other products were introduced. Other products which were to be sold across the globe but targeted at the more attractive country niches were developed.

Information technology

Developments in information technology in the financial services sector introduce major changes in respect of the link between consumers and firms, links between financial services firms, firms' international information systems and the generation of new products. Information technology links between consumers and financial services firms in the distribution of products may be categorized into electronic funds transfer at place of banking (EFTPOB, that is Automatic Teller Machines, ATMs), electronic funds transfer at place of living (EFTPOL, home banking) and electronic funds transfer at place of shopping (EFTPOS).

ATM networks are now well-established in the UK, with new generations of machines which provide a broader range of services being introduced (see Chapter 8 for trends). The substantial system costs, which have been shared between institutions, need to be balanced against the cost savings from using fewer bank staff to deal with routine transactions. ATMs may pose a problem in that individuals make less use of the inside of the bank branch, so that marketing opportunities may be lost. EFTPOL and EFTPOS have been slow to develop in the UK, although, as shown in Chapter 9, many of the initial problems are now being overcome.

Links between financial services firms may include shared networks to provide certain products in order to minimize costs. For example, shared ATM networks have developed, as shown in Chapter 8. A key point about such joint ventures is that they may be highly pro-competitive, as they keep in business firms that may otherwise disappear; they also make entry easier if exclusionary and other non-competitive factors are prohibited (Chiplin, 1986). Links between different types of financial services firms have also developed. For example, building-society, bank and independent broker branches may use a terminal link to obtain the best insurance-policy quotation for a potential purchaser.

An internal use of information technology which is of particular relevance for this book is the development of marketing information systems. Databases may be constructed from information contained in, for example, insurance-policy proposal forms, mortgage applications, and savings-account details. The information so collected, when suitably organized to relate to individuals, may be integrated for marketing purposes. For example, individuals with the characteristics of purchasers of a certain range of products may be selected to receive a direct mail shot of a new related product. However, in order to achieve such uses of information technology, great effort is required in obtaining information of sufficient detail and reliability. Some financial institutions may face major problems in converting computer systems developed on an account rather than individual basis and in training personnel to use information for marketing purposes at local levels (Watkins and Wright, 1986).

The changing boundaries of financial services firms

The changes in the general competitive and regulatory environment that have been analysed in the previous sections have direct implications for the boundaries of financial services firms. The changing boundaries which occur may be both internal and external as firms seek to restructure themselves so as to be better able to compete. Internally, there may be a need to shift from a functional-based organizational structure to a flexible one which focuses on products (Johne and Harborne. 1985). In retail banking, the traditional head office/branch relationship may need to be altered radically to reflect the need to market different products in different ways, as developed in more detail in Chapter 8. Major training and recruitment programmes may need to be introduced to develop a body of staff with the requisite skills. In addition, improved management accounting systems are required to enable product profitability and cost control to be effected. Internal cohesion may need to be increased in order that opportunities for cross-selling in diversified groups can be fully exploited. For example, in a typical small management buy-out proposal received by a bank branch there will be a need to introduce equity capital, key man insurance, industrial mortgage, leasing, factoring, etc. Traditionally, it would not be uncommon for these product opportunities to be offered to local outside providers, even though they were available within another part of the group. Internal marketing and communication may be required to increase awareness, reduce cross-activity jealousies, etc., to enable cross-selling to occur. Increased competition places particular emphasis on the need to make these changes. A survey by the Nottingham Institute of Financial Studies, undertaken as firms were implementing their strategic development plans, showed that the main internal organizational problems were as shown in Table 1.4. Recruitment of specialist staff was seen to be a major difficulty, together with the need to develop an appropriate organizational

27

Table 1.4 *Major management difficulties in the introduction*
of new products (%)

	Very important		Important		Not important		Not relevant	
	B.Soc.	Bank	B.Soc.	Bank	B.Soc.	Bank	B.Soc.	Bank
(a) Products introduced by acquisition								
Difficulties in combining management styles	31.7	36	29.3	36	9.8	5	29.5	23
Difficulties in combining computer systems	34.1	50	29.3	18	9.8	9	26.8	23
(b) For products introduced by internal product development								
Difficulties in recruiting specialist staff	41.5	32	41.5	68	17.1	–	–	–
Difficulties in dealing with change in the organization	43.9	36	46.3	50	9.8	9	–	5

Source: Ennew and Wright (1990b).

structure. The techniques of strategy assessment were also found to be limited, and to be in the process of development so as to permit financial services firms to better analyse their market positions (Ennew and Wright, 1990a). These issues have a profound impact on the marketing planning approach by such firms, which is addressed in Chapter 3.

External changes to a firm's boundaries relate to increased or occasionally decreased size, and may be undertaken to enable the firm to compete more strongly in existing markets or to enter new ones. These markets may be in the home country or, increasingly, of a cross-border nature, either within Europe or globally. The decision process as to which markets to enter and the position to adopt within them is analysed in Chapter 3. As firms seek to implement these strategic developments, three essential choices are available: the establishment of new outlets ('greenfield sites' or branch conversions), joint ventures and links with other service providers, or acquisition. The second half of the 1980s saw a sharply increased trend towards joint ventures and acquisitions carried out to enable diversification to occur. In addition, takeovers and mergers within institutional types continued, as will be seen in detail in the second half of this book. For example, the number of building societies fell from 273 in 1980 to 167 in 1985 and to 115 in 1989. Mergers occurred both among the smaller regional societies and between some of the very large ones – the former seeking to strengthen their niche market positions, the latter aiming to have sufficient resources to enable a broader range of services to be provided (Ennew and Wright, 1990, and Chapters 3, 4 and 10). Such mergers raise a number of well-known problems concerning the integration of management styles and computer systems, and the rationalization of personnel and branches. In addition, where societies are tied agents for the distribution of the products of different insurance companies under the provisions of the Financial Services Act, a choice has to be made as to which tie will be maintained. The direct acquisition cost has also begun to arise as an issue in the building-society sector. Hitherto, account-holders in societies were not compensated, as shareholders in a business whose ownership was transferred would have been. The acquisition by the Cheltenham and Gloucester Building Society of the Guardian Building Society in 1989 was the first case in which account-holders were compensated.

Such issues arise, perhaps to an even greater extent, in diversifying market entry, and are, for example, reflected in the different routes chosen by financial services firms entering estate agency (Ennew and Wright, 1990; and Chapter 8). Acquisition, franchising, joint ventures, partial acquisitions and new start-ups have all been used, often by the same firm as it seeks to build market share quickly.

This pattern in the UK market is being reproduced across Europe as financial services firms seeks to reconfigure their size and span of activities either as a pro-active move to take advantage of new opportunities or as a defensive move in the light of increased competition. Trends in the latter half of the 1980s are shown in Table 1.5, which relates to banking and insurance acquisitions involving at least one of the European Community's 1,000 largest firms. The substantial increase in the level of acquisition activity by banks in the same country is particularly noteworthy, reflecting the need for rationalization of large numbers of regional banks in some countries (see for example, Mottura and Munari, 1990, for the case of Italy). The growth of partial (minority) acquisitions and joint ventures across borders is also striking. Joint ventures may be useful in enabling insurance companies to sell their products in non-domestic branch networks to take advantage of the anticipated substantial growth in insurance in Southern Europe in the 1990s (Cockburn, 1989). In the banking sector, the French savings banks have pioneered a framework of cooperation agreements with other Community savings banks as a cost-effective alternative to establishing new branch networks or acquisitions.

Cross-border entry may further magnify the problems of entry and diversification found in domestic markets. For example, 'greenfield

Table 1.5 *Banking and insurance acquisitions in Europe involving at least one of the 1000 largest EC firms*

| | | Type of acquisitions | | | | |
| | | Majority | | Minority | | Joint ventures | |
		Banking	Insurance	Banking	Insurance	Banking	Insurance
National[1]	84/5	10	7	10	5	9	1
	85/6	12	5	10	4	10	0
	86/7	22	17	11	5	18	1
	87/8	53	14	38	8	16	10
EC[2]	84/5	6	7	6	3	2	0
	85/6	4	3	3	0	6	0
	86/7	3	7	9	1	5	1
	87/8	12	14	15	4	7	3
International[3]	84/5	2	1	5	0	2	0
	85/6	9	4	8	0	0	0
	86/7	10	4	13	5	1	0
	87/8	13	12	28	19	7	3

Notes: 1 Mergers of firms from the same member state
2 Mergers of firms from different states
3 Mergers of firms from member states and third countries, with effects on the EC market

Source: Comm. of EC, *Eighteenth Report on Competition Policy*

site' cross-border entry in banking may be unattractive in markets with existing branching capacity, and entry into retail insurance may only be feasible on a large scale with a tied sales force. Entry by merger also is not without its problems. Community merger policy has been notoriously problematical to establish (Chiplin and Wright, 1989) and national restrictions on takeovers may still pose problems of entry. Moreover, the attainment of economies of scale and scope from merger are by no means unambiguously clear, varying as they do between retail and wholesale sectors. In the wholesale (and corporate) sector, cross-border provision of services is less problematical, as there is no need for extensive local branch networks. In the retail sectors, economies of scale and scope may be outweighed by economies of specialization. The key financial service attributes of trust, security, confidence, branding, and consumer protection (Carter *et al.*, 1986) may be perceived by individuals as coming from those financial institutions established in their country with a local, familiar name. As a result, the structure of the European financial services industry may be more heavily influenced by the extent to which intermediation by retailers between wholesalers and customers is profitable. Inter-mediaries fulfil the role of monitoring a large number of providers of services which would be beyond the ability of individuals to under-take. If economies of scale and scope are limited, organizational forms other than those produced by merger may also be important for service provision. In particular, various forms of horizontal or vertical quasi-internal or managed market relationships may be more effective (Thompson and Wright, 1988).

Where there is experimentation in the nature and extent of market entry, some failures may be expected with a consequent need to undo arrangements which initially seemed correct. In the domestic market in the UK, divestments by some building societies of at least part of the estate-agency networks they have established by acquisition reflects the difficulties of integration. These problems are magnified where very high acquisition prices have been paid. The perceived need to build market share quickly in competition with other entrants contributed to this problem. However, where the rates of growth in the sector seen at the beginning of this chapter could not be sustained, prices may have been paid which more than discounted future benefits. Problems may also arise with joint ventures and other similar arrangements. Different managerial approaches may be difficult enough to resolve in straightforward acquisitions, where it is usually clear that the acquirer is the dominant partner (Jones, 1985). In joint ventures there may be no such clarity. One party may want dominance but be resisted forcefully by the other. Hence, great care and caution are required in selecting the appropriate partner and in defining the scope of the joint venture.

Many cross-border relationships have already been established in advance of the regulations to set up the EC single market. Evidence from the UK's financial services firms indicated that they generally feel well-placed to benefit from the increased opportunities which will be available (Bank of England, 1989).

Conclusions

This chapter has reviewed the changing environment affecting financial services firms in the UK and Europe and sets the scene for the development of marketing activity, which is addressed in the chapters that follow. It has been shown that the environmental changes have several dimensions and that the full implications of regulatory changes in the UK and Europe have still fully to be worked out. The appropriate actions to be taken by firms in the light of these environmental developments will vary according to circumstances, but seem highly likely to necessitate changes in both their internal and external boundaries. Such changes allow for the introduction of new management styles and skills and the provision of new products either within the firm, following acquisition, or outside in some form of joint arrangement with other institutions. Different market strategies will require a variety of entry methods. The market strategies adopted will be influenced not only by different managers' perceptions of future prospects, but also by the capital base available to individual firms to enable prudent growth policies to be introduced. It is also clear that with the high degree of uncertainty in financial services firms environments, caution and experimentation are required. By its nature, experimentation is likely to produce the need to undo failed actions. Hence, in considering entry strategies firms also need to weigh the costs and barriers to exit.

CHAPTER 2
The demand for financial services
Trevor Watkins

Introduction

Since marketing is a consumer-orientated approach to business, an understanding of the patterns and nature of demand for a product must be a central component of any marketing strategy. There are two key areas of demand which require consideration. First, it is important to consider the buying behaviour of the individual (typical) consumer and how such a person chooses a particular product and brand. Second, the individual's buying behaviour must be set in the broader context of aggregate demand patterns. This latter aspect requires an analysis of the broad trends in a particular sector as a whole and across different product classes.

This chapter deals with both these aspects of demand for financial services. The next section examines briefly a standard approach to the analysis of the consumer's buying behaviour and examines some empirical studies of both the retail and corporate sectors, in the context of this approach. The third section considers the pattern of demand for personal financial services, firstly, in respect of market share by product, and subsequently by discussion of broad changes in demographic, social and economic factors. The corporate sector is treated separately in the fourth section and this is followed by some discussion of the marketing implications of the trends which have been observed.

Consumer-buying behaviour

Developing an effective marketing strategy requires that an organization assesses the processes which govern the consumer's decision to buy a particular financial service. An understanding of the ways in which consumers actually make decisions can provide an insight into the most appropriate way to develop a marketing mix in order to have maximum impact on those decisions. There are various consumer-behaviour models which break down the purchase decision into a series of distinct stages. During each stage the consumer is subject to a variety of influences, both internal and external. While these models tend to be developed in relation to product purchases, they can readily be adapted to the financial services sector (Marsh, 1988).

A simple example of this type of approach is the model developed by Engel, Kollat and Blackwell (Engel *et al.*, 1987). Five key stages in the consumer's decision process are identified, as follows.

Problem recognition

At this stage, the consumer recognizes a need for a product or service in order to fulfil a particular set of wants or needs. A number of external and internal influences may create this feeling in the consumer. Social factors, such as a desire to match with reference groups or the need to convey a particular image, may encourage an individual to apply for a credit card. Economic factors (such as income and wealth) may affect the individual's need for credit or savings products. Personal factors, in particular the lifestyle and life-cycle stages, may affect the demand for mortgage and insurance products. Finally, psychological factors, such as attitudes to risk, attitudes to debt and need for security, will affect the extent to which different consumers perceive a need for a range of financial services.

Information search

Information search is the process whereby the consumer collects information on the ways in which a particular need can be satisfied. There are two sources for such information. First, the consumer may draw on internal sources, namely his/her past experience and existing knowledge of the service and the service provider. In this context, the concept of brand loyalty is of particular importance in governing choice, and in the case of financial services, it increases the opportunities for cross-selling. Second, the consumer may draw on external sources of information, the most obvious of which are advertising and promotion, personal recommendations and independent consumer reports.

Evaluation of alternatives

Evaluation of alternatives entails the analysis of the information collected in the context of the criteria which the consumer considers important in relation to the product. At one level, these criteria will be influenced by the factors which stimulated the consumer's recognition of a need for a particular product. At another level, they can, in some way, be influenced by the marketing campaign which the organization develops. In either case, a thorough understanding of the nature of consumers' evaluative criteria is a key component in the development of any successful marketing mix.

Purchase decision

This stage is the one at which the consumer, in the light of his/her evaluation of the competing products, makes the decision to purchase. In principle, purchase may be regarded as a natural conclusion to the process of evaluation. However, the realization of a purchase may still be influenced at this stage by the presence of negative attitudes from reference groups or unforeseen situational factors. Thus, a consumer's decision to buy from a particular insurance company or bank may be changed at the last minute if he/she encounters adverse publicity concerning the company's behaviour towards its customers.

Post-purchase behaviour

Post-purchase behaviour focuses on the consumer's reactions to the product and the extent to which it satisfies or exceeds his/her their expectations. From the marketing perspective, this stage is important for two main reasons: first, because satisfaction with the product can provide the basis for the establishment of brand loyalty and the communication of favourable information to other potential consumers; and, second, because consumers often experience feelings of doubt regarding the purchase decision (cognitive dissonance) which may adversely affect their perceptions of the product. This phenomenon is perhaps of particular relevance in relation to services because the consumer gets no real opportunity to experience the service before purchase. Effective marketing will seek to minimize the extent to which cognitive dissonance occurs by ensuring that the product is not represented in unrealistic terms and, more importantly, by relying on forms of marketing communication to confirm to the consumers that their decision to purchase was the correct one. The consumer protection components of the Financial Services Act may be of particular relevance in this context, since one requirement is that purchasers are allowed a 14-day 'cooling off' period following the sale of an investment product, to give them time to reassess their decision.

While models of the kind just discussed acknowledge the complexity of the consumer's decision process, it must be recognized that not every purchase decision will involve the consumer in all stages of decision making. In particular, a distinction is often drawn between low-, medium- and high-involvement decisions (Kotler, 1986). Low-involvement decision processes require minimal search and evaluation, while high-involvement decision processes entail more extensive search and evaluation and are more likely to display extensive post-purchase behaviour. In addition, while the nature of the decision process is thought to be common across all groups of consumers, it is recognized that the stimuli to problem recognition and the evaluative criteria will vary across different market segments.

There is comparatively little empirical work on using this type of framework to analyse buying behaviour in the financial services sector. A study of customer loyalty in retail banking in the US (Jain *et al.*, 1987) suggested that important distinctions could be drawn between loyal and non-loyal customers. The latter tended to be knowledgeable about financial markets, heavy users and risk-takers; they were found to be particularly responsive to economic factors such as interest rates, and to convenience factors. To attract and retain such customers would require particular attention to price, reliability, flexibility and quality. The loyal segment, by contrast, tended to be older, less affluent and typically blue-collar workers. Such customers placed particular emphasis on community orientation, reputation, size and quality of promotion, suggesting that particular attention should be focused on these criteria in developing marketing strategies to retain their business.

A different approach was used in a study of the factors influencing the choice of bank in a Canadian study undertaken by Laroche *et al.* (1986). Their results suggested that, in selecting a bank, personal customers were particularly concerned with location, convenience, speed of service and the competence and friendliness of staff. Similar results were reported by the *Nottingham Evening Post* (1987) in a survey of consumers' reasons for choosing banks and building societies. In the case of banks, convenience and family tradition were seen as important influences on the consumers' choice, and in the case of building societies, the key factors for savers were similar, with interest rates also cited as important. Mortgage customers tended to select the building society they currently saved with, or acted on mortgage recommendations from an estate agent.

In the corporate market, Teas *et al.* (1988) suggest that many organizations will look for their banks to be responsive to business needs and knowledgeable about the organization and its markets. In general, they found that the notion of the bank taking an active interest in the welfare of their corporate customers was a key element in building customer loyalty in the corporate sector. Channon (1986) focuses on some of the more objective factors which affect the selection of banks by corporate customers, although he stresses that emotional factors, while of less importance than in personal markets, should not be ignored. In the case of multi-nationals', global branch networks, the quality of foreign exchange services and the level of international knowledge and operating efficiency were seen to be of particular importance. Among the medium-sized organizations, greater emphasis was placed on the breadth of service, price and the level of the banks' understanding of the business. In both instances, the importance of identifying the decision-makers is stressed, as is the need to recognize that in many organizations the decision-takers or influencers may not necessarily be specialist finance personnel. Turnbull and Gibbs (1987), in a study of corporate customers in South Africa, suggest that the quality of service and staff, along with the quality of relationship with the manager, were considered the most important selection criteria, with convenience and speed of service being given generally low rankings.

Studies which have focused specifically on the small-business sector indicate that in many areas the reasons managers give for choosing and remaining with banks are similar to those discussed above. Particular emphasis seems to be placed on the banks' knowledge and under-standing of the business operating environment, although price and speed of service are also mentioned as important factors in businesses assessments of their banks (see, for example, Binks *et al.*, 1989). Other factors which have been cited as important include accuracy and confidentiality (Smith, 1989). The small-business sector is frequently treated as a single segment in bank analysis of their markets. However, a study conducted by National Girobank in relation to the small business segment (Roach, 1989) emphasized the differences between different types of small firms and the importance of understanding the needs of different segments within this grouping in order to develop products to meet the needs of these customers.

Market-share analysis

As a starting point, it is useful to consider the trends in patterns of demand for financial services. Table 2.1 illustrates the market penetration of various financial products by age, social group and gender classifications. A number of interesting factors emerge from these tabulated distributions.

Table 2.1 Holding of selected personal financial products (%)

| | Total | Male | Female | Social class | | | | | 16–20 | 21–24 | 25–34 | 35–44 | 45–54 | 55–64 | 65+ |
				A	AB	C1	C2	DE							
Population profile	100	48	52	2	16	24	27	33	9	8	18	19	14	13	19
Penetration															
Bank current account	69	73	66	93	91	84	72	45	50	70	76	81	75	69	55
Bank deposit account	25	25	24	31	26	24	27	23	25	24	23	26	27	26	23
Building society ordinary share account	42	41	42	38	44	46	46	33	43	47	50	46	39	35	33
Building society higher interest account	22	23	21	40	39	28	20	10	8	16	20	24	26	30	21
Stocks and shares	15	18	13	44	33	19	13	6	5	8	12	18	21	23	15
+ Bank credit card	35	39	31	72	64	48	31	14	13	29	42	49	41	34	19
+ Bank loan	8	10	6	10	10	9	10	4	7	13	12	12	8	4	*
+ Retail store account	14	12	15	37	29	17	11	6	8	12	18	21	18	11	4
+ Life assurance	61	64	59	65	66	63	68	53	26	46	70	77	72	63	47

Base: 28,663 adults aged 16+ in Great Britain
+ Base: 27,853 adults aged 18+ in Great Britain
Source: NOP Financial Research Survey, October 1988–March 1989
* Less than 0.5 per cent

Competition

It is increasingly difficult to make clear-cut product definitions as building societies and banks offer an increasingly differentiated range of interest-bearing chequeing accounts. The move by building societies into this traditional bank preserve was led by the Nationwide Anglia Flexaccount and by the Abbey National Cheque account, which, unlike bank current accounts at the time, offered interest on credit balances. These new products began to take a large proportion of newly opened accounts and grew quickly. Although the big four banks have many more current accounts in total, some of the take up would be by existing bank current account holders. Nevertheless, the banks responded by their own interest-bearing cheque accounts, offering better deals to customers.

The 16–20 age group

The 16–20 age group are regarded as the key market for chequeing services by banks and building societies. The simplistic underlying assumption traditionally used by banks is that there is very little account-switching between banks. Thus, getting the account of young people may not always be regarded as profitable in the short term but is expected to become so in the longer term, provided switching does not occur. The figures from Table 2.1 show that banks and building societies (ordinary accounts) have similar penetration of this market at about 46 per cent each. The switching assumption may well turn out to be unrealistic as financial literacy grows.

A particularly hotly contested sub-set of the 16–20 age group market is new students. At age 18 many students entering higher education leave home for the first time and have to run their own financial accounts based on their grants and/or parental contributions to their subsistence costs while at polytechnic or university. The marketing techniques currently used to attract the new student consist mainly of sales promotion gimmicks and special offers such as subsidized railtravel, book tokens, reduced overdraft costs and discounts. Interestingly, many of these offers can be regarded as product-demeaning, in the sense that they try to attract customers by peripheral features rather than through the inherent qualities of the brand itself.

Life-cycle and demand

The family life-cycle stages correlate well with demand for financial services. For example, comparing the 25–34 age group with the 55–64 age group is not dissimilar from comparing the 'young married with young children' and the 'empty nesters' (families whose children have grown up and left home). In simple terms the former are likely to be net borrowers (especially mortgage borrowing) and the latter net savers. It is not surprising therefore to see that 2 per cent of the former group hold national saving certificates compared with 8 per cent of the latter. Similar explanations account for differences in the penetration of building societies' higher interest accounts (15 per cent v 27 per cent), stocks and shares (8 per cent v 12 per cent), bank credit cards (40 per cent v 33 per cent), bank loans (13 per cent v 4 per cent) and retail store accounts (18 per cent v 8 per cent).

Social groups

Unsurprisingly, social groups A, B and to a lesser extent C1 are heavier users of financial services products than other social groups, especially DEs. ABs are much more likely than DEs to hold bank current accounts (90 per cent v 43 per cent), building society higher interest accounts (34 per cent v 7 per cent), national savings certificates (11 per cent v 3 per cent), stocks and shares (20 per cent v 3 per cent), bank credit cards (60 per cent v 13 per cent) and retail store accounts (23 per cent v 6 per cent).

Penetration

The penetration of life-assurance products is remarkably consistent across social and age groups (apart from the under-25s). One reason is that penetration is measured by volume not value. In insurance, industrial branch policies with very low sum assured amounts are held traditionally by C2DE social groups and older people. These are the policies sold by the traditional door to door insurance collectors calling each week for cash premium payments, usually of very small sums. Long-established insurance companies such as Prudential, Pearl and Co-operative insurance services are among the companies still offering industrial branch business. If the life assurance held had been measured in terms of the value (i.e. sum assured) rather than volume (i.e. owned or not owned), then a much more skewed distribution could have been expected.

As Table 2.1 shows only a snapshot of penetration at one point in time, it does not illustrate the current state of the competitive position between suppliers. Most of the rest of this book considers the strategic marketing responses which can be made by firms to try to gain competitive advantage.

It should be noted that any quantitative analysis of demand for financial products is fraught with measurement difficulties caused primarily because of the plethora of products of varying types. For example, there is a strong interaction between personal insurance and business insurance (personal and group pension schemes, individual and business motor insurance, for example). However, a number of qualitative trends can be identified, and they provide market opportunities for suppliers of financial services.

Marketing trends

The following social, economic and demographic trends describe patterns of change in the marketing environment which might be expected to create opportunities or pose threats for suppliers of financial services.

The growth in self-employment

During the first 10 years of the Thatcher government, with its avowed aim to create an enterprise culture, there was a growing trend to small-business formation. At the same time, the high unemployment levels of the early 1980s destroyed, at least in part, the 'jobs for life' security enjoyed in many professions and industries. Table 2.2 shows a recent breakdown of the economic status of the UK population.

Table 2.2 *Economic status of population of working age – 1985 (millions)*

	Women	Men	Total
Employed – full-time	4.9	10.9	15.8
– part-time	3.8	0.4	4.2
Self-employed	0.6	1.9	2.5
Unemployed	1.1	1.9	3.0
Looking after the home	3.5	0.1	3.6
Long-term sick or disabled	0.5	0.7	1.2
Students	0.6	0.7	1.3
Retired	0.1	0.4	0.5
Others	0.7	0.4	1.1
Total of working age	15.8	17.4	33.2

Source: *Social Trends, 18,* p. 69

Table 2.3 *Households by type*

	1961		1971		1981	
	Million	% of total	Million	% of total	Million	% of total
One person, under retirement age	0.7	4	1.1	6	1.5	8
One person, over retirement age	1.2	7	2.2	12	2.8	14
Two or more persons (non-family)	0.8	5	0.7	4	0.9	5
Married couple alone	4.1	26	4.9	27	5.0	26
Married couple + dependent child(ren)	6.1	38	6.3	34	6.0	31
Married couple + independent child(ren)	1.7	10	1.6	8	1.6	8
Lone parent + dependent child(ren)	0.4	2	0.5	3	0.9	5
Lone parent + independent child(ren)	0.7	4	0.7	4	0.7	4
Two or more families	0.4	3	0.3	1	0.2	1
Total	16.2		18.3		19.5	

Source: *Social Trends*, 15

These economic changes have far-reaching implications for personal financial planning, which could be exploited by financial institutions, particularly insurance companies. Responses have included the launch of flexible pension and life-insurance products, in which the proportions of the premium devoted to protection and to savings can be varied by the buyer as circumstances change.

Changes in the number and structure of households

An increase in the divorce rate is one of the factors which has led to an increase in single-parent families and a decline in the 'traditional' family of working husband, wife and dependent children (Table 2.3). The increase in unemployment in the early 1980s was weighted towards males in traditional industries, and the subsequent increase in employment in the late 1980s was weighted towards females in service-orientated sectors, often working part- rather than full-time. Thus, one would expect to find more households in which the sole breadwinner is female rather than male.

The financial services implications of these changes include a growing role for females in household decision-making. Indeed, some financial products aimed specifically at women were launched in the late 1980s, but many financial products are aimed at the 'traditional' family, if TV advertisements are to be taken as an indicator of target markets.

These household structural changes have been accompanied by a trend towards later marriage and delayed child-bearing. House-price rises have meant that newly formed households contain partners who both work. Maybe the 'enterprise economy' has encouraged a greater interest in career development. Greater financial independence for women is also a likely trend caused by the economic and social changes in the 1980s. Products aimed at the increased number of 'single person of pensionable age' households are also likely to increase.

The implications for financial services marketing are that new niche markets are likely to grow while traditional markets may be declining. The use of customer databases to direct more specific target marketing may be one solution, as may product proliferation. Figures 2.1–2.3 illustrates these trends.

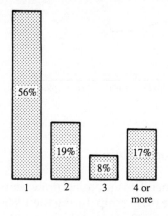

Source: *Sunday Times*, 24 December 1989

Figure 2.1 *Number of different shares held by private investors*

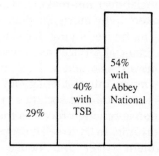

Figure 2.2 *Percentage of private shareholders who have only privatization shares*

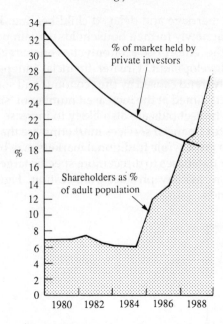

Figure 2.3   *Trends in share ownership*

Increasing home/share-ownership

Although it is again difficult to quote accurate statistical evidence, growth in home and share ownership during the 1980s is claimed. The privatization issues of the 1980s spread the ownership of shares into new categories, even if many of these new owners immediately sold to take a profit when open dealing began. A particular feature of home-ownership with financial services implications is bequeathed wealth, which has grown in significance as house prices have risen.

With this increase in house prices, the mortgage has taken a pre-eminent role in family financial decision-making. The proportion of family disposable income taken up by mortgage payments has grown rapidly for many families. The house-buying decision has long been recognized by suppliers of financial services as *the* crucial time when associated financial decisions are also taken. This link was a strong underlying reason for the move into estate-agency ownership by insurance companies, banks and building societies in the mid to late 1980s. The first stop in the house-buying process is the estate agency, which provides a good opportunity to try to sell mortgages and related financial services (endowment cover and house insurance, for example).

The house-price slump and the drop in the turnover of properties in the late 1980s after the general rise in interest levels, made the high price per branch paid for estate agencies seem very costly indeed. It remains to be seen how well the purchases can weather the storm.

It is possible that recent developments are leading to growing financial literacy. The plethora of financial advice columns in newspapers and magazines (and the surrounding advertisements) certainly suggests a growing sophistication. It has been argued that consumer sophistication, along with convenience, has become an increasingly important demand influence (Watkins and Wright, 1986). It is difficult to quote convincing statistical evidence, although it is worth noting that recently introduced pensions and life products are more sophisticated and include flexibility to switch between protection and savings, as noted above.

Bequeathed wealth offers marketing opportunities for lump-sum investment – a very competitive market place with a whole range of options and the wide availability of specialist portfolio management services to provide specialist advice.

The North-South divide

There is strong statistical evidence (*Social Trends*, 1988, for example) of geographical variations which have financial services opportunities. It is well-known that there are political differences, income and employ-

Table 2.4 *Economic data by region*

Region	Population (millions)	Total personal disposable income (billions)	Total consumer expenditure (billions)	Total personal savings (billions)	% of UK personal savings
Scotland	5.2	19.3	17.1	2.2	8.5
North	3.1	10.9	9.3	1.6	6.2
North West	6.4	24.1	20.9	3.2	12.3
Yorks and Humberside	4.9	17.0	15.1	1.9	7.3
E. Midlands	3.9	14.8	12.5	2.3	8.8
W. Midlands	5.2	18.7	16.4	2.3	8.8
Wales	2.8	9.6	8.5	1.1	4.2
E. Anglia	1.9	7.3	6.4	0.9	3.5
S. East	17.1	76.3	68.9	7.4	28.5
S. West	4.5	17.3	14.9	2.4	9.2
N. Ireland	1.6	5.3	4.6	0.7	2.7
UK	56.5	221.0	195.0	26.0	100.0

Totals may not add up, due to rounding
Source: *Regional Trends*, 21, HMSO (1986), p. 120

ment differences, home-ownership and house-price differences between North and South in the UK.

Geographical segmentation of financial markets can be coupled with other segmentation bases, notably socio-economic ones, to provide a more sophisticated and narrowly targeted marketing approach. Financial products targeted at 'the family' are likely to be replaced by a much more specific set of products targeted more precisely at particular market niches. Table 2.4 shows economic data by region and illustrates the potential importance of each market for financial services suppliers.

Demographics

The UK has an ageing population, as Table 2.5 shows. About 15 per cent of the UK population is aged over 65, with women outnumbering men in the ratio of about 3:2. The number of people in their 60s will actually decline in the 1990s, owing to the low birth rate in the 1930s, but in the early years of the next century the 'baby boom' of 1947 will produce a 'granny boom'. By 2031 about 25 per cent of the UK population should be aged over 65 on current trends. As might be expected from the previous section, the distribution of pensioners is skewed. In the south-west over 20 per cent of the population is of pensionable age and over-75-year-olds are more prevalent in Sussex, Dorset and Devon than anywhere else.

Consumer debt

The level of consumer debt rose during the 1980s. Much of the debt is mortgage debt but the rise in non-mortgage debt (unsecured loans, credit card accounts) is causing problems. One indicator of the problem is the number of house repossessions because of persistent

Table 2.5 *United Kingdom population projections (millions)*

Age	1981	1986	1991	1996	2001	2011
0–14	11.6	10.8	11.0	11.7	12.0	11.0
15–44	23.8	25.0	25.0	24.2	24.2	24.0
45–64	12.4	12.3	12.4	13.2	13.8	15.8
65–74	5.2	5.0	5.0	5.0	4.8	5.2
75+	3.3	3.7	4.0	4.2	4.4	4.4
Total	56.4	56.8	57.5	58.3	59.0	59.4

Totals may not add up, due to rounding
Source: *Social Trends*, 18, HMSO (1988), p. 24

Table 2.6 *Repossession by building societies, 1979–89*

	Year	Number
	1979	2530
	1980	3020
	1981	4240
	1982	5950
	1983	7320
	1984	10870
	1985	16770
	1986	20930
	1987	22930
	1988	16150
(first half)	1989	6352

Source: Building Society Association

default on mortgage repayments, and the trends in this area are illustrated in Table 2.6. These numbers are still very small as a proportion of total mortgages, but have strong social implications. The negative public relations possibilities for a financial firm seen to be turning families out of their homes are undoubtedly a cause for concern. Building societies are moving into much more of a pro-active debt-counselling role. For example, when interest rates on mortgages moved up to 14.95 per cent in late 1989, the Abbey National announced that it would be approaching all its customers with large mortgages (defined as being over £100,000) to discuss any repayment problems that may have arisen.

Debt-counselling facilities are provided by local authorities and citizens' advice bureaux on a relatively limited scale, but reported increasing demand in the mid to late 1980s. The moral responsibilities of lenders have been called into question on occasion. The pressure to make sales can lead to marginal cases being allowed credit, mortgage facilities or other financial services which may turn out not to be in the borrowers' best interests. As discussed in Chapter 1, the Financial Services Act, which grew out of a perceived need for consumer protection, has provided some safeguards for buyers by requiring suppliers to offer best advice. The provisions of the Act only apply to a limited range of financial investments and insurance products. The potentially negative media coverage may be a potent force in ensuring that financial product suppliers do not make irresponsible decisions in their choice of customers.

Table 2.7 gives more details of mortgage provision by region.

Financial literacy

Despite the difficulties, already observed, in measuring financial

Table 2.7   *Building society mortgage advances, 1986*

Region	Average income of borrower	Average purchase price	% of advances over £30,000	Price of housing land per hectare
Scotland	12,400	28,200	13	NA
North	10,800	24,300	5	130,600
Yorks and Humberside	10,600	25,600	6	107,400
North West	11,100	27,500	9	96,100
East Midlands	11,300	28,500	9	127,000
West Midlands	11,200	28,400	11	178,000
Wales	11,000	27,400	8	74,300
East Anglia	12,400	36,100	20	129,700
South East	15,800	50,400	52	561,800
South West	12,500	38,500	22	230,600
N. Ireland	11,600	25,700	9	NA

Source: *Regional Trends*, 23 HMSO (1988), p. 64

sophistication among buyers, there is some evidence that users of retail-store cards and bank-credit cards are becoming more aware of the extremely high APRs which have to be paid if full repayment is not made within the appropriate interest-free period. This evidence is authenticated by the suppliers of the bank-credit cards, who are said to be contemplating the introduction of a fixed annual fee for each card because an increasing proportion of holders repay their total debt within the interest-free period, thus reducing the profit of the suppliers.

Certainly, the availability of financial advice from the media is increasing. Coverage of personal financial services is particularly strong in weekend 'quality' newspapers, radio, and some TV shows, both popular (of the investigative type) and of minority appeal (the business show type). It is more difficult to assess the demand for such provision. Traditionally, financial advice has been provided in the UK at the cost of the supplier rather than the buyer. Thus, insurance brokers and other financial intermediaries receive commission on sales from suppliers and usually make no charge to buyers. Attempts to provide advice services independent of these commission charges, that is by charging buyers, have not been particularly successful.

There is little hard evidence of substantial shopping around by the majority of buyers in choosing financial services, nor of switching between suppliers on a large scale, although the example of building-society chequeing accounts is a significant exception. Convenience of access to branches of particular banks and building societies and to provision of financial services in the home (direct mail, direct response advertising and home calls by sales people) have been found to account for a significant proportion of supplier choice decisions (Watkins and Wright, 1986).

The Financial Services Act's requirement to match products to specific customer needs has led to the offer of financial planning services by some insurance companies. The sales presentation is preceded by a customer-needs analysis. This 'advice' provision is intended to avoid high-pressure selling techniques, which have been associated with the life-insurance industry in the past.

The corporate market

The corporate market for financial services has been subject to a number of broad structural developments. With increasing industrial concentration, the number of corporate customers has declined, but the value of the business associated with these customers has increased correspondingly. The growth in business activity at an international level has also meant that the needs of corporate customers have become increasingly varied. The policy-promoted expansion in the small-firms sector has meant that financial institutions have had to face the problem of designing products for a group of small-scale corporate customers with quite different needs and often limited experience of business. As a sector, the corporate market realized the benefits of deregulation and increased competition much earlier than the personal sector. The 1970s, for example, saw an increase in international activity by the major UK and overseas banks; competition for corporate accounts increased and split banking became more common.

There are many areas in which the corporate market differs from the personal market, and these differences will have important implications for marketing efforts. The needs of the corporate market tend to be more complex, and this requires matching skills from the sales force dealing with such customers. At the same time, corporate buyers usually have a much more complete understanding of their financial requirements, and the scale on which they tend to operate gives the supplier much greater scope to tailor products to specific requirements. The international dimension is of much greater relevance in the corporate market, requiring that institutions offer a much broader product range to their corporate customers, and those customers tend to be much more closely influenced by the state of the economy both nationally and internationally. It can also be argued (Turnbull and Gibbs, 1987) that the idea of the supplier developing a 'relationship' with the customer is of particular importance to the corporate sector.

Table 2.8 *Segmentation by parts of corporate financial structure*

Sector	Fixed assets	Working capital	Product need
Primary	High	Medium	Long-term mainly non-bank debt at fixed rates. Interest rate exposure management. Limited demand for short-term bank debt and money transmission
Manufacturing	High	High	Long-term, non-bank debt. Short- and medium-term bank debt. Interest rate and foreign currency management. Efficient money transmission service. Debtor collection and exposure management
Services	Low	Medium	Relatively low usage of bank products. Greatest need probably understanding of business, due to low level of security available for borrowing
Retail	Medium	Low	High cash flow requires efficient and cheap cash-handling services and money transmission. Premises, if not rented, provide acceptable security for medium-term lending if required
Wholesale	Low	Medium/high	Short-term and, to a lesser extent, medium-term bank loans, but access to short-term tradeable paper market an increasingly attractive source

Source: Carey (1989)

Since the nature of financial service provision can have a significant impact on the development of a particular business, it is important for both parties to develop a good working relationship.

Although there are a number of broad features which can describe the corporate customer, patterns of demand and the nature of services required will vary across sectors. Carey (1989) examines the demand characteristics by industry type for the banking sector, and his analysis, outlined in Table 2.8 highlights the diversity of services required.

The marketing implications of demand trends

A number of marketing implications can be identified from the above analysis of demand issues and trends.

Market-share battle

The deregulation of financial services provision, as discussed in Chapter 1, has contributed to the breakdown of the traditional boundaries between banks and building societies and to a lesser extent insurance companies. Growing internationalization has occurred, especially in relation to the 'big bang' in the City of London, when the stock market was liberalized, and to 1992, when easier access to pan-EEC markets should be available. Merger and acquisition activity in the sector has grown, and financial conglomeration has been a growing trend. The polarization requirements of the Financial Services Act have led to a number of joint venture deals, which may progress into more permanent arrangements, between insurance companies and building societies.

In these circumstances supply capacity is greater than demand capacity, and a battle for market share is the result. As an example, a house-buyer could in some circumstances hope to obtain a mortgage from any one of a whole range of suppliers, including building societies, banks, insurance companies, specialist mortgage companies and local-authority sources. Reference has already been made to the battle for chequeing account services between banks and building societies. In addition, a plethora of savings vehicles exists for the personal saver. Long-term savings could be made via insurance policies, building society or bank deposit accounts, unit trusts, investment trusts, stocks and shares, national savings certificates and many other outlets.

In this market-share battle suppliers are likely to make increasing use of marketing techniques. Marketing is becoming an increasingly

Table 2.9 *Length of time marketing and marketing research departments established in personal financial services*

Time	Marketing	Marketing function (%)	Research function (%)
Function absent	16.4		71.8
Less than 1 year	8.2		3.6
1–2 years	19.1		4.5
3–5 years	20.9		8.2
6–10 years	20.9		6.4
Over 10 years	11.8		5.5
Not known	2.7		–
Total	100.0		100.0
No. of respondents	110		110

Source: Davison *et al.* (1989)

important activity in financial services provision. It is a relatively recent phenomenon, as shown in Table 2.9.

Market research is less common as a function but is growing in importance and is discussed below. Unsurprisingly, the study referred to in Table 2.8 found that it was the larger suppliers which had the longest-established marketing departments. Other studies have found similar results (Morgan and Piercy, 1988).

Attractive market niches

Some of the legislation affecting the financial services sector has opened up new market opportunities. The Social Securities Act, 1986, which liberalized the provision of pensions, is one example; and the scheme for personal equity plans (PEPs), enabled and extended in various recent budgets, is another. The demand analysis earlier in this chapter illustrates various attractive market niches – products aimed at women, the self-employed, the elderly, single-parent families could, if successfully adopted, hit growing portions of the population. The identification and targeting of such niches is made possible by the growing availability and sophistication of customer databases, which can be used in conjunction with direct mailings to specified individuals.

The sales force in advisory role

If the Financial Services Act is effective in that it gives confidence to consumers that they can trust the financial advice they receive, the role of the sales force as advisers will develop (see Chapter 7). In the past, financial services, particularly insurance-sales forces, have not had a very positive image. The image is polarized in popular conception into either hard sell or soft sell. The hard-sell image relates to the commission-only sales forces who need to sell to earn and who often have reputations for unscrupulous tactics to achieve sales not in the customer's best interests. The soft-sell image relates to the industrial branch insurance collectors who have regular contact with their client base but as collectors of premiums rather than as cross-sellers of other financial products. In the former case any advice given is unlikely to be trusted because of the perceived self-interest of the seller. In the latter case advice may not be offered because the seller is not well-trained to spot sales opportunities, even though advice could well be trusted because the seller is well-known to the buyer.

The requirements of the FSA on best advice (see Chapter 1) could lead to the sales force offering more impartial advice. This implication is much more likely to occur in distributors which have made polarization decisions in favour of being independent rather than tied distributors. It is noteworthy that the FSA requires a preliminary needs analysis to be conducted before customers are offered financial products covered by the Act. Some insurance suppliers have incorporated the needs analysis into their marketing approaches, promoting free advice sessions, guaranteeing that no sales approach will be made during this meeting. Personal financial planning services have been built around this approach.

The underlying motivations which result in purchases of financial services are held to be deeply rooted. Concepts such as 'future-orientation' and 'looking after the family' are built on complex psychological and sociological influences. Culture, upbringing, family, social class, motivations, attitudes to saving, are influences which, when combined with economic considerations, produce idiosyncratic approaches to financial services purchasing which can be influenced, *inter alia*, by the sales force.

Product proliferation, which has been one result of deregulation, has produced a need for more consumer advice. As noted in the previous section, the levels of sophistication among financial services consumers are difficult to measure, and historically 'paid for' advice has not been common in this sector. Positioning the sales force as advisers may be one way in which suppliers can exploit this latent consumer need.

Multi-channel marketing

Traditionally financial services organizations have each used only one route to their customers. Banks and building societies have used their extensive high-street branch network. Insurance companies have used insurance brokers or their own direct sales force. In the new environment, suppliers have forged new alliances and started using more than one channel each. New channels include:

1 Estate agencies
2 Direct mail
3 Direct response advertising
4 Joint ventures
5 Moves from independent to tied agencies
6 Setting up direct sales force

Joint ventures have become a common response to the FSA

polarization requirement, in that building societies and insurance companies have latterly and now commonly opted for the tied route, as noted in the previous chapter. More specific detail on the current arrangements is contained in Chapter 8, Table 8.1. Building societies have become very important retailers of insurance products and have exploited their buying power to secure good commission levels from insurance companies desperate to avoid being excluded from market access. It is interesting to note that some leading building societies have set up a separate arm to offer independent advice from leads from the branch network.

The insurance companies who have not been 'selected' by building societies for a joint venture have distribution problems. They have reacted in a number of ways, most commonly seeking new routes at the risk of upsetting their existing broker relationships. Sun Alliance has become a major user of direct response advice, spending £10m+ per annum on national newspaper advertising.

Most financial services suppliers have begun to use direct mail. Banks and building societies have begun belatedly to exploit their mailings of statements to customers to make direct-mail offers to their client base. Customer databases have been used to make these mailings much more of a rifle than a shotgun approach, and more sophisticated targeting of market segments is becoming possible.

The distribution element of the marketing mix of financial services suppliers has become very important because of the demand and supply pressures affecting the sector.

Corporate positioning

A further demand implication is the need to establish a corporate image and strategy which differentiates the organization from its rivals. While the major banks have been consistent high spenders on corporate image advertising and have clear, well-defined logos which are well known to the public, insurance companies and building societies have not been in such a happy position. Up until the early 1980s the building societies operated a price cartel in which all charged common rates on mortgages and saving accounts, and changes were announced by the Building Societies Association. Since this cartel broke down, the societies have competed much more between themselves, predominantly using mass media advertising to create name awareness and price (i.e. interest-rate) based appeals. They have actively tried to create corporate positions which could give them a competitive edge over their rivals.

Insurance companies have traditionally been anonymous

monoliths, unrecognized by a large majority of the public. In the new competitive environment, especially when wishing to sell direct to the public, a need for corporate identity has arisen. As we shall see in Chapter 4, spending by insurance companies on mass-media advertising rose rapidly in the late 1980s.

A wider product portfolio

Suppliers have reacted to the new deregulated environment and the demand trends discussed earlier in this chapter by broadening their product portfolios. The most common source of new product ideas in the sector is copying from competitors (Davison *et al.*, 1989). Little strategic thought seems to have been given to the preferred product portfolio, but piecemeal additions to the range have been made and, less commonly, deletions to the range if not successful.

All these marketing implications are developed further later in the book. Here the objective has been to try to link the implications to demand and supply trends in the sector. Thus, the aim in the following chapters is to identify marketing strategy responses to the changing competitive environment.

Market research

Before moving to this marketing strategy analysis, it is necessary to give brief consideration to market research. Such research can be seen as the process by which suppliers obtain information on the changing competitive environment, particularly:

1 Monitoring competitor activity
2 Monitoring market shares, i.e. consumer behaviour
3 Identifying consumer needs

These will be treated separately.

Monitoring competitor activity

The financial services sector is in many ways very parochial. For many years it was almost unknown for executives to be recruited from outside the sector. This situation changed first of all with the advent of large-scale data-processing and outside experts were widely recruited. In the mid to late 1980s a similar trend occurred with marketing staff.

There are several long-established industry bodies, e.g. the ABI and the BSA, and intermingling of executives from different companies is frequent. In this environment intelligence on competitor activity is not too difficult to obtain. Collecting product information from competitors is commonplace; the trade press is one major source, and annual reports of competitors can also provide useful information.

Secondary information may also be obtained from competitors. While it is difficult to approach competitors directly for information, their annual reports can give useful leads as to future intentions. Another source of information is trade journals, which will often give early indications of sales successes or forthcoming new products. Trade bodies, such as the Association of British Insurers and the British Insurance and Investment Brokers Association in the UK, are other possible sources of summarized data.

In addition, much secondary information can be obtained from government publications. The Census of Population and Product data can be used to identify market potential, growth rates and macroeconomic influences. In the UK, such reports as *The Family Expenditure Survey, Social Trends and Economic Trends* are other easily available sources of socio-economic and demographic data.

In an attempt to persuade advertisers to use their media vehicles, all the media owners publish a vast array of data relating to their audiences. These data cover not just media accessibility but also socio-economic data, and attitudinal and consumer-durable ownership data. The obvious application is in advertising campaign planning, but other uses are also feasible.

Finally, from time to time, syndicated market research studies are undertaken and sold 'off the shelf' to interested parties. These can be on the impact of particular events, in specific attitudes or on particular market segments, and may or may not be relevant to market-intelligence needs. Other studies are conducted on a regular basis with a panel of respondents, the reports being available to subscribers.

Monitoring market shares

Trends in market shares are most usually obtained from syndicated research studies, which carry out interviews on a regular basis on financial product purchases and/or sales and thus provide trend data on market shares. One example is the National Opinion Polls *Financial Research Survey* (Whitmore, 1988), which carries out regular surveys of consumers and investigates their ownership of various financial products. Other surveys of insurance brokers and other financial intermediaries are available (e.g. Taylor Nelson Monitor Service,

where a representative panel of 400 insurance brokers is ir
quarterly to investigate marketing effectiveness of
companies, company image, advertising and promotions).
hoc surveys of the sector are undertaken from time to
Euromonitor, which investigates the major suppliers and ca
primary research data.

Identifying consumer needs

Insurance companies and brokers have the potential benefit of a rich
seam of customer information in the proposal form. The exact
information will vary according to the specific proposal form, but
typical examples of data which could be available for marketing use
include the following: name and address of customer, postcode and
telephone number, occupation (and, from this, social class), age,
marital status, place of birth, medical history, house type and
ownership status, ownership of specific consumer durables (e.g.
freezer), and car details; and for business customers, type and location
of business, value of stock, profits, payroll, etc.

Banks and building societies also collect much customer data when
new accounts are opened and mortgage applications are made. These
sources are a very useful starting point. They provide information on
the company's 'successes' – their existing customers for their existing
products. But what about the 'failures' – the ones that got away and
presumably bought rival products from rival suppliers? One source is
applications made for services but not subsequently taken up. However, the reason for non-take-up may not be obvious from the
application form and a follow up telephone call may be necessary.
Although this information is negative, it is useful in helping refine
marketing strategy to avoid losing customers in the future.

Secondary sources of information can be supplemented by trade
gossip, feedback from salesmen, agents, complaints analysis, exhibitions and conferences, and a range of other low-cost sources to add to
the understanding of buyer behaviour. In many cases, however,
specific information will be required, in which case primary sources
must be used. The company must then decide (1) how to specify and
interpret terms of reference and objectives for the research; (2) what to
ask (questionnaire development); (3) who to ask (sample size and
structure, sampling procedure); (4) how to contact respondents; (5)
how to ask for information, e.g. self- or interviewer-completed
questionnaires, dichotomous (yes-no), polychotomous (multiple-
choice) or open-ended questions; (6) short or in-depth interviews; how
to analyse the resultant data (which statistical method to use); (7) how

57

to interpret the results in terms of the original terms of reference; and (8) how best to present the findings with appropriate recommendations.

Typical uses of primary research in the financial services sector include:

1 *Advertising research.* To plot a proposed advertisement campaign by testing it on a small sample of customers
2 *Direct-mail research.* Testing a direct-mail offer on a small sub-sample of the intended audience to assess effectiveness
3 *New-product research.* In depth interviews with potential customers to assess their reaction to a proposed new product

Market segmentation – the development of customer databases

The availability of detailed customer information in financial services companies can lead to the systematic use of computer-based data in marketing activities. The most common use to date is in targeting direct-mail shots, but more elaborate methods are being developed (Cornell and Bond, 1988). Software now available allows for a customer database to be accessed by any one variable, or combination of variables, known about the customers. Thus mail shots to all existing male customers in the 35–9 age range living in Oxfordshire with a mortgage over £30,000 could be customized from a database. The sophisticated use of customer data can lead to higher return rates from direct mailings and can ensure that the product offering can be very specifically tailored to the needs of the customer segment selected.

Thus the use of customer databases can facilitate the segmentation of the market, and could, for example, reflect some of the qualitative trends discussed earlier in the chapter.

Setting up a customer database is costly and time-consuming. In practice it is likely to be a subsidiary activity to the need within the financial services organization to administer accounts/policies/product efficiently. When financial services organizations were first computerized in the 1970s, for administrative reasons it was common to hold data by account or policy rather than by customer. Thus a customer with several accounts or policies would, if the database were used unamended for a mail shot, potentially receive several letters. Such an occurrence is unsatisfactory. Because large financial services organizations can hold details of several million accounts/policies, the task of switching to a customer-based system is complex. However, such a move is now thought to be worthwhile because of the increased competition in the sector.

It is important, because of the competitive situation in the sector, that marketing considerations are given the first consideration. The need for customer orientation is best expressed through a database based on customers rather than products.

While a database for existing customers is an excellent starting point in the financial services sector, it is possible to augment these data by using some or all of the other sources discussed earlier in the chapter. Consumers receiving quotes not subsequently taken up could be recontacted systematically. Mailing lists can be bought, so that selling through direct mail to non-customers can be attempted. A word of warning: any list purchased needs to be checked against the customer database for duplication – what the Americans call 'purging the dups' – otherwise an existing customer may receive a mail shot which presumes that he/she is not a customer, and that will hardly contribute to harmonious customer relations.

Conclusions

This chapter has considered the demand for financial services in both quantitative and qualitative terms. It is the foundation for the chapters to come, in that it has identified the implications of these demand pressures in terms of marketing strategy opportunities.

The chapter has also considered how market research and customer databases can be used to inform organizations about the market place and competitive pressures and to add sophistication to the marketing segmentation process.

CHAPTER 3
Marketing strategy and planning
Christine Ennew

Introduction

The financial services sector has undergone considerable change in the last decade; the traditional institutional divisions which characterized financial markets are disappearing as organizations seek to take advantage of environmental change to offer their consumers a more integrated range of financial services. Financial markets themselves have become increasingly international, technology has developed to improve the speed and variety of service provision, and a trend towards deregulation has widened the potential product range for the majority of suppliers. In periods of rapid change, whether legislative, institutional or technological, the need for a planned approach to marketing becomes increasingly important to guide the organization in its approach to an increasingly unknown and uncertain future.

Planning at both strategic and operational levels is a key element in the successful management and marketing of products and services. The strategic component of marketing planning focuses on the direction an organization will take in relation to a specific market or set of markets in order to achieve its objectives. Marketing planning also requires an operational component which details specific tasks and activities to be undertaken in order to implement the desired strategy. Developing such a planned, strategic approach ensures that the marketing efforts of any organization are consistent with organizational goals, internally coherent and tailored to the needs of identified consumer markets.

This chapter will consider the role of marketing planning in the financial services sector. The first section will deal with the key concepts of strategic marketing, and the rest will consider the development of marketing strategies. The focus throughout will be on the strategic aspects of marketing planning, including strategies for growth, sources of competitive advantage and methods for planning the product portfolio. Subsequent chapters will confront more specific

operational issues relating to the development of appropriate marketing mixes.

Strategic marketing

Within any organizations, strategies develop at several levels.
Corporate strategy deals with the development of an organization's
business activities, while marketing strategy focuses specifically on the
organization's activities in relation to the markets served. It has been
suggested that organizations in the financial services sector have been
slow to adopt a strategic approach to their marketing activities. As a
business function, marketing has tended to play a largely tactical role.
However, Clarke *et al.* (1988) suggest that, in the banking sector at
least, there is a move towards recognizing the integral role of
marketing in organizational strategy. Their views are supported by
Hooley and Mann (1988), who observed a clear trend towards market-
driven strategies in a recent survey of financial service providers.

There are many forms which strategy can take; two commonly
identified forms are deliberate and emergent strategies. The concept of
deliberate strategy is based on the notion of strategy as a process, i.e. a
strategy which exists as the result of conscious planned activities. The
concept of emergent strategy is based on the notion of strategy as a
pattern, i.e. activities and behaviour which develop unconsciously but
which fall into some consistent pattern. In practice, it is frequently the
case that most strategies which are pursued by firms are part deliberate
and part emergent. To the extent that they are deliberate, they are
usually the outcome of some planning process. In the context of
developing a marketing plan, the notion of strategic marketing can be
seen as having three key components:

1   Designation of specific, desired objectives
2   Commitment of resources to these objectives
3   Evaluation of range of environmental influences

From the point of view of the organization, strategy is not just about
being efficient; it is crucially concerned with enabling the organization
to be effective. The efficiency component simply relates to doing a task
well: the effectiveness component relates to doing the right task –
having the right products in the right markets at the most appropriate
times. Thus, for example, from the perspective of a bank, strategy goes
beyond simply ensuring that money transmission activities are performed in the most cost-effective manner; it requires that the bank is

supplying the *right* type of money transmission facility – that which best meets the needs of the bank's customers.

The organization can only be effective if it is aware and responsive to the environment in which it operates. In a sense, it can be argued that marketing is, by definition, strategic, since to be able to market a product successfully ultimately requires that the firm has the right type of product and is operating in the right markets. However, it is perhaps worth emphasizing that the concept of strategy has a dynamic component: it implies effectiveness and efficiency, but it also implies responsiveness – developing an awareness of environmental change and identifying appropriate and effective reactions to that change.

Developing strategy

There are numerous variants of marketing plans, but a key feature of any particular format that is used is that it should follow a logical structure, from historical and current analyses of the organization and its market, on to a statement of objectives, then to the development of a strategy to approach that market, both in general terms and in terms of developing an appropriate marketing mix, and finally to an outline of the appropriate methods for plan implementation. While offering a coherent set of clearly defined guidelines to management, the plan should remain flexible enough to adapt to changing conditions within the organization or its markets.

In principle, the methods of marketing planning which have been developed extensively in relation to products can be transferred to the marketing of financial services. However, in practice, there are some features of financial services which necessarily add an additional dimension to the planning problem. In particular, we should recognize the dependence of financial services on the individuals (branch employees, sales staff) who deliver them, the difficulties associated with quality control and the problems associated with presenting essentially intangible services to a consumer. While this need not alter the necessary stages associated with the planning process, it may alter the relative emphasis placed on those stages. An outline of a possible format for a marketing plan is contained in Figure 3.1.

Company mission and objectives

The mission statement essentially requires that the organization defines the areas of business within which it operates, and defines it in a way which will give it focus and direction. In effect, the mission

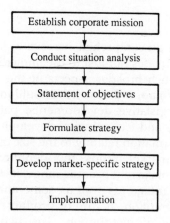

Figure 3.1   *Marketing planning*

statement defines areas in which the organization has distinctive competences. The nature of the corporate mission depends on a variety of factors. Corporate history will often influence the markets and customer groups served – thus Crédit Agricole retains strong links with its farming depositors (Channon, 1986) while Coutts concentrates primarily on high-income consumers in its retail banking activities. Corporate culture may also influence the ways in which an organization approaches its markets and customers.

The commonest approach to determining the corporate mission is to rely on the *product/market scope*. This entails defining the business in terms of customer groups, needs served and technology employed. This approach seems particularly beneficial from the marketing perspective, since it forces managers to think of the customer groups and the particular set of needs/wants the firm is looking to satisfy. The importance of this idea has its roots in the concept of marketing myopia (Levitt, 1960). It is not sufficient for a firm to identify its mission as being 'insurance' – it would be more appropriate to identify that mission as being 'meeting consumer needs for risk reduction and financial security'. A mission statement of this nature can offer guidelines to management when it considers how the business should develop and in which directions. With the benefits of a clear mission statement, future growth strategies can look to rely on what are regarded as distinctive competences and aim for synergies by dealing with similar customer groups, similar customer needs or similar service technologies.

Situation analysis

This entails presenting a comprehensive review of the current marketing environment. It relates not just to the immediate market environment but also to much broader aspects of the macro environment (Sanderson and Luffman, 1988), which should include an analysis of economic trends, legislative developments, patterns of social and demographic change and technological developments. At the market level, it requires information relating to the size of the current market, market shares and market trends, the identification of major competitors, statements of current product range, its features and its basis for competitive advantage, as well as some analysis of patterns of distribution and promotion, nature of product, market share, sales trends and patterns of distribution. The two previous chapters reviewed the key aspects of the external environment which affect the strategies of organizations in the financial services sector. The main source of such information relating to the organization's external environment is marketing research, either in-house or from off-the-shelf reports. Additionally, to develop a suitable strategy, an organization will require some analysis of its internal environment in order to assess its capabilities and limitations in relation to a particular market/product/customer group. Information of this sort will usually be collected as a result of an internal audit of an organization's marketing activities.

This process can generate a considerable volume of information, which, despite its importance, may be of limited practical use to planners. Accordingly, there is a need to organize the main points of any situation analysis in order that management may be presented with analytic summaries to guide future strategy decisions. Gap analysis and SWOT analysis are two of the most commonly used techniques for organizing the information collected in relation to the firm's marketing environment.

Effective situation analysis is increasingly dependent on the development of efficient mechanisms for the collection and analysis of information, particularly in an environment which is rapidly changing and thus difficult to monitor. Technological developments have undoubtedly led to improvements in data-processing capabilities, and in many financial services organizations have created the opportunity for the development of increasingly sophisticated customer databases. However, recent research (Mitchell and Sparks, 1988; Morgan, 1989) suggests that organizations in the financial services sector still have some way to go in terms of developing fully integrated marketing information systems.

Statement of objectives

Any plan must be guided by a coherent set of objectives, which are indicated or determined by the nature of the firm's corporate strategy. The objectives set for any marketing plan must fulfil three important criteria: they must be achievable, they must be consistent and they must be stated clearly and preferably quantitatively.

Strategy formulation

Given the available information and the targets which have been set, planners must develop suitable strategies in order to identify which markets the company intends to enter and the way it anticipates entering them. This process will often be conditioned by corporate strategy, and requires some assessment of how the organization is to develop its business in relation to its particular markets. Key features of this exercise will include an examination of the extent to which there are different segments present in the market, identifying which of those segments to focus attention on and how to position the service within those segements.

Market-specific strategy

The market-specific strategy constitutes the set of policies and rules which will guide the marketing effort for a specific service or group of services in relation to a specific set of markets. There will be two key components:

1   Determining the appropriate level of marketing expenditure. The extent to which the marketing division can control this will obviously vary according to firm-specific policies and the company's financial position. However, any marketing plan would require a statement of the budget required to implement it.
2   Developing the marketing mix, i.e. the combination of product, price, promotion and place which will ensure that the service is appropriate in terms of its features, its image, perceived value and availability. In the context of services, it has been suggested that the marketing-mix elements should be broadened to include featues such as personnel and the physical environment in which the service is delivered (Cowell, 1984). However, the need to make this distinction is open to debate, since these features, which are aspects of the delivery system, can readily be considered as components of the 'place' element of the marketing mix.

Implementation

This requires an identification of the specific tasks which need to be performed, the allocation of those tasks to individuals, and the establishment of a system for monitoring their implementation, e.g. identifying the nature of any short-term marketing research which needs to be undertaken to determine how appropriate the product is, the nature of customer reactions, etc. The implementation procedure may also include some elements of contingency planning. However well thought out the marketing plan may be, the market is always changing. Consequently, certain planned activities may turn out to be inappropriate or ineffective; it is important to be aware of these and be in a position to respond, i.e. to modify the strategy as new information becomes available.

Aspects of the marketing environment facing the suppliers of financial services and the development of the marketing mix for financial services are considered in depth elsewhere. Accordingly, the focus of the rest of this chapter will be on the formulation of a broad marketing strategy.

Strategy formulation

The formulation of an organization's strategic approach to its marketing activities is essentially concerned with developing some 'match' between the organization and its operating environment (Piercy and Peattie, 1988). The resulting strategy must enable the organization to meet the specific needs of its consumers, and to do so more effectively than its competitors. While there are a number of analytical techniques which management can employ, the role of these techniques is not to offer definitive statements on the final form that a strategy should take, but rather to provide a framework for the organization and analysis of ideas and information. No one technique can always provide the most appropriate framework, and those discussed below can and should be regarded as complementary rather than competitive.

Growth strategies

A common framework for the analysis and determination of growth strategies is Ansoff's Product/Market opportunity matrix (Ansoff, 1965), which is discussed in the context of the banking sector in Chapter 9. In developing a strategy for growth, the organization must determine whether to concentrate on existing or new products and existing or new markets. This suggests four possible options – market penetration, market development, product development and diversification – the first three of which are regarded as intensive growth strategies, and the last as a form of extensive growth.

Market penetration

The organization aims to sell more in its current markets by persuading existing users to use more (increasing the extent of life coverage, offering higher rates of return for increased levels of savings), persuading non-users to use, or attracting consumers from competitors. Barclaycard's 'Profiles' scheme, which allocates points to consumers for the use of the card, with these points then entitling the user to a variety of free gifts, is a simple strategy to encourage existing users to increase usage. By contrast, American Express, in order to encourage non-users to use, offer free gifts to existing card-holders who introduce new members. As a strategy for growth, market penetration will only work where the market is not saturated.

Market development

This requires that the organization looks to sell its existing products in new markets. These may be new markets geographically, new market segments or new uses for products. As a strategy, it requires effective and imaginative promotion, but it can be profitable if markets are changing rapidly. The various marketing strategies used by the clearing banks to attract student accounts, including a variety of 'special offers', provides a simple example of an exercise in market development. Movements into new markets geographically is probably the most common form of market development, and the 1992 programme may present particular opportunities for UK insurers in this respect. Barclays for example envisage that movements into the credit-card market in Europe will be an important strategy for maintaining levels of profitability in this increasingly competitive market.

Product development

This entails developing related products and modifying existing products to appeal to current markets. The key features of a product-development strategy are restyling service products, the addition of new features and quality changes. Recent developments in the mortgage market provide a good example of product development.

The traditional standardized mortgage account is rapidly being supplemented by variants which offer lower starting rates, special terms for particular types of customer, particular mixes of fixed and flexible repayment rates, etc. A strategy of this nature relies on good service design, packaging and promotion, and often plays on company reputation to attract consumers to the new product. The benefit is that, by tailoring the products more specifically to the needs of some existing consumers and some new consumers, the organization can strengthen its competitive position.

The advantage of intensive growth strategies is that they tend to be low on risk. Diversification tends to be a more risky strategy, with the risk increasing as the organization moves into areas where it has limited experience. However, it may be the only suitable strategy if existing products and markets offer few growth opportunities. Perhaps the most common form of diversification among providers of financial services has been concentric diversification, which means developing new products that are related to existing products in terms of both markets and technology, such as the movement by the banks into mortgage provision. However, with the recent deregulation and the increase in competition, there has been an increase in the levels of contiguous (horizontal) diversification, which involves services that are technologically dissimilar but appeal to the same broad customer groups, e.g. building societies moving into money transmission and estate agency. Conglomerate diversification, which covers both new markets and new technology, is a comparatively rare phenomenon in the financial services sector because of the limited opportunities for synergy and the greater risks.

Competitive strategies

One of the most widely used approaches to the development of strategies to maintain a competitive position is based on the work of Porter (1980, 1985). The strategy adopted by a firm is essentially a method for creating and sustaining a profitable position in a particular market environment. Two key factors determine the profitability of an organization:

1 The inherent profitability of an industry
2 The organization's competitive position *vis-à-vis* its rivals

The organization in an inherently profitable industry may perform badly with an inappropriate strategy, while the organization in an inherently unprofitable industry may perform well with the appropriate strategy. Industry attractiveness and profitability depend (as economic theory would suggest) on the structure of the industry and specifically on five key features:

1 Bargaining power of suppliers
2 Bargaining power of consumers
3 Threat of entry
4 Competition from substitutes
5 Rivalry between firms

These factors affect costs incurred and prices received, thus also affecting profitability. Success does not depend only on being in the right industry, because the strategy which the firm pursues can influence industry structure and profitability. In determining strategy, Porter suggests that the firm must consider whether to adopt a broad or narrow competitive scope and whether to aim for competitive advantage based on differentiation or cost advantages. A typology of strategies is presented in Figure 3.2 and the significance of these strategies is discussed in more detail in the context of the Building Societies in Chapter 10.

Cost leadership

The aim is to control industry structure by being the low-cost producer,

Competitive scope

	Broad	Narrow
Competitive advantage / Differentiation costs	*Cost leadership* E.g. specialist mortgage supplier	*Cost focus* E.g. regional building society with savings and mortgage facilities only
	Differentiation leadership E.g. national/international bank with money transmission, mortgage and insurance	*Differentiation focus* E.g. insurance broker offering wide range of financial advice

Figure 3.2   *Competitive strategies*

and it requires up to date and highly efficient service delivery systems. Generally, the product is undifferentiated, but a firm cannot ignore differentiation, since the cost savings for the consumer must compensate for the loss of product features, while the discount offered by the firm should not be so high as to offset cost advantages. It can be argued that cost leadership was a traditional strategy in many areas of financial services before deregulation, as suppliers tended to take an institutional- rather than consumer-orientated view of their markets (Ennew *et al.*, 1989).

Differentiation

Essentially the firm seeks to offer products which can be regarded as unique in some dimensions that are highly valued by the consumer. It is the product's uniqueness and the associated customer loyalty that protects the firm from its competitors, from the threat of entry and from substitute products. The differentiator cannot ignore costs – the costs of differentiation must be less then the premium charged for the firm to remain profitable, but, at the same time, the customer must feel that the extra features more than compensate for the price premium. In the light of deregulation and the opportunities it offers, many organizations are moving away from their traditional narrow product range to offer a much greater range of products, both differentiating their traditional products and expanding into new product areas.

Focus/nicheing

This strategy uses either costs or differentiation but concentrates on specific segments of the market. The aim is to identify part of the market with distinctive needs which are not adequately supplied by major producers in the market. Differentiation focus is the most common form of focus strategy, and implies producing highly customized products for very specific consumer groups. A number of smaller building societies have opted for differentiation-based strategies, resulting in the appearance of specialist savings products for children (Peckham Building Society's 'Jumbo Savings Account' and Greenwich Building Society's 'Adopt a Duck' scheme) and equity release plans for retired home-owners. However, cost-focus strategies are not uncommon in the financial services sector, particularly where markets are segmented geographically. For example, many of the regional and local building societies appear to be selecting a cost-focus strategy, even in the light of deregulation, concentrating specifically on the provision of a traditional service range in a narrowly defined geographical market (Ennew and Wright, 1990b).

Porter's analysis stresses the importance of avoiding a situation where the organization is 'stuck in the middle', i.e. trying to be all things to all consumers. The firm trying to perform well on costs and on differentiation is likely to lose out to firms concentrating on either one strategy or the other. Equally, it should be recognized that, in a period of rapid market change, the strategy selected as a basis for establishing competitive advantage may not be sustainable if all other organizations are reassessing their strategic position at the same time. Accordingly, an element of experimentation may be part of strategy selection (Thwaites, 1989).

Matching environment and strategy

The process of SWOT analysis is one that is widely used by firms for organizing information relating to the marketing environment and providing guidance on strategy development. The basic principle of SWOT analysis is that any statement about the organization (derived from a marketing audit, for example) or about the environment (derived from marketing research or sales forecasts or consumer analysis) can be classified as a strength, weakness, opportunity or threat.

An opportunity is defined as any feature of the external environment which created conditions which are advantageous to the firm in relation to a particular objective or set of objectives. By contrast, a threat is any environmental development which will create problems for a firm in achieving its specific objectives. What consistutes an opportunity to some firms will almost invariably constitute a threat to others. An increased presence in domestic financial markets by overseas banks might be regarded by domestic banks as a threat, particularly in relation to the corporate side of their business (Lewis, 1984). By contrast, the recent changes relating to state pension schemes might be regarded as an opportunity for building societies, banks and insurance companies in relation to personal customers.

A strength is considered to be any particular skill or distinctive competence within the organization which will aid it in achieving its stated objectives. These may relate to experience in specific types of markets or specific skills possessed by employees either in relation to production, R&D or marketing. It may equally include aspects of corporate culture/image, e.g. a firm's reputation for quality, customer services, etc., may all be regarded as strengths. A weakness is simply any aspect of the company which may hinder the achievement of specific objectives, and may include limited experience of certain markets/technologies, nature of reputation, or extent of financial

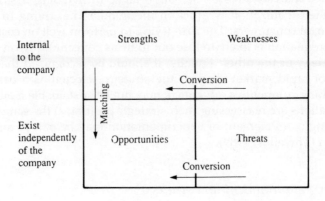

Source: Piercy and Giles (1989)

Figure 3.3   *SWOT analysis*

resources available. The lack of experience within building societies of money transmission facilities could be regarded as a weakness when considering the development of current accounts, while banks may consider their experience in wholesale money markets to be a strength in relation to the development of mortgage services.

These data are commonly presented as a matrix of strengths, weaknesses, opportunities and threats. There are several points to note about the presentation and interpretation. First, it should be recalled that effective SWOT analysis does not simply require a categorization of information, it also requires some evaluation of the relative importance of the various factors under consideration. In addition, it should be noted that these features are only of relevance if they are perceived to exist by the consumers (Piercy and Giles, 1989). Listing corporate features that internal personnel regard as strengths/ weaknesses is of little relevance if they are not perceived as such by the firm's consumers. Equally, threats and opportunities are conditions presented by the external environment, and they should be independent of the firm. Thus, it is inappropriate to identify the potential for price-cutting as an opportunity, for it is not – it is a strategy which may be implemented by the firm if the opportunity exists. When the opportunity is highly price-sensitive consumers, the strategic response could then be price-cutting.

Once a matrix of strengths, weaknesses, opportunities and threats, with some evaluation attached to them, has been constructed, it then becomes feasible to make use of that matrix in guiding strategy formulation (see Figure 3.3), as follows:

1 *Matching*. The need to try to match the particular strengths of the company to the opportunities presented by the market environment. Strengths which do not match any available opportunity are of limited use, while opportunities which do not have any matching strengths may require the firm to reconsider its internal situation, if they are to be capitalized on.

2 *Conversion*. Developing strategies which can be used to convert weaknesses into strengths in order to take advantage of some particular opportunity, or converting threats into opportunities which can then be matched by existing strengths.

This process should not exclude the development of completely new strategies, which may occur simply as a result of SWOT analysis encouraging a systematic approach to the analysis of the marketing environment.

Selecting the product portfolio

As has been indicated earlier, diversification has become an increasingly common trend in the financial services sector. In response to an increasingly competitive and deregulated environment, the major suppliers of personal financial services have been expanding their product ranges. While the nature of product strategy is discussed in greater depth in Chapter 4, this trend poses important questions which require attention at the level of market planning and strategy. In particular, they raise the issue of how, in a strategic sense, the organization should manage its product portfolio. Managing the product portfolio raises broad issues. What role should a product play? How should resources be allocated between products? What should be expected from each product? Of particular importance is the notion of maintaining some balance between well-established and new products, between cash-generating and cash-using products, and between growing and declining products. Two common approaches which are used to plan product portfolios are the matrix-based approaches of the Boston Consulting Group and the General Electric Business Screen, and the concept of a product life-cycle.

Matrix-based approaches

Both the BCG and the GE matrices require a classification of products/ business units according to the attractiveness of a particular market and the strengths of the company in that market. The BCG matrix bases its classification scheme purely on market share and market

73

growth, while the GE matrix relies on more subjective measures of market attractiveness and business strengths. In both cases, the appropriate strategy is determined by the position of a product in the matrix. A simple example of the GE matrix is presented in Figure 3.4; each market is represented by a circle with the diameter proportional to the market size and the shaded segment representing the organization's market share. The matrix approach is not unrelated to the concept of the product life-cycle, as has been illustrated by Barksdale and Harris (1982), who suggest that the patterns of product development implied by the BCG matrix are consistent with the notion of some form of product life-cycle. The use of matrix-based approaches has been subject to some criticism, particularly the BCG matrix, because its rationale is the existence of a strong and positive relationship between profitability and market share. Further problems arise with the rather arbitrary nature of the classification procedures (O'Shaughnessy, 1988), which tends to suggest that, although these techniques can offer some useful insights, their results need to be interpreted with care.

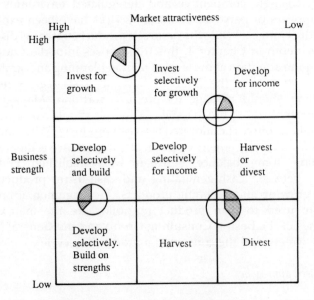

Note: Circles represent particular businesses; their size is proportional to the market size and the shaded area represents the company's market share

Figure 3.4 *The General Electric Business Screen*

The product life-cycle

The notion of a product life-cycle is one that is widely used as a tool for market planning, in that it can be employed both to guide an organization in the determination of the appropriate balance of products and in the development of a suitable strategy for the marketing of those products. Although a familiar concept in the marketing of products, there is no reason to believe that the basic principles are not applicable to services in general (Cowell, 1984) and to financial services in particular (McIver and Naylor, 1986; Marsh, 1988). However, Black *et al*. (1985) suggest that there are some difficulties in considering the life-cycles of certain types of financial service, because the cash flow from the product can easily be confused with the product itself. They cite, in particular, loan products, which will require cash for their launch but will initially also be net users of cash, since that is the basic feature of the product. They argue that this adds some complexity to the use of life-cycles in product planning but does not invalidate the basic concept.

It is argued that a service, like a product, will pass through four basic stages, from introduction, through growth to maturity and eventually into decline. The concept is not, however, one that is universally accepted; indeed the notion of a life-cycle is often seen as an exercise in attributing biological laws to inanimate objects. While the idea of a life-cycle should perhaps not be taken too literally, the basic idea which underlies this model can be useful in guiding marketing decisions.

The role of marketing is generally considered to be one of prolonging the growth and maturity phases, often using strategies of product modification or product improvement, which are frequently regarded as less risky than new-product development. While the basic life-cycle pattern (see Figure 3.5) is stylized, it gives some indication of the patterns of development. In particular, we should note that the life-cycle is longer for the product class (e.g. loans) than it is for the product form (e.g. car loans), and longer for the product form than it is for the specific brand. Given the increased level of competition in the financial services sector, Watkins and Wright (1986) argue that organizations should be aware of the potential for increasingly short life-cycles, and be prepared to adjust their strategies accordingly. They cite the example of the variety of savings accounts which developed as a result of the competition between banks and building societies. The resulting array of products had the potential to create confusion among customers, and, in response to this, a number of building societies opted to rationalize their range of accounts to give consumers a clearer indication of the type of account and the benefits available.

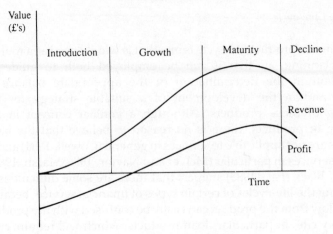

Figure 3.5   *The product life-cycle*

Assessing the existing product range according to life-cycle position can give some indication of the balance of the existing product portfolio. Furthermore, according to stages in the life-cycle, the organization can obtain some guidance as to the appropriate marketing strategy, as follows:

1   *Introduction.* A period of slow growth and possibly negative profit as efforts are made to obtain widespread acceptance for the service. Cash flows are typically negative and the priority is to raise awareness and appreciation of the product, with the result that the marketing mix will place a high degree of emphasis on promotion. In the financial services sector it is of considerable importance that new products are introduced quickly and that this phase of the life cycle is shortened, because of the ease with which new products can be copied. Building society cheque accounts might be regarded as products which are at present in the introductory stage of their life-cycle.

2   *Growth.* Sales volumes increase steadily and the product begins to make a significant contribution to profitability. Increase in sales can be maintained by improvements in the features, targeting at more segments or increased price-competitiveness. It is at this stage that the new service product will begin to attract significant competition. Growth services include personal pensions and unit-linked life insurance.

3   *Maturity.* Sales begin to stabilize, with replacement purchases becoming more common than new purchases. The market itself is mature and the marketing campaign and product are well established. Competition is probably at its most intense at this stage, and

it may be necessary to consider modification and rejuvenation of the service to arrest future decline. Building society ordinary share accounts and bank current accounts are products which can be seen as having reached maturity and in many cases are being modified in attempts to prolong their life-cycles.

4 *Decline*. Sales begin to drop away noticeably, leaving management with the option of withdrawing the product entirely, although often with long-term investment products this may not be feasible; in this case the alternative is a withdrawal of support but maintenance of the product. Alternatively, if the product is seen as one with a potential long-term future, then the appropriate strategy may be one of rejuvenation. In the financial services sector it should be noted that barriers to product withdrawal are often high; some products such as life insurance cannot simply be withdrawn from the market, because some customers will still be paying premiums. Consequently, the more appropriate strategy may be to minimize the marketing effort rather than formally withdraw the product (Davison *et al.*, 1989).

The use of the product life-cycle in marketing planning can provide some guidelines for the allocation of resources among service products, enabling the organization to attach high priority to growth products and medium priority to mature products, and consider possible withdrawal of declining products.

Market segmentation

A key element in any process of strategy formulation is market segmentation, the process of identifying and even creating distinct segments within the market to which specific financial services can be targeted. The most obvious segmentation issue in relation to financial services is the distinction between wholesale (corporate) and retail (personal) markets. Increasingly, however, this form of segmentation is not sufficient. Within the corporate market, distinctions can be drawn between firms on the basis of geographical coverage, types of business, turnover and also perhaps on the basis of the degree of financial sophistication within the firm (see Carey, 1989, for a more detailed discussion of segmentation issues relating to the banking sector). There is no reason why segmentation should end at these broad levels; Roach (1989) reports on the more detailed segmentation exercise undertaken by Girobank specifically in relation to small businesses. By carefully segmenting this market, Girobank was able to identify how best to launch its new services for small businesses and which groups to target.

In the retail market there is an equal diversity of market segments. One of the more traditional approaches to market segmentation in the financial services sector was based on income and wealth. While this type of segmentation remains important (Stanley *et al.*, 1987), it is by no means the only basis for market segmentation. Many suppliers of financial services have found that segmentation based on lifestyle and life-cycle offers significant opportunities for product development and differentiation. Students, for example, are increasingly targeted as a distinct segment by the banks, Midland launched its Vector account specifically to appeal to the 'yuppie' market and many building societies are targeting the 'retired' segment of the market with mortgages to release equity holdings in property.

In developing an effective pattern of market segmentation, a number of important criteria must be recognized. First, the segments must discriminate between groups on the basis of their purchasing behaviour. Second, the segments must be identifiable and measurable. Clearly this is much easier when segmentation is based on objective variables such as income. Psychographic segmentation, based on attitudes and behaviour, is increasingly seen as more appropriate for distinguishing between consumer groupings, although the measurement process is rather more complex. Third, the segments identified should be sufficiently large to justify the development of specific products, and organizations should be able to communicate with those segments in a cost-effective fashion.

The significance of segmentation is probably greatest for firms looking to pursue a market nicheing strategy and tailor its financial services to the needs of a specific group of customers. At the same time, it cannot be ignored by organizations competing across a much broader area of the market, since successful differentiation is ultimately based on being able to tailor products to the needs of particular groups. In the context of the financial services sector, it is important to note that differentiation arises not only from the features of the service product. Given the particular significance of service delivery and the inseparability of production and consumption in services, the quality of service provision can be equally effective as a basis for differentiation (Lewis, 1989).

While many of these techniques discussed above are extensively used in relation to product markets, their application in the financial services sector appears to be rather less well developed. A survey of financial institutions in 1987–8 found that the most popular technique for formulating corporate strategy was brainstorming. Banks did indicate that SWOT analysis was important in their strategy formulation, but generally growth-share matrices, life-cycle analysis and similar techniques tended to receive rather low rankings (Ennew and

Wright, 1990a). However, it would appear that this results from a lack of familiarity with such techniques, rather than from the unsuitability of the techniques themselves.

Conclusions

The environment facing the suppliers of financial service has changed dramatically over the past decade. Deregulation, in conjunction with developments in information technology and fluctuations in economic performance, has resulted in an increasingly competitive market environment. The traditional institutional boundaries which existed between suppliers of financial services are breaking down; banks, insurance companies and building societies are all competing across the same broad markets. In such an environment, success requires a planned and strategic approach to marketing. The organization must be clear about its products and the markets it serves, and it must develop a thorough understanding of their various facets. It must have a clear statement of where it plans to go in the future and a clear indication of the most appropriate route to get there. That strategy itself is one that should be consistent with the distinctive competences of the organization itself and must match the environment in which it operates. Neither of these is immutable; strategy can be used to modify the environment either internally or externally. However, in a period of environmental turbulence it is becoming increasingly important to recognize that strategies are not fixed; they can be adjusted and often need to be adjusted as the pattern of environmental change becomes clearer.

CHAPTER 4
Product strategy
Christine Ennew

Introduction

The product is the central component of any marketing mix; however competitively priced, imaginatively promoted and effectively distributed that product may be, if it does not offer the key features that consumers expect, the organization lacks an effective basis for long-term success in a competitive market. The product component of the marketing mix deals with a variety of issues relating to the development, presentation and management of the product which is to be offered to the market place. As such, it covers issues such as developing an appropriate product mix and product line as well as considering decisions relating to the attributes and features of individual products. It also, and perhaps most importantly, deals with aspects of new product development. Extending product ranges, either by new product development or through the modification of existing products, is a commonly observed strategy in the rapidly changing and increasingly competitive financial services sector. In particular, the banks (Rothwell and Jowett, 1988) and the building societies (Ennew and Wright, 1990b) have already taken advantage of opportunities to develop and extend product ranges.

In order to examine the product component, it is important to define clearly what is meant by the term 'product'. This chapter begins by examining the concept of the service product and the factors which will influence the development of the product strategy. Subsequent sections deal specifically with aspects of the product-range strategy and the process of new-product development in the financial services sector.

The concept of the service product

Like products, any service is purchased by consumers not for itself but for the benefits it offers, i.e. for the basic customer needs it fulfils. The intangibility of services makes the definition of what constitutes the service product a potentially complex exercise (Cowell, 1984). The marketing literature presents a variety of frameworks for the analysis of the components of a product, and these provide a useful framework for examining and defining the service product in general and the financial service product in particular. Kotler (1986, 1988), for example, distinguishes between the core, tangible and augmented product, while Levitt (1980) focuses on the products generic, expected and augmented components. In each case the analysis is based on the idea that any product can be seen as offering a basic set of featues which might be considered as its essential features from the consumer's viewpoint. Beyond this, products are augmented by a variety of additional features which associate it with a particular supplier, differentiate it from competing products and make it in some sense distinctive.

In the case of services, we can consider the core or generic element as being composed of those features which provide for certain broad consumer needs. Thus, for example, a unit trust would constitute a core or generic service which fulfils investment needs on behalf of the consumer. The tangible or expected elements give a service a more specific identity by adding shape and features to the core or generic product. In the case of a unit trust, this would include an association with a specific supplier (branding), choice of investment realization method (income v capital growth), projected returns, accessibility, etc. The augmented element would then incorporate features which go beyond those that would be expected by the consumer. In the case of a unit trust, this might include the option to invest only in 'socially responsible' companies.

While these frameworks are useful in conceptualizing the components of a financial service, and establish a link between product and service marketing approaches, there is one further element which is of relevance in defining the service product. The nature of service is such that the basic product cannot be distinguished from its delivery system, and that delivery system must also be included as a component of the service. Certain aspects of the delivery system can reasonably be considered as components of the expected or core service, while others may usefully be characterized as part of the augmented service.

Service strategy in the marketing mix concentrates on identifying the core features required in any basic service and on developing the most appropriate peripheral features to augment that service. However, in the services sector there are a number of features of the product which complicate the process of developing and presenting it to the market:

1 *Services are intangible.* A service cannot be seen, touched or displayed. A customer may purchase a particular service but has nothing physical to display as a result of the purchase. Money transmission is a service which customers pay for and is performed by banks, but the customer does not obviously have anything to show as a result. The same can be said of insurance, savings and investment services.

2 *Services are inseparable.* In general, it is impossible to separate the production and consumption of a service. Most goods are produced and subsequently sold to consumers; by contrast, the service product is sold and then produced. As a result, services are perishable – they cannot be stored, they must be produced on demand and often can only be produced in the presence of the customer.

3 *Services are heterogeneous.* The quality of the service product is usually highly dependent on the quality of the personnel conducting the transaction. As a result, the potential for variability is high. The quality of service a customer receives from a bank when making a loan application will be dependent on the performance of the loan assessor; the bank will be judged on that rather than the quality of the resulting loan. The reduction of quality variability requires standardization in service delivery, such as the use of ATMs.

These features are present to varying degrees in financial services products. A key aspect of product strategy for any financial services organization is to confront these issues and attempt to resolve them. A common strategy is to develop a tangible representation of a product, e.g. credit cards and cheque cards are tangible representations of money transmission and credit facilities. Indeed, the credit card goes one stage further and provides a facility which actually enables the consumer to store credit. When the process of direct association is not feasible, an alternative is to rely on developing associations between the service and other tangible items which represent stability. A particular variant is to focus on the organization and the nature of the relation between buyer and seller (e.g. Listening Bank). A further advantage of such a tangible representation is that it makes the process of differentiation and the establishment of brand loyalty more straightforward. Furthermore, as we shall see later, the notion of developing a tangible representation of the service is crucial in the development of an effective promotional strategy.

Influences on product strategy

Products, particularly service products, are not immutable. The successful organization will undertake a process of monitoring products, their performance and the requirements of the market place to give them the information necessary to modify existing products and develop new products. Regular market research is crucial in this respect to provide the organization with the necessary information regarding market developments and market reactions to the organization and its products. Monitoring the environment is necessarily an ongoing process and should be part of any planned approach to marketing. In the context of product strategy, it is of particular importance to monitor:

1 *Customers* – their tastes and preferences, life styles, demographic change
2 *Competitors* – their marketing mix, new and modified products
3 *Distributors* – new threats in distribution and new opportunities
4 *Legislation* – opportunities and threats created

The legislative aspects of the environment have been of particular importance in relation to the financial services sector, and their impact on product ranges is discussed in some detail in Chapter 1. Chapter 2 discusses some of the trends in consumer markets and their implications for product development and marketing.

Throughout the analysis of influences on product strategy, a key issue is the most appropriate pattern of response. It is not operationally or financially feasible for an organization to react to every change in the marketing environment; at the same time, no organization can afford to miss key opportunities which may be presented by legislative, social or economic change.

Product-range strategy

The majority of organizations offer a range of products to a variety of customer groups; the product strategy concerns itself with the management and development of this range to ensure that the organization maintains and improves its competitive position in the various markets in which it operates. The range of activities which constitutes product management is potentially very broad (see, for example, Stevenson, 1989, for a discussion of aspects of product management in corporate banking).

The first key issue in relation to product strategy is the determination of an appropriate product mix, which describes the range of products an organization chooses to offer. Decision-making in this area is frequently a component of the strategic plan, because of its implications for diversification and patterns of growth. Traditionally, in the financial services sector, organizations have been characterized by a limited product mix – banks concentrating on money transmission, building societies on savings and housing finance, and insurance companies on insurance products. In part, the narrow mix was determined by legal restrictions on the products that could be supplied by particular types of organization, but it was reinforced by the traditionally conservative nature of financial institutions. The combination of deregulation, developments in information technology and the resultant increase in competition have led many organizations to expand their product mix considerably.

In the context of the marketing mix, the components of product strategy range from decisions on the attributes and presentation of individual products, through decisions regarding the most appropriate mix of products to offer, to decisions relating to the development of new products and the withdrawal of existing products. While each of these aspects of product strategy will be considered separately, it should be recognized that they are necessarily interdependent; product-attribute decisions have implications for the product mix and decisions relating to the product mix will also have implications for aspects of the new product-development process.

Product attributes

In development, a variety of attributes are attached to the generic product in order to differentiate it from the competition and tailor it more specifically to the needs of customers. These attributes normally include quality, style features, brand name, packaging, labelling and after-sales service. In the financial services sector, marketing managers face similar decisions. The generic service product (money transmission, for example) has to be developed into some tangible or augmented form (the Midland Vector Account or the Nationwide FlexAccount). The importance of developing a suitable set of product attributes was highlighted in a recent survey of financial organizations (Hooley and Mann, 1988); the features of the product – its design, performance and its match with customer requirements – were cited as the most important determinant of success or failure in new-product launches.

One of the key issues in developing the service product is to attempt to overcome the problem of intangibility. When purchasing a financial service, the customer cannot see or examine the product and can only accurately judge its performance once the purchase has been made. An important aspect of the organization's attribute decisions is to overcome this problem of intangibility by developing some physical representation of the service product. The most obvious tangible representations of service products are the chequebooks and cards which accompany current accounts; building society passbooks and well-presented insurance certificates may also be regarded as tangible representations of intangible products.

Quality, which is regarded as an increasingly important product feature, refers to the ability of a product to perform its intended task. In financial services, the quality aspects of a product are inextricably linked with the actual provision of the product, which is in turn usually highly dependent on the individual who deals with the consumer. As a consequence, quality control can be a difficult exercise, requiring investment in staff training and the establishment of a quality-orientated corporate culture. The recent developments in 'relationship banking', particularly in the corporate market, can be regarded as an attempt to improve the quality aspects of banking services (Watson, 1986; Turnbull and Gibbs, 1987).

The range of features offered as part of a particular service product is important as a mechanism for differentiation to appeal to specific market groups. Again, in relation to the range of features offered, it is important to stress the aspect of personal service in relation to financial products; the range of actual distinct features which can be attached to a particular financial service is limited and may not provide a long-term basis for differentiation, since such features are easily copied. Offering interest payments on chequeing accounts might constitute an extra product feature which can be attached to a money transmission product; if successful, it is easily copied and may not generate much increased business for the innovator. By contrast, improvements in the quality of service provision in general, and customer care in particular, are recognized as being important key strategies for successful product differentiation (Lewis, 1989).

Branding is an attribute which is often regarded as being central to the marketing of products, but is less common in the service sector (Cowell, 1984). The obvious problem associated with branding services is the difficulty of maintaining a consistent level of quality. Yet branding is important as a mechanism for conveying information to consumers and as a means of establishing a degree of customer loyalty. In the financial services sector, it is probably the customer's image of the organization which is the most important type of branding available (Howcroft and Lavis, 1987). Casual empiricism tends to support this conclusion, since most financial products are identified primarily by the supplier's name; there is some evidence to suggest a move away from the company trade-name brand to individual product brands – thus Midland's decision to brand the Vector account and Nationwide Anglia's decision to brand their Flexaccount. Even with these developments, it seems unlikely that the use of the organizational name will disappear, since it remains perhaps the most important source of information and indicator of quality available to customers.

Product modification/product development

Irrespective of the attributes that may be assigned to service product initially, some adjustments may be required at later stages in the product's life. Product modification is often pursued in the maturity stage of the life-cycle to attract new customers and differentiate the product from the competition. Product modification does not add to the product line, as such, but implies effectively replacing an existing service with a new and improved version. Related to the process of product modification is the process of product development, which constitutes a process of modification resulting in the appearance of new but related products. Essentially this will call for some form of product-line stretching or product proliferation.

Product modification in financial services aims to improve the performance of an existing product. This may entail making the service easier to use (fixed annual repayments on existing mortgages, for example), improving the quality of the service (personal account managers for corporate clients) or improving the delivery system (the introduction of ATMs). The importance of product modification is considerable in an increasingly competitive market place. With financial services suppliers diversifying and the number of products proliferating, significant improvements in existing products can be an important strategy for maintaining and expanding the existing customer base. There are clearly risks associated with devoting additional resources to existing products, particularly at the maturity/ decline stage of the life-cycle, but these risks may well be small in comparison with those associated with new product development and diversification.

Product-line stretching or product proliferation entails adding new services to an existing service line, and has traditionally accounted for much of the new-product development activity in financial institutions. The Midland Vector account described below is a simple example of adding a new service to an existing service line. The rationale for any line-stretching exercise is to differentiate existing products further in order to appeal to more specific segments of the markets. Since line-stretching entails a form of new product development in a market with which the organization is familiar, the risks tend to be relatively low, although there is the danger of over-segmenting in the line-stretching process. The potential to identify a large number of segments among the consumers of financial services exists, but many of those segments may be small or insufficiently distinct to justify the addition of a new service line. Excessive product proliferation can then result in overly long service lines, which can cause confusion among consumers. Consequently, line-stretching exercises must consider not only the potential to add new lines but also the scope for rationalizing existing lines. With the increased competition between banks and building societies, both in personal savings and money transmission, a large range of different accounts appeared, but consumers experience considerable difficulty in distinguishing between the products on offer. Accordingly, a number of building societies, recognizing this problem, opted to rationalize the relevant service lines in order to clarify the range of products on offer to their customers (Watkins and Wright, 1986).

Case Study 1
Service line-stretching:
The Midland Bank Vector Account

Segmenting personal customer markets provides a basis for product differentiation and more accurate targeting of customer needs. The Midland Vector Account, launched in May 1987, was an attempt by Midland Bank to extend the range of accounts available to its customers, offering a current account with a number of new features targeted at a specific group of consumers. The Vector account was based on lifestyle segmentation, concentrating on the young, affluent independent consumer – the 'yuppie' market. It was targeted specifically at the 25–44 age group with salaries in the region of £12–25,000 and the typical customer was considered to be someone who was well-educated, confident, with a sophisticated and easy lifestyle.

This particular segment was seen to have considerable growth potential; the number of Bs and C1s in society was forecast to grow, and they were expected to become increasingly affluent as inheritance windfalls from property continued to rise. Furthermore, the bank recognized the importance of trying to break down the traditional view of the banks and the 'superior attitudes adopted by many branch managers'. The importance of relationship banking was growing on the personal side as well as on the corporate side.

The account offers a moderate rate of interest, free overdrafts up to £250 and no unexpected charges. In return, the account holder pays a fixed fee of £10 per month. The account was essentially designed to run itself, provided that a monthly salary cheque appeared, to cater for the needs of consumers who are willing to incur the monthly charges in order to save themselves the time and effort associated with running their finances. The monthly charge provides Midland with a guaranteed income, which contributes to the estimated 9 per cent costs of running current accounts. The initial take-up was in the region of 70,000, which provided Midland with a fee income in the region of £8.4m.

Recognizing the ease with which financial products can be copied, Midland elected to brand the new account heavily to establish emotional as well as rational appeals to their customers. The promotional package was developed using a common set of images in a 'modern style' format, and included cheque book holder, filing box and Filofax style wallet. The theme used was that banks should treat their customers with respect.

Prior to the launch of the Vector account, Midland recognized the need to launch the product to its staff. One of the key dangers with the approach that was being taken is that the product image could be undermined if branch managers and staff failed to live up to the image that Vector was presenting. Accordingly, prior to the launch, some 500 managers attended a one-day conference to familiarize them with the product and its image. This was complemented with the preparation of a training video and information packs to be used to familiarize branch staff with the new product.

(Source: *Marketing*, 1987.)

New-product development

One of the most important aspects of product strategy relates to the issue of the development of new products, a strategy which is becoming increasingly important as the intensity of the competitive environment increases. In many organizations, the resources devoted to new-product development (NPD) are substantial, yet it should be remembered that much of the work carried out under this heading is not always the production of brand new products; frequently, it relates to the development and modification of existing products. In this section we will consider two specific types of new product development:

Major innovations

These are products which are new to the organization and new to the market. As such, while they offer great potential in terms of returns, they are inherently more risky, since they will require a much higher level of investment, the use of different and new technologies, and possible moves into areas in which the organization is comparatively inexperienced. Major innovations in the financial services sector, as in many sectors, are comparatively rare.

New service lines

These refer to products which are new to the organization but not new to the market. Since there are competing products already established in the market, the potential returns may be lower, but, at the same time, the organization is moving into an area with which it is considerably more familiar, either in terms of the technology or the markets. It is one of the more common forms of NPD in the financial services sector, particularly so as deregulation has removed many of the barriers which had in the past restricted certain types of organization from offering certain types of product. Thus, for example, the decision by many building societies to move into estate-agency services, insurance and pensions can be regarded as the addition of new service lines rather than as major innovations. The process of adding to existing service lines and modifying existing service products can also be regarded as a form of NPD, although for the reasons indicated above these are treated separately.

There are a variety of frameworks proposed to guide new product development. The approach suggested by Booz *et al.* (1982) is widely accepted as an appropriate framework, although a number of alternatives specific to service industries have been suggested by Donnelly *et al.* (1985), Cowell (1984), and Scheuing and Johnson (1989). Despite the various formulations suggested, the basic components of any new product development process are essentially similar and are outlined in Figure 4.1.

New-product development strategy

Any exercise in new-product development must be systematically organized in order to ensure that effort and resources are devoted to the development of new products in areas which the organization regards as strategically important. The motivations for new-product

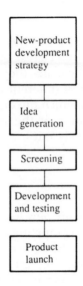

Figure 4.1 *New-product development process*

development should be clearly defined in order to provide some guidance in the process of formulating ideas. Thus, for example, it should be made clear whether the process of NPD is to be orientated towards taking advantage of new market segments, whether it is seen as crucial to the continued competitiveness of the organization, whether it is required to maintain profitability, whether it is designed to reduce excess capacity or even out fluctuating demands. There are numerous strategic factors which may underlie any process of NPD, but it is of considerable importance that these are clearly stated at the start of an NPD exercise.

Idea-generation

The process of generating ideas can take many forms both inside and outside the organization. Inside many organizations, there are often distinctive groups or individuals with particular responsibility for NPD; however, Scheuing and Johnson (1989) suggested that this particular management function was relatively underdeveloped in the financial services sector. Of equal importance in generating ideas may be the feedback that reaches management from the experiences of staff in their dealings with consumers. The results of market-research studies and information collected from consumers have traditionally been seen as an important breeding ground for new product ideas, although recent research would tend to suggest that this facility is relatively under-used in the financial services sector (Davison *et al.*, 1989). A significant number of new product ideas are developed from external sources, which may include the use of specialist new-product development agencies, learning from overseas or simply copying the competitors. Survey work reported by Davison *et al.* suggested that copying from competitors was a major source of NPD in the financial services sector, primarily because of the ease with which products could be copied and the lower risks and costs associated with doing the same as the competition but attempting to do it rather better.

Screening

The variety of ideas produced at the idea-generation stage must be screened to ensure their consistency with the organization's existing strategy, the extent to which they fit the image of the organization and its capabilities, their appeal to particular segments and their cost and profitability implications. In any NPD exercise, the evaluative criteria should be determined in advance of the process of idea-generation and should constitute, at least in part, the strategic guidelines to be used in NPD. Screening requires thorough evaluation: the application of weights to the different criteria and the development of rankings for the various ideas in terms of the suitability. Often the screening process passes through several stages. Initially all ideas are screened, using simple low-cost screening to eliminate any obviously un-attractive suggestions; as the screening process moves on, it becomes rather more complex and rather more expensive. Examples of first- and

Table 4.1 *Example of a first-phase screen for new-product development*

	Yes	No
1 Can the service be marketed through the existing delivery system?	x	
2 Is the service hard to imitate?		x
3 Will the service assist in building good customer relationships?	x	
4 Is the service compatible with corporate image?	x	
5 Is service quality easily maintained?	x	
6 Is the service compatible with existing skills?	x	
7 Is the service compatible with resource availabilities?	x	
8 Is there the opportunity to build a strong base in the relevant market segment?	x	
9 Is the service simple to understand?	x	
10 Are the income-generating opportunities good?	x	

Minimum score to advance is 6 'yes' responses
Source: Adapted from Donelly *et al.* (1985)

Table 4.2 *Example of a second-phase screen for new-product development*

Criteria	Raw score Poor(1)	Average(2)	Good(3)	Weight	Total
Extent to which target market needs service		x		x2	4
Potential profitability		x		x2	4
Compatibility with company strengths			x	x2	6
Opportunity for long term competitive advantage	x			x1	1
Durability (length of life-cycle)		x		x1	2
Total					17

Minimum score of 16 required to proceed
Source: Adapted from Donnelly *et al.* (1985)

second-phase screens which could be employed by financial services organizations are presented in Tables 4.1 and 4.2.

Following on from these preliminary screenings, a number of product ideas would be selected and subjected to a more detailed examination of their operational and financial viability. This process often requires a degree of product-specific market research.

Development and testing

Those ideas which have survived the screening process must then be translated into specific service concepts, i.e. into a specific set of features and attributes which the product will display. A particular feature of this process is that of establishing an appropriate position for the product *vis-à-vis* competing products, i.e. determining the way the product should be conceived by the customer. The two basic options are whether to position the product in direct competition with existing products, trying to offer something extra, or position it away from the competition to ensure that the new product is perceived as something quite different, although still fulfilling the same basic needs.

At this stage it is common to test this newly defined product and to identify consumer and market reactions in order to make any necessary modifications to the product before it is launched. The problem with test marketing in the financial service sector is that it gives competitors advance warning of an organization's latest ideas, and, given the ease of copying products, if offers competitors the opportunity to imitate. As a consequence, test marketing of financial services is comparatively unusual, being avoided by many organizations because the actual costs of developing new product are often low but the losses from giving advance warning to competitors may be quite high (Davison *et al.*, 1989). However, Donnelly *et al.* (1985) argue in favour of more extensive test marketing for financial services despite these perceptions of cost. They argue that there are significant benefits, not only in terms of feedback but also in terms of developing an appropriate marketing campaign to guide the product launch, and that it is 'better to be second with a good service – one that is thoroughly tested, and debugged – than it is to be first with a faulty service' (p. 153).

Product launch

The product launch is the final stage and the true test of any newly developed product; it is the point at which the organization makes a full-scale business commitment to the product. At this stage, the major decisions are essentially of an operational nature – decisions regarding the timing of the launch, the geographical location of the launch and the specific marketing tactics to be used in support of that launch.

The use of a structured and integrated framework for new product development will not, by itself, guarantee success. In a study of product innovation in commercial banks, Johne and Harborne (1985) identified a number of other general factors which they consider central to the success of NPD programmes. First, they suggest that it is important to maintain regular contacts with the external environment to identify changes in market characteristics and customer requirements. Second, the organization should develop a corporate culture which is receptive to innovative ideas – what Donnelly *et al.* (1985) describe as 'creating a climate of trying'. Third, they stress the importance of flexible management which stimulates and encourages the NPD process. Finally, they mention the benefits of identifying key individuals with specific responsibility for the NPD process. In this latter respect, recent studies by Scheuing and Johnson (1989) and Davison *et al.* (1989) suggest that few financial service suppliers have specialist NPD groups, and both studies also suggest that the use of market-research techniques is limited, which may in turn imply that many organizations are not maintaining the close degree of contact with their environment that is necessary for the effective and efficient development of new products.

Case Study 2
Developing a new service line:
The Nationwide FlexAccount

The Building Societies Act 1986 presented opportunities for the development of new service lines in this particular sector of the financial services industry. It was one that many societies were keen to take advantage of, not least because of the increased competition they were experiencing from the banks in their traditional area of business –the mortgage market. Nationwide Anglia saw the opening up of the market for money transmission as an opportunity to strengthen their customer base and reassert their competitive position against the banks. A money transmission facility was seen to be crucial to the society maintaining a competitive position in the financial services sector defined in its broadest terms. Furthermore, with the growing dependence of consumers on money transmission facilities, the development of a good working relationship with consumers based on such a facility was seen as the key to developing markets for related financial products. The problem they faced in offering money trans- mission facilities was their lack of experience in aspects of the technology associated with this facility combined with a degree of uncertainty regarding consumer reactions.

At an early stage in the development of this product, it was decided that branding was likely to be an important marketing tool, particularly since research had suggested that consumers did not easily differenti- ate between individual banks or building societies. The choice of brand name was a simple development from the features of the product. Four specific groups were identified as targets for the launch. First, the society's own staff who would sell the account to customers and so should be convinced of its benefits. Second 'high potential' and 'special potential' customers who were considered to be the most likely users of the account and, finally, the retail trade whose acceptance of the account would be crucial to its success among consumers. The launch was supported by carefully targeted advertising, extensive point of sale literature and staff training and motivation programmes to emphasize not just the features of the product, but also, to emphasize FlexAccount as a brand name. (Source: BSG, 1989.)

Conclusions

The intangibility, heterogeneity and inseparability of services inevitably create some difficulties in the process of developing an appropriate product strategy. Particular strategies to deal with these problems include the association of tangible items with the intangible service and focusing attention on the relation between the service-provider and the service-consumer. In this context, the development of a corporate image is becoming increasingly important and will be discussed in more detail in the following chapter.

The key to a successful product strategy is the development and maintenance of an appropriate product range. This requires that a financial service is developed with a set of features which correspond to consumer requirements, and that this range is constantly monitored so that existing services can be modified and new services can be developed. The process of new-product development in the financial services sector had tended to concentrate on the redesign of existing products within an organization's portfolio and the development of products which are new to the organization, though not necessarily new to the sector. The perennial problem which faces the provider of financial service products is the ease with which such products may be copied, and the consequent importance of ensuring rapid market penetration in the desired segment when new products are launched.

CHAPTER 5
Advertising and promotion
Christine Ennew

Introduction

Promotion as a component of any marketing mix is the mechanism by which an organization communicates with actual and potential customers, its own employees and other interest groups. The communications process in marketing has traditionally stressed the attributes and benefits of a particular good or service in order to create awareness, stimulate interest and encourage purchase. However, in practice, its role is much broader than this, encompassing all aspects of the image of an organization and the way that image is presented to a variety of interest groups within society. Communicating effectively with these interest groups requires a thorough and systematic approach to promotional planning to ensure that the message is correct and consistent with the desired image of the product or organization.

The promotion of financial services has many similarities with the promotion of physical products, although, as has been pointed out by Cowell (1984), some differences do characterize service promotion, either as a result of the nature of the service industries themselves or as a result of the characteristics of services. In developing a communications strategy, the particular problem facing suppliers of financial services is that they have no physical product to present to consumers; the task of promotion then focuses on developing a message and a form of presentation which allows the organization to present a product which is essentially intangible in a tangible form.

Trends in promotion

Among the various promotional tools available to financial services, perhaps the most visible is advertising. In recent years, the role of media advertising in the marketing of financial services has increased substantially, reflecting a growing recognition of the need to increase

Table 5.1 *Advertising expenditure (£m) by financial services organizations, 1981–8*

Year	Banks	Building societies	Insurance companies	Unit trusts	Total
1981	22.604	31.964	18.088	15.201	77.857
1982	31.485	44.295	24.410	6.121	106.311
1983	44.851	62.814	35.223	8.928	151.816
1984	51.962	60.196	37.962	10.581	160.701
1985	65.002	71.434	49.111	13.439	198.986
1986	68.135	68.573	62.896	25.624	225.228
1987	77.912	86.849	67.315	47.617	279.693
1988	–	–	96.346	–	–

Source: Media Expenditure Analysis Limited (MEAL)

consumer awareness of products and organizations in the financial services sector. Patterns of expenditure in relation to the marketing of financial services are detailed in Table 5.1, which confirms the increasing role played by advertising in this sector. Despite the fact that the financial services sector now outspends many of the traditional heavy advertisers in the fast-moving consumer goods sector of the market, a recent survey (*Marketing*, 1989) suggests that advertising by financial institutions has been less than successful as a result of the lack of a clear strategy for developing communications with customers. Yet, it is widely recognized that in an increasingly competitive market place effective communication will have a significant bearing on the success of an organization. The problem that faces many organizations is the difficulty of measuring the effectiveness of advertising (O'Shaunghnessy, 1988); pre-testing attempts to predict the likely effectiveness of a campaign and eliminate weak spots, and commercial market research, are widely used to determine levels of recall and comprehension, while econometric analysis is often used to assess the impact of advertising on the level of sales. General techniques of this nature are often unsatisfactory. Pre-testing does not guarantee effectiveness and many successful advertisements have failed pre-tests. Commercial recall and comprehension surveys can indicate whether a communications link has been established, but are less suitable for assessing how effective a campaign has been in terms of encouraging purchase. Equally, econometric and other techniques, which entail some element of comparison of sales on a 'before and after' basis, will be able to identify correlations but not necessarily indicate whether advertising has actually 'caused' an increase in sales. Ideally, evaluation of advertising should be organization/product specific, with clearly defined objectives and statements of what is to be measured and how; in practice, the costs of this approach often lead to a reliance on general, commercial studies and an acceptance of some loss of detail and relevance in the evaluation.

The communications process

The essence of the communications process can be described in terms of who says what to whom, through which channels and with what effects. The elements of a simple model based on this framework are presented in Figure 5.1 and described in greater detail in general marketing texts (e.g. Kotler, 1986). There are basically nine components:

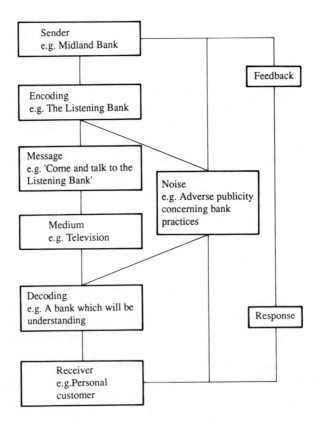

Figure 5.1   *The communications process*

1   *Source*: The party sending the message, either the organization or a quasi-independent body

2   *Encoding*: Finding some verbal or symbolic representation for the concepts used

3   *Message*: The set of words and symbols that the sender transmits

4   *Medium*: The channel through which the message is transmitted, either personal (sales staff) or non-personal (advertising, publicity or sales promotion)

5   *Decoding*: The process whereby the receiver assigns meanings to the message that has been transmitted

6   *Receiver*: The party receiving the message

7   *Response*: The receivers' reaction to the message

8   *Feedback*: Information on the receivers' response, which is transmitted back to the sender

9   *Noise*: Unplanned interference with the communications process, which distorts the message

This basic model highlights many of the important components of effective communication: the need to identify an audience, to develop an appropriate message, present it in a form which will attract the attention of the target audience and minimize the effects of noise. The presence of noise in the marketing environment is unavoidable, and there will inevitably be some distortion in the message – the target audience may receive only part of the message being communicated, they may interpret it in accordance with their own preconceptions and they may recall only parts of the message. Effective communications will aim to minimize distortions of this nature by keeping messages brief, distinctive and unambiguous.

Promotional planning

Planning the promotional effort calls for much more than simply developing advertising campaigns. As the financial services sector becomes increasingly competitive, and expenditure on promotions, particularly advertising, increases, effective communications will require a systematic and planned approach to promotional activity. The stages of promotional planning are outlined in Figure 5.2.

Objectives

In most instances, the desired outcome of any promotional strategy is to increase sales of a product; however, as mentioned earlier, an increasing number of promotional campaigns are targeted at creating, reinforcing or changing an organization's image in relation to specific

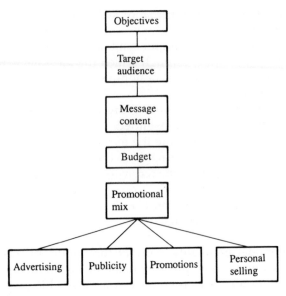

Figure 5.2 *Promotions planning*

groups. These can perhaps be considered the two key objectives of any promotions campaign:

1 *Stimulating demand*. Promotional campaigns aimed at stimulating demand from final consumers will have as their ultimate objective an increase in sales. However, given the complexity of the consumer's decision process, it is not sufficient simply to identify an increase in sales as an objective. In developing promotions it is important to be aware of the stage in the buying process which characterizes consumers.

2 *Corporate image*. Promotional campaigns in the financial services sector are increasingly being directed at corporate image. Recognizing the problem of product intangibility has led many oganizations to view the development of a positive image with society in general as being important in establishing brand loyalty and developing some tangible representation of the intangible product. The importance of image has been discussed in relation to banks by Howcroft and Lavis (1989), Morello (1988) and in relation to Building Societies by Smith and Harbisher (1989). For the financial services sector in general, Ennew *et al.* (1989) found that most organizations placed greater emphasis on image-orientated promotion. An additional advantage of this approach in relation to financial services is that it eases the burdens imposed by the FSA in relation to information requirements of advertisements.

Target audience

Planned promotion requires a clear statement of exactly who the target audience is. This will in turn be determined by market-segmentation decisions taken at an earlier stage of market planning. As well as defining who constitutes the target audience, it is also important to be aware of the position of that audience in relation to the product or the organization. The nature and extent of the consumer's knowledge and attitudes will condition both the formulation and presentation of the message. In considering the state of the target audience, simple buyer-response models can offer some guidelines. The best known is perhaps the AIDA model, which suggests that consumers pass through four stages from Awareness, to Interest to Desire and finally to Action. The precise formulation and presentation of a message will vary according to the perceived position of the consumer, and it has been suggested (*Marketing*, 1989) that advertising in the financial services sector has been less than successful because many organizations have not clearly identified their target audience.

Message content

The message content relates to the ideas and information that the sender wishes to convey to the receiver. This requires that the sender establish the theme of promotion or the unique selling point of the product. The message itself can then be broken down into two parts: first, the buying proposal, which is the basic content of the message and, second, the creative presentation, which refers to the form in which the message is presented (Killough, 1978). While buying proposals and creative presentations are distinct, they are not independent. The buying proposal should incorporate ideas, features and images of the product/organization which the sender considers to be most relevant and effective in relation to a particular target audience. The creative presentation then concerns itself with the actual process of presenting these ideas, features and images. A simple example might be the Sun Alliance campaign. The buying proposal revolves around the image of the company as caring and concerned, cautious and yet innovative. The creative presentation centres around the personality of an individual employee – 'the place where Norman works'. The form of a message can easily be varied for different target audiences, while retaining the same basic content in order to maintain consistency in the campaign.

Budget

A budget is required for the whole promotional exercise and for the individual components of the promotional mix. There are a variety of methods available for determining the appropriate budget for a particular promotional exercise. Ideally, the objective–task method should be used, since this provides a systematic approach to budgeting based on stated objectives and costings of the mechanisms employed to achieve those objectives. In practice, many organizations rely on simple percentage of sales methods, on matching the advertising expenditure of their competitors or simply on what can be afforded.

Promotional mix

The decision relating to the promotional mix requires that the organization determine the appropriate balance between the four promotional tools available. In developing this balance it is important to stress that the various tools available are in many senses complementary and certainly should not be regarded as competitive.

Advertising

While advertising is the method of promotion that has been most extensively used in the financial service sector, the results it can generate by itself are becoming rather limited in an increasingly competitive market environment. Financial services are complex products for which considerable information (often consumer-specific) is required before purchase. Media advertising as a promotional tool is limited in the volume of information and the degree of detail it can present, particularly given the requirements of the Financial Services Act in terms of the information content of advertising. Furthermore, where the product is dependent on the consumer's financial situation, the benefits from conveying such detail are in any case limited. Finally, the product itself is intangible, which will complicate the process of developing a message. This is not to suggest that media advertising has a minimal role to play in the promotion of financial services; rather, it suggests that it should be regarded as the first stage in any promotional campaign, with its prime objective being that of creating and raising the consumer's awareness of the institution and its product. A particular feature of advertising and promotion in general in the financial services sector is the need to attempt to develop tangible representations of the product or, if this is not possible, develop some method of presentation which associates the product with a tangible object. In many cases, the tangible object is the organization itself, but it could equally well be a 'Flexible Friend' or a 'Black Horse'.

A variety of media are available for advertising and the choice of the most appropriate ones will depend upon the nature of the market being reached and the complexity of the message. Television advertising has the advantage of reaching a large number of people at a relatively low cost. Its disadvantages stem from the fact that it is not easily targeted – the message may often be wasted because it reaches many consumers who are not in the target audience or because it becomes increasingly difficult to get access to the peak-time slots, when the advertisements might be expected to have maximum impact. A further problem arises in scheduling advertisements to avoid confusion with other financial services, particularly as the volume of advertising for these products increases. Furthermore, the volume of information that can be conveyed through this particular medium is restricted by the need to keep the message relatively simple. By contrast, with press advertisements it is rather easier to reach the target audience by selecting particular newspapers, magazines or journals to carry the advertisements.

Following the introduction of the Financial Services Act, the nature of advertising began to change; television advertisements generally fall into category A (see Chapter 1) and must concern themselves with simply announcing and drawing attention to the product or the company. Advertisements which actually attempt to sell a product are required to give full details of the small print surrounding an investment product. These compliance requirements create substantial problems for the preparation of copy, particularly for press advertisements. As a consequence, many such advertisements are moving towards category B, namely advertisements which invite consumers to respond for further information, thus reducing the compliance costs for the sponsors.

Recent years have seen a substantial increase in direct response advertising and direct mail in the financial services sector, and a recent survey (Ennew *et al.*, 1989) suggested that these methods of communication and distribution are likely to increase in importance over the next few years. In terms of targeting, direct mail is perhaps the most accurate form of advertising, since an organization can identify precisely which group it wishes to direct its campaign towards and can convey a relatively large volume of detailed information to prospective consumers. However, in terms of numbers of consumers reached it is relatively expensive, and requires the construction and efficient management of a comprehensive customer database. The advantage of direct mail for relatively complex products such as financial services is that it gives the consumers time to consider thoroughly before deciding to buy and, as such, is regarded as increasing their confidence in the product. With an increasing number of organizations looking to cross-sell new products to their existing consumer base, direct mailing, either independently or 'piggy-backed' to monthly or annual statements, is likely to become an increasingly important marketing tool. Recent research on the use of direct mail by financial services organizations (*Marketing*, 1989) suggests that the subtle personalization of direct mail increases the power of the message and thus tends to improve response rates. Furthermore, it was argued that direct mail from banks in particular was generally not perceived as 'junk mail', but rather as a serious business communication, and that this would also tend to improve the quality of the response.

In developing advertising for financial services, the following guidelines suggested by Cowell (1984) are useful:

1 Use clear and unambiguous messages. Given the extent of advertising in all media and the potential for noise to distort a message, simplicity and clarity considerably improve the chances of consumer recognition and recall of the message. In the case of press and television advertisements for financial services, this would suggest minimizing the amount of technical detail that is included to avoid information overload. Technical detail is more easily conveyed via promotional literature or preferably personal selling.

2 Advertise to employees. An organization's employees are a key component of the service; advertising should therefore not only encourage customers to buy, it should also encourage employees to perform.

3 Build on word-of-mouth communication. In the services sector, personal recommendations from friends are often an important influence on the consumer's buying decision. Advertising should therefore encourage satisfied customers to communicate their satisfaction to others or encourage potential customers to talk to existing customers.

4 Develop tangible cues. Given the intangibility of financial services, advertising should make full use of any tangible links which can be developed.

5 Develop continuity. The continued use of a common theme (the Black Horse, the Listening Bank) helps keep the image of a service provider in the consumer's memory and distinguishes that organization and its products from its competitors. This is perhaps particularly important in the financial services sector, where many purchases are made on an irregular basis.

6 Minimize post-purchase anxiety. The phenomenon of cognitive

dissonance in buying behaviour – the feelings of doubt a consumer experiences about the choice of a particular product – is well documented. In the case of physical products, the consumers can at least attempt to judge the wisdom of their purchase by evaluating the product purchased. With financial services, the customer lacks a tangible object to evaluate, which reinforces the importance of advertising to provide existing consumers with reassurance that their choice was the correct one.

Personal selling

Personal selling is in many respects central to any service delivery system; it is perhaps equally important as a method of promoting financial services, particularly in the light of the increasing complexity of the product. When dealing with a complex product, despite the obvious importance of advertising in creating an awareness of the product, effective personal contact becomes of paramount importance in explaining the product to the potential consumer. In addition, personal selling is of central importance in dealing with corporate clients, for whom the cost-effectiveness of mass advertising is extremely poor.

There are several advantages that personal selling has over other elements of the promotions mix in both the personal and the corporate sectors of the financial services market. Unlike other aspects of promotion, it is a two-way form of communication, giving the customer the opportunity to query aspects of the product and the sales staff the opportunity to deal with the specific needs of each customer. As a consequence, the message itself becomes much more flexible, and service provision can more easily be tailored to the needs of the consumer. By contrast with other aspects of promotion, it is rather more expensive and requires a high degree of expertise, both among the members of management who coordinate and motivate sales staff, and among the sales staff themselves, who require a variety of interpersonal skills combined with in depth knowledge about an organization's product range. The organization, training and motivation of the sales force is discussed in detail in Black *et al.* (1985), Donnelly *et al.* (1985) and Marsh (1988).

While the principles of personal selling and the management/ development of a sales force are similar, whether that sales force is dealing with goods or services, there is some evidence to suggest that the selling of financial service may pose some particular problems. In a study of the life-assurance industry, George and Myers (1981, quoted in Cowell, 1984) outlined the following difference between selling goods and selling services:

1 *Customer perceptions of services*
   (a) Services are seen to be less consistent in terms of quality
   (b) The purchase of a service is more risky than the purchase of a good
   (c) Buying a service is a less pleasant experience than buying a good
   (d) The image of the service provider has a significant impact on the buying decision.
2 *Purchase behaviour*
   (a) There is less price comparison with services than with goods
   (b) The particular seller has a considerable influence on the consumer's decision
   (c) The influence of advertising is less than it is for goods while the influence of personal recommendations is greater.
3 *Personal selling*
   (a) There is greater customer involvement in service purchasing
   (b) Customer satisfaction is influenced by the attitudes of sales staff
   (c) Sales staff often have to spend a considerable time reducing customer uncertainty.

Considering these differences, we can develop a number of guidelines which are central to the success of personal selling for financial services. Given the significance of contact with individual staff, it is clearly important to ensure that sales staff develop good personal relations with their customers. To alleviate any doubts or risks which the customer may feel requires a professional orientation on behalf of sales staff to illustrate their competence and familiarity with all aspects of the relevant products. This in turn requires the organization to ensure good training and motivation for such staff. Finally, the personal selling approach should ensure that the actual purchase decision is made easy, and minimal demands are imposed on the customer.

Promotions

Sales promotions are perhaps most commonly associated with 'money off' coupons or product samples. Standard promotional techniques such as these are of limited relevance to financial services as such, but this does not exclude the use, by suppliers, of promotional material. The most common form is point-of-sale promotions, but there is evidence to suggest the increasing use of free gifts to encourage the take-up of certain products. Northern Rock Building Society found that in selling insurance products, offering a free calculator or radio alarm to consumers who took on certain policies was much more effective than offering short-term reductions in premiums and considerably cheaper. The consumers perceived themselves to be getting something of greater value, something of more interest and something which provided a tangible link with their purchase (BSG, 1989b).

Public relations

Publicity in any form is regarded as any non-paid form of mass communications, and traditionally was expected to concentrate on gaining favourable press coverage relating to new activities or developments within an organization. However, the traditional view of public relations as being centred around producing regular, informative press releases and building up good contacts with journalists misses the variety and complexity of activities undertaken in the public-relations arena. Two broad aspects of public relations require specific attention in relation to the financial services sector – corporate image/identity and sponsorship, with the latter constituting a particular aspect of an organization's corporate image.

Although customer perceptions of the character of an organization are seen to be of increasing importance in the marketing of both products and services, their significance in relation to services is considerable. In the financial services sector, it is widely recognized that consumer reactions to the organization are critical in terms of their perceptions of service quality (Howcroft and Lavis, 1986; Smith and Harbisher, 1989). When faced with a variety of similar products of a highly technical nature from competing suppliers, consumer choice is frequently motivated by the perceived image of that organization. Indeed, Howcroft and Lavis (1987) suggest that image is perhaps the most important form of branding available to the suppliers of personal financial services. Consumer perception of a service can be thought of as having two components – technical quality and functional quality (Richardson and Robinson, 1985). The former refers to specifically technical aspects of the service and its delivery, including product features, sales staff knowledge of those features and the efficiency of computer-based systems. The latter is more image-orientated and focuses on the attitude and appearance of staff, the branch environment, etc. It is often suggested that it is from aspects of functional quality that customer dissatisfaction is most likely to arise.

The factors that contribute to the creation of a favourable image are many and varied. A clear corporate identity is important to give the organization a coherent face in its dealings with consumers and make it instantly recognizable. An organization's corporate identity can be represented by a variety of visual symbols associated with promotional material, branch layout and design and staff appearance. This can be reinforced by advertising, which can emphasize identity and create images. Indeed, as has been suggested earlier, a large volume of financial services advertising has been concerned with imagery rather than specific products. Thus for example, advertisements built round slogans such as 'TYesB – the bank that likes to say Yes' and 'Commercial Union – we won't make a drama out of a crisis' are all concerned with creating a particular image of the organization. Simply advertising and preparing corporate logos will not be sufficient to create and maintain a desirable corporate image. It is essential to ensure that this image is then reflected in aspects of the service presented to consumers, as is clear from the case study below.

One increasingly important aspect of public relations and the creation of a desirable corporate image has been the growth in sponsorship. The market for television advertising has become increasingly competitive; media costs have risen and with the rise in the number of newspapers/magazines and expansion in the television networks, reaching a target audience has become increasingly difficult. As a consequence, many organizations, particularly financial service suppliers, are beginning to see sponsorship as an increasingly effective mechanism for reaching a target audience, not least because in many cases it is seen as being more cost-effective than advertising. In the sports arena, the financial services sector accounts for some 25 per cent of all sports sponsorship; while some of this is directed to the sponsorship of large-scale national or international events, a significant volume is also directed to what are currently minority sports and to the sponsorship of local and regional activities (BSG, 1989). Sponsorship is not confined to sport but has spread to many cultural activities as well. The advantage of sponsorship, apart from its cost-effectiveness, tends to be that it is viewed less cynically by the consumer than more orthodox forms of advertising. At the same time, organizations engaging in sponsorship should be aware that it can only effectively promote a name rather than a specific image, and that there is always the danger that, as with Gillette and its sponsorship of one-day cricket, the organization becomes better known for its sponsorship than for its products.

Case Study
Corporate image:
Town and Country Building Society

Town and Country Building Society was described as being the 'undoubted star' in a Phillips and Drew efficiency analysis of building societies published in August, 1988. Despite this relatively strong position it has still decided that it needs to undertake a radical overhaul of its corporate image. Management in the society recognize the importance of creating and maintaining a favourable image for the society as an integral component of the marketing strategy; in the financial services sector the quality and reliability of a product is inextricably linked to the customer's perception of the quality and reliability of the supplier. Creating a favourable image for the society should create a favourable image for its products resulting in an increase in the potential market and an increase in profitability. Furthermore, Town and Country recognize that their corporate image should be created not just in relation to individual customers, but also in relation to much broader groups within societies including professional intermediaries and related corporate organizations.

Management identified three underlying motives for the change in corporate image. First, they noted the importance of ensuring that any social group or 'public' which had any direct or indirect connection with the society, had a favourable image of the society. Second, they stressed the increasing importance of competition in the mortgage market, particularly in the light of 1992 which created the potential for competition for lower cost continental providers of housing finance. Third, they recognized that the financial services sector in general and the mortgage markets in particular had moved from being sellers' markets to being buyers' markets. In developing their new corporate image Town and Country recognized that corporate image should be directed at both an internal and an external audience; the image may be created by management, but it must be projected by staff throughout the organization and those staff must be supportive and in tune with the image being created.

In the light of these environmental changes, they implemented an eight point strategy to alter and improve the society's corporate image:

1 *Wider press coverage*: A public relations consultancy was engaged as part of a more systematic programme of disseminating information about the society to the press. As a result, Town and Country experienced a 274 per cent increase in the number of references to the society in the press.
2 *New promotional material*: The society's promotional material was redesigned to improve quality and present a consistent visual theme.
3 *New branch design*: Town and Country aimed to increase the flow of customers through their branches by creating an attractive and welcoming image. Their approach was to reverse the traditional branch layout in which the majority of space was reserved for administrative staff; instead the bulk of the branch space was to be

made available to customers with window displays being opened up to give customers a clearer view of activities within the branch.

4 *Staff appearance*: The existing staff uniform was redesigned, with the aim of providing a more up to date and friendly image. To accommodate staff preferences, two different styles were offered.

5 *Staff training*: With the increased role being played by branch staff in the personal selling of the societies services a comprehensive staff training programme was implemented. The key features of this programme were to emphasize first, that to the consumer, the service itself will only be as good as the person who is selling it. Second, that effective selling requires that the consumer is given a full range of information relating to the product and, third, that successful selling requires familiarity with the services and their features to be able to deal with specific consumer requirements.

6 *Computerization*: Computer equipment throughout the society was to be updated, both to improve productivity and to project the image of Town and Country as a modern and forward looking society.

7 *Positioning statements*: In order to convince both staff and member of the public that the Society was a cohesive organization, a clear mission statement was composed as part of the five year corporate plan and a copy distributed to all staff to ensure that they were aware of how the society perceived its role and would be able to explain this to interested customers.

8 *Arrears counselling*: To reinforce its customer care programme and re-emphasize the centrality of the customers, irrespective of their position, an arrears counselling service was developed with a leaflet on the subject prepared in consultation with the Citizens Advice Bureau being prepared and distributed to all customers.

The development of this new corporate image has begun; the redesign of branches began with a pilot exercise in 1989 and Town and Country is looking to review its corporate logo style. The management view is that a positive corporate image can have significant business benefits and is an important tool in an increasingly competitive market environment. (Source: BSG, 1989a)

Conclusions

In the marketing of financial services a key problem is that the product being marketed has no physical appearance; financial services are basically intangible. Accordingly, promotion is of considerable importance in creating an image for the product in the mind of the consumer, often through the creation of an appropriate image for the supplier. Despite the large-scale expenditure by suppliers of financial services, there is evidence to suggest that their promotional activity has been less effective than it might have been. An effective promotional campaign for a product or an organization must be carefully planned. The objectives of promotion must be clearly stated and the target audience must be accurately identified. The message that is to be communicated must be clear, and an appropriate balance of promotional tools must be developed to communicate this message.

CHAPTER 6
Pricing
Malcolm Hughes

Introduction

The price component of any marketing mix has a number of important roles to fulfil for any organization. First, and perhaps most importantly, it affects revenue and therefore profitability. Second, it is a competitive tool which can be used to exploit market opportunities and, third, it contributes to the image created for the product within the marketing mix. In broad terms, the role of pricing in a marketing context is to determine a price which will produce the desired level of sales in order to meet the objectives of the business strategy.

In general, costs will inevitably play an important role in determining price, but, at the same time, price-setting cannot ignore the willingness of consumers to pay (the price–quantity relationship) and the nature of the competitive environment. In the context of services in general and financial services in particular the influence of these factors in pricing is often complicated by the intangibility of the product and the difficulties associated with the concept of price (Cowell, 1984).

If we consider financial services, price as a competitive tool is becoming increasingly important, and yet the concept of price is not always clear, certainly from the perspective of the consumer. For example, what is the 'price' of a building society ordinary share account? It clearly has a price, since the user of an ordinary passbook account receives a range of benefits from the society (convenient branches, efficient administration, security of capital, annual or semi-annual payment of interest, the facility to draw cheques, use ATMs and the availability of mortgage funds), which cost the society significant resources to provide; and these costs have to be over-recovered if the society is to remain in business. It can be suggested that the user of the ordinary account is 'trading-off' the opportunity to maximize the interest on his or her capital in return for other benefits.

This principle of 'trading-off' or accepting lower than maximum return on investment in exchange for other attributes or benefits is a key concept in the pricing of financial services. These relationships can be examined by means of a research routine known as 'conjoint' analysis, in which consumers or potential consumers of a product are interrogated via a PC-driven research questionnaire as to considerations of benefits and attributes, including price, which they find attractive and purchase-motivating. As well as the 'trade-off' or 'conjoint' concept of price, many financial services are obtained by the purchaser in return for a straight fee, interest charge or premium payment (direct pricing). Examples of this area are household contents insurance; personal loans; mortgage finance; accident, sickness and unemployment insurance; and motor insurance. In some of these categories, price is a more important purchase selector than in others. For example, some 30 per cent of motor insurance policy-holders change their insurer each year in a search for cheaper premiums. Motor insurance therefore demonstrates 'commodity behaviour', wherein price is the *major* determinant of volume and market share (bread, milk, petrol are examples of goods where price is a dominant component in purchase decisions). Household contents insurance is a type of financial service where price (or premium level) is becoming increasingly important and commoditized.

Furthermore, the measurement of costs associated with particular products and the distinctions between fixed and variable costs often present problems. A rational pricing policy across a range of products requires some consideration of these factors, not only for purposes of price-setting but also to evaluate the relative strengths associated with individual products. However, in many financial services sectors, particularly banking, a limited knowledge of costs combined with oligopoly condition in the market place has tended to lead to extensive cross-subsidization (Howcroft and Lavis, 1989). As competition increases, and as price competition becomes important, more detailed information on cost structures and consumer reaction will become crucial to an effective pricing strategy.

This chapter focuses on the issues surrounding pricing in the financial services sector, and pays particular attention to the impact of regulation on these decisions. The second and third sections consider the impact of regulation on the pricing of savings and investment products and credit, respectively. The fourth section examines the impact of competition on pricing, and the fifth the relationships between risk, return, and liquidity in the context of price-setting.

Pricing and regulations – savings and investment

The introduction of the Financial Services Act provided a comprehensive framework of control over the methods of marketing of pensions, life assurance and investments (excluding deposits) in the United Kingdom. The essential aims of the legislation are twofold; first, to ensure that the purchaser of a controlled product is sold a product suitable for his or her needs (this is referred to as 'best practice' or 'selling to needs'); second, clearly to establish that a salesperson is acting either for one company only (a company representative) or can offer a choice of products from all sources (independent intermediary). There is a great deal more to the Financial Services Act than this, of course, and it is dealt with at greater length in Chapter 1; but it is restated here because the role of pricing changes depending on the channel of distribution.

The price for a life-assurance policy or pension paid to an independent intermediary (i.e. the premium) will contain a substantial element of discount or commission as a payment to the independent intermediary (or broker) for his or her services. Usually for a life-assurance policy taken out in support of a mortgage, the whole of the premium for the first year will represent such a payment. Various attempts have been made by the regulatory authorities to control the levels of commission paid by life investment and pension companies to intermediaries (or brokers). This is referred to in the literature as 'ROLAC' (for Regulation of Life Assurance Commission). Moves also continue to provide details to the customers of the proportion of premiums which are absorbed by commission and expenses in a life, investment or pension contract. This is referred to as 'disclosure'.

As may be imagined, the financial services industry is less than enthusiastic to agree to control of commission (a key marketing variable) and positively unenthusiastic at the prospect of the customer being made aware of commission and expense levels for life-assurance products, either generally or specifically. However, commission and expenses are a significant part of the 'price' paid by a consumer, and it can be argued that the purchaser has a right to be able to compare such expenses as between for example, endowment policies, mutual funds (or unit trusts), Personal Equity Plans, direct investment in common stocks and investment trusts. This issue is further complicated by important companies such as Prudential, Pearl and Co-op, which operate their own dedicated sales forces selling only the products of the company ('company representatives'). While the price of the policy bought from a company representative is paid direct to the company, and not via an intermediary or broker, it also contains elements of commission paid to the salesman and company operating expenses.

Regulation of price is notoriously difficult, and this is especially the case in the financial services industry, where the price paid has a number of components usually encompassing the basic fee or investment plus other elements representing commission and expenses. Moves are also being made to bring the selling of 'general insurance', i.e. the insurance of things (cars, houses, possessions), under a regulatory regime similar to that already operating and under consideration in the market for life pensions and investment contracts.

Pricing and regulations – credit

There are differential prices charged for loans of all kinds. Loans are priced differently, depending on:

1   The status of the borrrower. Checks are made on age, homeownership or tenancy, address, previous history of credit, other relationships with the lending institution, income and occupational group, court orders, etc. These status checks are routine for virtually all lending and are referred to as 'credit scoring'. This credit scoring may take the form of a sophisticated on-line computer system with direct lines to special agencies who keep records of county court judgments for non-payment of debt and other unreliable debtor histories (debtors now have the right to see and challenge such records).
2   Whether the loan is *secured*, i.e. on property, shares or other assets, or *unsecured*, i.e. not supported by assets but simply on the basis of the borrower's agreement to repay capital and interest. A well-known example of a secured loan is a mortgage for house purchase and of an unsecured loan an overdraft on a bank current account.

The price of credit will be higher the greater the risk of bad debts or unrecovered losses on the portfolio of loans. Unsecured loans always cost more than secured loans, since in the latter case the lender is able to recover the debt by obtaining a court order against the borrower and sequestering the assets used to secure the loan. Court orders to pursue default on unsecured loans are also issued, but the level of recovery is lower, and the incidence of defalcation significantly greater.

The Consumer Credit Regulations recognize that the price of a loan will be shown in two ways – the flat rate and the APR (annual percentage rate). The flat rate is taken by the simple application of interest to the whole loan over the period of the loan, e.g. a customer borrows £5,000 at a flat rate of 10 per cent per annum over 3 years. The total interest due is 3 (years) × 10 per cent × £5,000 = £1,500 (or 30 per cent of £5,000). Monthly repayments are:

Capital interest (£5,000 + £1,500) divided by 36 months = £180.55 per month for 3 years.

However, over the 3 years, the borrower is progressively repaying the capital month by month at the rate of £138.88 per month. Thus at the start of the third year of the loan only £1,666.66 is left to pay off the capital, but the interest charged on that during the third year is £500 (one-third of the total interest) or an interest rate of 30 per cent! The Consumer Credit Act sought to remedy this confusion between flat rates and real rates by introducing the concept of annual charge for credit or APR. This is calculated according to a set (and complex) formula, and for a loan at a flat rate of 10 per cent would typically be 19.4 per cent.

Price and competition

The setting of a price is based on the considerations shown in Figure 6.1. Profit arises from the over-recovery of fixed and variable costs and in the figure occurs at point A of sales output. Beyond that point the business activity is 'profitable', although the level of profit beyond point A will depend on the need to produce a satisfactory return on shareholders' funds.

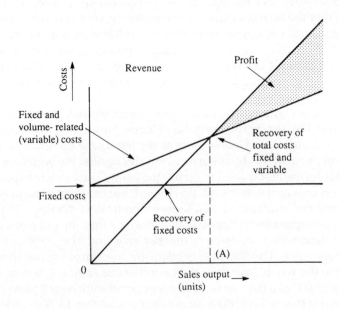

Figure 6.1 *Considerations in price-setting*

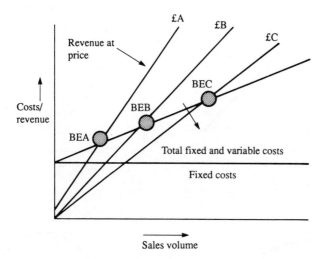

Figure 6.2   *Lower price/higher volume contrasted with higher price/lower volume.*

From the general analysis of the role of price we can more specifically consider the effect on unit sales of different levels of pricing. This is known as sensitivity – the response of sales unit volume (e.g. number of household contents policies sold at particular premium levels) to the price (or fee or premium).

Figure 6.2 is a development of Figure 6.1, in that it suggests a relation between a lower price (£C) and a higher volume contrasted with a higher price (£A), with a consequentially lower volume of sales. The breakeven points (BEA, BEB, BEC) for the business at which recovery of fixed and variable overheads takes place are different for the three price levels shown. Thus it can be demonstrated in theory that the price and volume of a financial service are related, and that these variables are in turn related to the ability of a business to recover its fixed and variable costs and then to generate a return on shareholders' funds.

However, this is a considerable over-simplification of the relation between price and sales in financial services. As Figures 6.3(a)–(d) show, many sales/price relationships can be detected in financial services from the simple linear decline (6.3(a)) found in established markets to non-linear relationships (6.3(b) and (d)), where sales may rise as price rises due to extra commission payments, sales-force incentives and consumer advertising. In highly competitive markets (6.3(c)) even a small increase of price outside the established framework may produce significant falls in volume (e.g. motor insurance).

Competition therefore has a strong influence in price-setting, since it

117

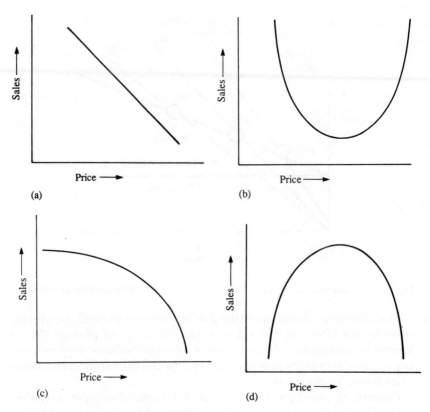

Figure 6.3   *Sales/price relationships*

controls the relation between price and volume. But this relation may not be simple, and, in particular, may be influenced by incentives aimed at the distributive system, such as sales commission, advertising and promotion.

Price and other relationships

The price of a financial service is related to three other main variables: return, risk and liquidity. These variables are themselves related, in that, as an obvious example, the highest returns from investment are available only at higher risks and/or for limited 'liquidity' (ability to withdraw the investment speedily). For general insurance the lowest price may be associated with restriction of benefits (e.g. a household contents policy which contains a number of clauses limiting the circumstances in which a claim will be accepted) or with a focused or segmented market (e.g. motor insurance for the 55+ age group). These restrictions can be compared to liquidity with investment products. It is the case in financial services that 'there is no free lunch', but the purchaser buying a product whose price is out of line with the general market statement should beware of restrictions on the use of the product. This is true in all markets: financial markets are no exception to the rules of price/value and supply/demand.

Some of these relationships can be expressed in diagram form (Figures 6.4(a) and (b)). As with general insurance, investment, life and pension products whose price is outside the market framework should be examined with care. The skill of the independent intermediary lies in selecting those products which offer good value for money and still protect the purchasers' long-term interests and need for a secure investment and reliable cover.

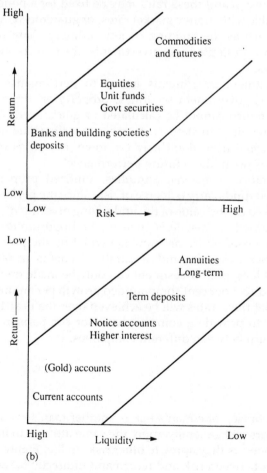

Figure 6.4 *Return/risk relationships*

Return

As Figures 6.4(a) and (b) indicate, the return on an investment product is related inevitably to risk and liquidity (or withdrawability). What is return and how may it be measured? For fixed-interest investments, such as ordinary share accounts, deposit accounts, term (or time) deposits, the return is clear to see. It is the payment of interest (annually, semi-annually or monthly), which is made to the investor in return for the investment. Rates for accounts where the money is immediately available for withdrawal (call or sight deposits) without notice usually pay lower rates of interest than accounts where notice of withdrawal (28, 60 or 90 days) has to be given. Higher rates are available for investors prepared to commit capital for 1 to 5 years (term or time deposits) and these rates may be fixed for a period (usually 1 year), variable with money market rates, or guaranteed over a variable base rate such as the building society ordinary share rate. Because these are low- or limited-risk investments, the returns are in line with market rates.

For investment instruments linked to performance of common equity stock, government securities, property or commodity prices, the future return cannot be calculated or guaranteed. As advertisements are required to state, 'remember that the value of investment and the income from them may go down as well as up' and 'past experience is no guide to future performance'.

All insurance, pensions, annuities, unitized property and gilt-edged-based funds carry a degree of risk, since the performance of the funds is based on the value of the underlying investment. They should all be regarded as *long-term* investment opportunities. However, projected rates of return are now governed by the provisions of the Financial Services Act, and illustrated benefits available on the maturity of long-term investment can only be made on the basis of 7 per cent and 10.5 per cent compounded growth per annum. This is not to imply that these rates will be achieved over the next 10 years, say, but simply to provide a common basis for comparison of projected rates of return between different companies.

Risk

To coin a phrase, 'one man's risk is another man's certainty'. Savers and investors will generally apply the same attitude to the placement of their money as they apply to other risks in life. Figure 6.4(a) shows the relation between risk and return and indirectly between risk and liquidity. Risk in the context of *investment* is usually understood as risk to capital. This might be the prospect of a collapsed share price (remember October, 1987!) or a failed commodities contract. Higher than normal market rewards are almost always accompanied by some element of risk to the underlying capital value. Alternatively the placing of a sum of money in a bank, insurance company or building society carries only a small risk of loss of capital, and this could only be brought about by the failure of the bank or building society as a trading business. It is fair to observe that these institutions have had failures, but these have tended to be smaller examples and due to fraud or mismanagement (e.g. State Building Society, London Indemnity Assurance). Investment in a large and reputable bank, insurance company or building society on deposit for payment of interest effectively carries no risk, but the returns offered will not and cannot be spectacular. For life and general insurances, the risk factor is dependent on the company selected, and this in turn is based on reputation and trading history. An unusually low price for motor insurance, house-contents insurance or simple life cover (e.g. term assurance) may indicate a less than sound company which might prove difficult to deal with in the event of a claim. The most notable post-war example was the collapse of Dr Emil Savundra's Fire Auto Marine Insurance, which left uninsured many motorists who had originally been attracted to the company by the very low prices charged for cover.

Liquidity

Price and liquidity are closely linked, since money deposited for a committed time will earn a higher rate of interest than money on call or demand. It therefore follows that a saver or investor is paying a 'price' for immediate availability of cash. For many people, the ability to get at their money instantly is an important product feature, and, for example, nearly £30 billion is invested in building society or bank ordinary share passbook accounts, paying 4–5 per cent net interest per annum. Thus a major benefit to the customer cannot be the rate of interest paid but must be the convenience of a passbook showing the current balance and the comforting certainty that this money is available on demand. Since these same customers could, at very little trouble and no cost, transfer their funds to accounts within the same bank or society paying up to 10 per cent net interest per annum, with the trade-off of only 30, 60 or 90 days' loss of liquidity or notice of withdrawal, then the availability of funds on demand must be a very powerful marketing proposition. This is so much the case that many fixed-interest passbook deposit accounts provide for instant withdrawals over a certain waterline (e.g. over £10,000), permit one or two withdrawals per year up to a defined maximum, or will allow withdrawals from high-interest term deposits at the loss of several months' interest. It is well-established that a significant minority of customers for higher-interest term deposits make penalty withdrawals so frequently that the actual rate of interest they earn on their total investment can be reduced to the level of the ordinary passbook account and below.

Long-term endowment assurance provides the main example of an investment with virtually no liquidity. Indeed, reputable insurance companies go to great lengths to stress that a 10, 15 or 20 year endowment assurance policy must be treated as a commitment for that period of time. The 'cashing-in' of policies after only a few years is a major problem for the insurance industry, and can result in a return of only, or less than, the premiums paid. However, if the saver is prepared to pay the price of loss of liquidity for the period, then the real returns from long-term assurance policies are highly attractive, and compare favourably with all other long-term investments. The pub-lication *Money Management and Unitholder* publishes comprehensive tables of performance for long- and short-term investments.

Price and marketing

Marketing expenditure in financial services has increased dramatically over the last 13 years. See Table 6.1.

'Above-the-line' expenditure, e.g. advertising in press, television, radio, outdoor and transportation, is approximately half of all sales costs. The 'below-the-line' component generally covers market research, sales promotion, special deals and discounts, sales incen-tives, sales literature and brochures, sponsorship, gifts, branch displays, magazines for customers and staff and other 'non-advertising' sales development techniques. Therefore it can be seen

Table 6.1 *Marketing expenditure, 1975–88*

Institution	Total advertising expenditure measured by independent audit (£m)*		
	1975	1980	1988
Banks	5.6	17.9	99.5
Building societies	5.5	20.9	100.9
Insurance companies	4.3	12.5	96.4
Other financial services/companies	6.7	22.0	109.7
Total	22.1	73.3	406.5

* Press, television and (some) outdoor

that very large and growing sums of money are spent on the proselytization of financial services. These sums do not include the basic costs of operating a sales force in terms of salaries, benefits, cars, pensions, commission payments and regional and district sales offices. It will come as no surprise that for major direct selling companies, such as Prudential, Pearl and Co-operative, nearly half of all premium income is swallowed by expenses, and even for companies selling through independent intermediaries the proportion can be as high as 35 per cent.

Marketing costs clearly have to be paid for by the customer of the business, whether it be a bank, insurer or building society. It might be concluded that the shrewd purchaser of financial services should deal only with those companies with low total management expenses, so that a higher proportion of the price (or premium or fee) is used by the company to provide for investment or protection or growth. As with other areas of industrial and commercial enterprise, however, this conclusion would be entirely wrong. In fact it tends to be the dynamic, vigorous and successful companies who spend heavily on marketing and business development. In this way they attract good quality managers and salesmen who ensure a healthy flow of new customers and new investment. This in its turn can produce more effective fund management and underwriting positions, and hence better long-term performance. Unfortunately for the customer for financial services there is no simple relation between price and marketing expenses. The only advice must be to look at the track record of the company in terms of investment performance, claims handling and reputation. It is in this area that the role of the 'independent financial intermediary' can be valuable.

The Financial Services Act, however, has had the inevitable consequence of increasing the power and coverage of the 'company representative' at the expense of independent distribution. In fact the great majority of banks and building societies have decided to sell the life pensions and investment products of only one supplying company, because of the very high training and administrative costs of providing 'independent' advice through a large branch network. In this way the real choice to the purchaser of financial services is becoming more limited – surely not the intention of those who framed this important legislation.

Pricing and distribution

Financial services in the UK can be bought in more places and more ways than any other services – and all these different methods have significant implications for the price of the product or service. Figure 6.5 sets out the many ways in which a customer can obtain financial services and draws particular attention to the availability of financial services in different environments. (Note: the figure shows ways in which financial services may be purchased or where financial service transactions which yield actual or potential revenue for the supplier may be carried out, not necessarily where financial services are available.) For example, a *bill payment* may be effected at home via a telephone banking service; in a branch of the supplying bank or building society (own network); in a shared network, such as an outlet of the utility which offers payment handling services; by postal cheque; via an ATM network providing settlement service features; by direct debit; by credit or debit card, etc. The cost of each transaction varies according to the method selected. See Table 6.2.

While the cost of the transaction varies as shown in Table 6.2, the bearer of the cost (the bank, building society or utility) may choose not to pass on all the cost of (in this case) money transmission to the customer. Therefore, although the *cost* of providing financial services to the customer is probably not greatly different as from supplier to supplier, as a matter of marketing policy various distributors may choose to under-recover these costs. Why should this be the case? In the retailing of goods and services generally it is common practice to

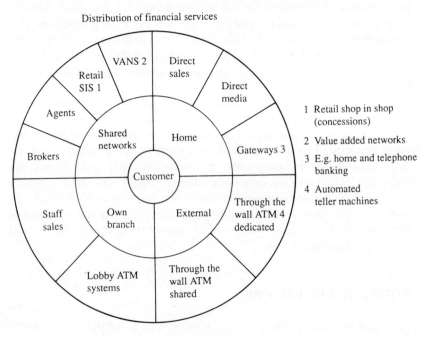

Distribution of financial services

1 Retail shop in shop (concessions)

2 Value added networks

3 E.g. home and telephone banking

4 Automated teller machines

Figure 6.5   *Distribution of financial services*

Table 6.2 *Transaction costs*

Method of payment*	Approximate cost (p), 1989 prices	
Postal cheque	20	Debit in item
Debit card	12	Excludes any retailer transaction charge
Credit card	11	" "
Telephone banking	11	Speedlink bill payment
Bank Giro credit	41	Cash over branch counter
ATM network	15	ATM bill payment
Direct debit	21	

* Say of an electricity bill

offer special low prices on certain popular lines to attract new customers. This may be done on a permanent basis, e.g. with the prices of key commodities, such as bread and sugar, or on an occasional basis in heavily promoted markets, such as canned soups, fabric detergents, soft drinks. Exactly the same pricing principles apply in financial services, although the expression of such practices may be less overt than in grocery retailing. A good example can be found during those periods when mortgage finance is in abundant or over supply. At these times it is common to experience 'sales' and 'special offers' from the major suppliers and distributors, during which the price of a mortgage (or interest rate) is discounted or reduced for all customers, or more usually for new customers and first-time buyers. Fixed rate offers, gift schemes, low start, cap and collar, free valuations and surveys abound – all methods of reducing price and attracting new customers. An attractive price for sugar or some other basic commodity is designed to lure the shopper to a particular store, and the intention is that the shopper will stay on to buy other and more profitable items during the visit. Such heavily discounted products are referred to as 'loss leaders' or traffic builders, and the store operators will not expect anything more than the thinnest of margins from such merchandise, even given the fact that many special offers are heavily subsidized directly and indirectly by the manufacturers.

In financial services, it may be well worthwhile to offer mortgage loans at or near cost, and to offset such apparent generosity from the attractive commissions for the good quality life and general insurances that accompany the sale of a mortgage. It is true that the financial services industry is moving away from simple considerations of product profitability toward customer profitability, so that the total relationship with a customer over a period of time yields profit for the supplier or distributor. There may be parts of that relationship which are unprofitable or periods of time during which the profit may be zero or negative.

For example, most banks scramble to attract university students, with attractively priced services and promotional schemes (free overdrafts, cash vouchers, free railcards, etc.). Since the typical student account must be unprofitable for several years, it can only be the case that the banks are persuaded that students are a profitable longer-term prospect. Since over 35 per cent of students change their banking arrangements on graduation, it seems that even this strategy has elements of doubt. As in the purchase of other goods and services, we might expect that the consumer will 'shop around' for the product which most closely matches his/her requirements in terms of features, availability, image and price. Research conducted in relation to the buying process for financial services (see Chapter 2) indicates that this process is complex and as yet imperfectly understood. Price is simply one variable which can influence this decision process. Price in financial services is sometimes less variable than in other services and in goods. But it is no less a component of the marketing mix and in some areas is assuming greater dominance.

Conclusions

The importance of price competition in the financial services sector has been increasing in recent years; the progressive dissolution of various interest-fixing agreements has given organizations much greater scope to use price as a component of their marketing mix, and the breakdown of barriers between organizational types has limited the opportunity for oligopoly conditions to de-emphasize price. As has been illustrated, pricing financial services is a complex exercise. Effective pricing requires a thorough evaluation of costs of the relevant products to avoid cross-subsidization. The interrelations between risk, return and liquidity necessarily mean that cost assessment is much more difficult than it might be for the producer of other products. Furthermore, costs alone will not be the only determinants of price, since any pricing strategy must also incorporate some assessment of consumers' willingness to pay, along with considerations of competitors' prices and the requirements of the various distribution channels.

CHAPTER 7
Direct distribution
Julia Kiely

Introduction

Direct distribution concerns itself with ways in which the product can be supplied from producer to consumer without the use of a specific intermediary. Direct distribution methods essentially fall into two categories: those using media such as the press, leaflets and telephones to invite response and purchase by the consumer; and those using a salesforce to contact consumers on a face-to-face basis. Despite the costs of ensuring compliance with the Financial Services Act, personal selling is likely to remain of considerable importance in the distribution of financial services, particularly insurance and investment products. In the first category, direct mail and direct response advertising are of particular importance in the financial services sector and their usage seems likely to increase in future years. A particular advantage of these methods is that they can be regarded as complementary to other methods of direct distribution – primarily personal selling.

This chapter focuses on direct distribution, with indirect channels being considered in the following chapter. In particular it will examine the nature and suitability of direct mail and direct response advertising. It will also consider in some detail the selling function, giving particular attention to issues surrounding the recruitment retention and motivation of sales staff.

Direct mail

Of the media-based methods of direct distribution, direct mail is perhaps one of the best known and most widely used. The objectives of direct mail may be confined simply to informing the consumer and stimulating interest in a product or it may be concerned with more directly soliciting a purchase. This latter function is commonly described as direct response advertising and will be discussed in more detail in the next section.

As mentioned in Chapter 5, there has been a noticeable increase in the use of direct mail in the financial services sector. This is in part attributable to the various restrictions which operate with respect to the advertising of financial services, but also reflects the fact that direct mail possesses a number of characteristics which make it particularly suitable for the communication and distribution of this type of product.

Firstly, when dealing with products which are relatively complex and often difficult to understand, an initial mail communication will give the consumer time to consider the product and his/her reaction to it prior to moving into a buying situation. As such, it is thought to increase consumer confidence in the organization. Furthermore with the opportunities to personalize and tailor the message to specific individuals and groups, the image of direct mail as 'junk mail' is reduced and the power of the message increased.

Secondly, direct mail allows an organization to be highly selective in terms of which consumers it approaches. It is often argued that some 80 per cent of an organization's sales come from 20 per cent of its consumers (the 'Pareto Law'); if this group can be identified, they can be specifically targeted via direct mail. Despite the higher costs associated with mail shots, the ability to target directly reduces the level of wastage in the communications process. That is to say, the consumers reached by direct mail campaigns, although smaller in number than those reached by alternative methods, are typically much better prospects. Thus, in terms of business generated, direct mail can be highly cost effective. In addition, with organizations increasing their product ranges, direct mail is becoming an increasingly effective mechanism for cross selling.

A third feature of direct mail is that it is a more versatile and controllable medium for communication and distribution. The organization has a high degree of discretion regarding the quantity and layout of information available to the consumer which is of particular importance in the light of the Financial Services Act and its information disclosure requirements. Furthermore by allowing the organization to control which consumers receive which types of information and when they receive it, direct mail presents an organization with the opportunity to monitor with a high degree of accuracy the effectiveness of communication and distribution campaigns. At the same time, one important implication of this degree of control, is that the message reaches the consumer at a time chosen by the organization rather than at a time chosen by the consumer. This would tend to suggest that a proportion of direct mail may be 'lost' because it does not coincide with a period of information search instigated by the consumer. However, it can be argued that direct mail will have the potential to generate responses until it is physically disposed of by the consumer; indeed, some building societies have reported that some mail shots still generate responses two years after their dispatch (BSG, 1989b).

The organization of an effective direct mail campaign requires that considerable care is taken in selecting the target group of consumers, identifying the product to be promoted and formulating the offer. Although a direct mail campaign may be undertaken in house, it is common for organizations to employ specialist agencies (see, for example, Simmonds, 1988).

In terms of choice of mailing lists and customer targeting, there are obvious advantages in using 'in house' lists. For long-term success in direct mailing it is preferable to build up specific lists which are customer based; the disadvantage of account-based lists arises from the fact that multiple account/product customers will receive multiple mailings and this will tend to damage the quality of the message. The benefits of combining customer based lists with specific information on purchase patterns is discussed in some detail by Worthington (1986) and this study illustrates some of the particular gains which can be made from the precise targeting of direct mail.

Direct response advertising

Direct response advertising covers both direct mail and press/leaflet advertising. In its direct mail form it essentially involves providing the consumer with all the information required to make a purchase with minimal further assistance from sales staff. In the press/leaflet format, the product is distributed by a two-stage process which requires the consumer to respond to an initial offer and collect further details prior to the actual purchase. The essence of direct response in each case is that the distribution of the product occurs largely without the involvement of an agent – either in the form of an intermediary or a salesperson.

Through press and leaflet advertising, direct response presentations can target specific groups of customers, although typically with a lower degree of accuracy than that achieved by direct mail. Although there is a loss of accuracy through the use of these media there is, nevertheless, a cost saving and it has been suggested that the increased use of direct response advertising for financial services products is as much cost driven as market driven (Watkins and Wright, 1986). At present, the financial services sector is probably the largest single user of press-based direct response advertising and in the context of press advertising by financial services organizations, direct response is the most common format used (*Marketing*, 1989).

Although a tremendous variety of products are presented to the customer via direct response advertising, this method of distribution has tended to be most successful for 'low advice' or standardized offerings. However, with the recent developments in information technology and the growing flexibility of information systems, direct response advertising is increasingly being used in a two-stage format to provide personalized quotes for products such as non-life insurance.

Direct sales forces

Within financial services, the role of personal selling is of paramount importance. While direct mail and direct response are increasingly used to sell financial products, it is through the personal selling medium that the majority of sales are negotiated and sealed. A salesperson's personal contact with a customer is, and is likely to remain, the most effective method of making a sale. If anything, the importance of personal selling is likely to increase as competition within the financial services sector intensifies and product ranges both expand and become more complex. The opportunity to adapt presentations to each individual customer is an advantage unique to personal selling. Direct mail and direct response, are more appropriate for conveying a standard message targeted at the typical customer in a particular market segment. The opportunity to modify sales strategies and approaches according to the needs and nature of the customer: the customer–salesperson interaction and the specific selling situation means personal selling and the part played by the direct sales force is, and will remain, crucial.

There has recently been a considerable increase in the numbers of salespeople employed in financial services (see Table 7.1). This is

Table 7.1 *Sales forces in insurance*

Company	Estimated end-1987 sales force (personnel)	Estimated current sales force (personnel)
Legal & General	1550	2500
Britannic	3500	4500
Abbey Life	2700	3200
London & Manchester	1020	2100
Sun Life	450	700
GRE	300	850
Sun Alliance	450	580
Allied Dunbar	n/a	5300
Royal Life	1000	1200

Source: Industry Estimates

130

partly because of the growth of owner–occupation in the 1980s and, accompanying this, a rapid growth in endowment mortgages. The increase in also related to the falling number of independent inter- mediaries, as the cost of compliance with the Financial Services Act impacts severely on the small independent broker. Many of the major sales force groups wishing to develop their sales forces have been approached by, or have themselves approached, small independents who are at least partly trained in the sale of life products. The continued build-up of sales force by both traditional life offices, such as London & Manchester, and unit-linked operations, such as Allied Dunbar, means that in some institutions the sales force had increased by 15 per cent between 1988 and 1989. Additionally, the traditional independent offices, such as Sun Life, have built up their sales forces. Of even greater impact is the decision by many banks and building societies to employ a sales force that can work closely with and from their own branches. The sales force is becoming an increasingly vital asset to all financial service organizations.

However, the development and management of an effective sales force requires that considerable attention is paid to the attraction, retention and motivation of salespeople. Implicit in such issues are matters of ensuring continuity of high performance by adopting appropriate financial and non-financial remuneration packages along- side performance monitoring and career development considerations.

Recruiting and selecting the sales force

As with all jobs there is a requirement to match the individual to the job specification. In respect of the selling function, both in general and in relation to financial services, successful recruitment and retention requires that full consideration is given to the following factors. Firstly, it should be recognized that the organizational work environment is very different from that of most other employees. Secondly, it is important to clearly define the primary job activities and, thirdly, it is necessary to identify and counteract the factors which lead to a high labour turnover.

Organizational work environment

Direct sales forces occupy a boundary-spanning role between their customers and their employers (Churchill, *et al.*, 1974; Winer and Schiff, 1980) and their unique position at the interface between the organization and customer requires them to be capable of fulfilling a wide range of roles. Such a position may give rise to the problems of role conflict, role ambiguity and physical and psychological isolation. Role conflict (Miles and Perreault, 1976) may arise as a result of salespeople being expected to work simultaneously in the best interests of their customers and their employers. This problem may be particularly acute with respect to financial services where customers place a high degree of importance on trusting the individual and organization supplying the product.

Role ambiguity is the degree to which a sales representative is unclear about others' expectations regarding the job, the best way to fulfil expectations and the consequences of role performance. There are numerous potential sources of role ambiguity within the job of salesperson. Some of these areas of ambiguity emanate from the nature of the work itself, others may spring from the sales organization itself. As salespersons typically spend a large proportion of their time away from their work base they may be unclear about matters such as communication procedures and the internal functions and politics of the company. Direct sales representatives may be particularly susceptible to the problem of role ambiguity as they are typically self employed. In such cases, questions are raised as to the extent to which the company they represent can legitimately expect loyalty and conformity of behaviour.

More than most other employees, the sales force is physically and psychologically isolated from the organization. The lack of peer group cohesion can have detrimental effects on productivity. Research studies have shown that members of highly cohesive work groups experience fewer work related anxieties and are better adjusted in the organization than those in non-cohesive work groups. They have higher levels of job satisfaction, lower rates of tension, absenteeism and labour turnover. Better adjustment partly comes from the psychological support of the group. In addition, members often learn from the group improved ways of working. This source of learning can be particularly important for jobs such as that of a direct sales force who must otherwise rely on the quality of company training and assistance from their immediate supervisor.

In addition to being physically and psychologically isolated from the organization, members of a direct sales force are highly visible and their actions are subject to continual scrutiny.

Performance evaluation based almost entirely on personal effort is one of the characteristics which distinguishes sales from other types of occupations (Bagozzi, 1978). Any discrepancy between managers' expectations and selling performance are tangible, rapidly visible and readily measurable (Jolson *et al.*, 1987).

For most people, financial services are a marginal part of their lives.

Products tend to be similar and there is a confusing amount of choice. As a result, choice is influenced by the image they have of companies and contact with sales representatives may serve to cement that image. As far as the consumer is concerned, the sales representative may be the only direct contact with the company. This places the sales force in the position of being the company spokesperson and representative while at the same time having to bear the brunt of any customer dissatisfaction with the services offered or support backup provided. It is the salesperson who has to face direct rejection not the organization being represented.

Primary job activities

Selling 'intangible' services such as insurance, stocks and bonds requires a higher level of skill than that needed for many other selling jobs. Such selling is primarily, though not exclusively, to final consumers. Direct sales forces must be able to master basic sales activities of reaching the prospect and making the sale by converting the prospect's interest into buying intentions and actual purchase. In many instances, they also need to develop a continuing relationship with the customer after the first sale by encouraging additional purchases or continued loyalty.

The financial services market place, deregulated and increasingly technology-driven, has become very competitive and changeable. In this changing environment, customer service becomes a key factor in retaining existing consumers and attracting new ones (Lewis and Smith, 1989). In this sector, where customers cannot easily see important differences in the choice of services offered to them, service quality can be the deciding factor. The key brand starts to be the company itself rather than the products. Customers start to feel that certain companies are more suited to them than others and to act accordingly. The direct sales force plays a key role in determining the customers' assessment of the company and service quality. As such their training and commitment to customer service is vital in influencing the current and future success of a company.

An important factor in ensuring quality of service is the ability to communicate. The sales force must be able to extract information, listen and express technical concepts in layman's language. They must be able to control situations by taking charge, instilling confidence and overcoming objections. Key influences impinging on a sale need to be identified, their importance assessed and appropriate responses made. Interpersonal skills, empathy and flexibility in dealing with potential clients and customers are crucial. The sales force must be able to perceive others' needs, points of view and problems, and respond appropriately. They must also master skills such as overcoming objections, planning and making sales presentations.

Furthermore, a sales representative must have a good understanding of the full range of products and services on offer. New products can be introduced at regional or area seminars and sales representatives must be both familiar with the products and willing and able to offer the services or products which are most suited to their clients. In companies where different products carry different commission rates, a conflict of interests may arise. There must be a complete understanding of legislative requirements.

Finally, members of the sales force must have a full awareness of administrative procedures and policies within the organization and be capable of managing their own time effectively. Personal freedom and autonomy are characteristics of sales jobs. This is perhaps more true of sales agents in the financial services sector than other sales jobs. Their jobs are somewhat more autonomous with weaker ties to higher levels of management. This means that sales representatives must be sufficiently self disciplined to manage their time and undertake all necessary aspects of their work regardless of their opinion of them.

Studies of sales force turnover

In attempting to recruit and select the most effective sales force, some guidance can be obtained from the analysis of sales force turnover. Sales force turnover in financial services tends to be more related to tenure and age than to attitude. The longer a salesperson has been with a company, the less likely he or she is to quit. Age and employment tenure are frequently positively related. With increased length of service, employees' specialized skills and general orientation become more specific to their employer. Hence, their opportunities to get other jobs may be reduced. In addition, as people grow older, they tend to have more personal commitments, such as a mortgage and children, which reduce their opportunities for mobility. The longer people stay in a job, the greater investment they have made in getting to know and understand the work system; building contacts with prospects, customers and colleagues; developing informal contacts, networks and power bases; retirement benefits, pension plans or company reward systems.

Turnover is also influenced by alternative job opportunities. The popularity or acceptance of the products and company affects turnover. Prestigious organizations with successful products or a good reputation provide the salesperson with benefits in the form of wide acceptance by prospective customers, voluntary enquiries and referrals, automatic reorders and non-effort earnings.

Being aware of the predictors of tenure places management in a better position to introduce measures to avoid high turnover. Financial, structural and strategic considerations though, may limit the use of this knowledge. A company may not find it feasible or desirable to recruit veteran salespersons. It may be difficult to do much about alternative job opportunities. Nor may it be possible to make sub-stantial short-term improvements to the popularity or acceptance of a company or its products. Nonetheless, there are steps which companies can take to utilize this information.

To reduce turnover, the salesperson should be viewed as a valuable asset, requiring investment and maintenance. Time needs to be spent on training and supporting salespeople rather than trying to change their attitude. With regard to general economic conditions and job opportunities elsewhere, management should be pro-active, anticipat-ing changes in their external environment and taking action to minimize turnover resulting from these changes. Finally, not all turnover is necessarily bad for the company. A weak relationship between turnover and job attitudes – except for salespersons whose performance is low – casts doubt on the value of focusing on job attitudes as a way of reducing turnover. It does, though, suggest that management should consider selecting target groups for special attention. For instance, they might wish to target high performing salespersons with short tenure for special attention as a way of investing in quality staff who, if appropriate action is not taken, are most likely to leave.

Rewarding the sales force – financial and non-monetary rewards

To a degree, the methods companies use to reward their direct sales personnel will affect the type of candidate they attract and their attitudes and behaviour. In reality, the method chosen is usually influenced by the service being offered and the norm for the financial services sector rather than an evaluation of the advantages and disadvantages of alternative options.

There are five main remuneration methods in this sector:

Commission only

This is a highly cost-effective way of rewarding sales personnel as companies only have to pay on results. The attraction for the sales person is that it offers unlimited income to those who are highly successful. Companies operating with a commission only salesforce experience high levels of turnover. There are two main reasons for this. Firstly, such companies tend to be less selective in who they set on and more willing to take a chance on candidates. Secondly, working on a commission only basis puts job holders under a considerable strain. Even those who are suited to the type of work can find the insecurity too much for them.

Aside from the problem of labour turnover, commission only has other effects. Salespeople usually reach an income level with which they are satisfied and decide that the extra effort to get more money is not worth it. Many commission only salespeople are self-employed. This can make it difficult for companies to gain commitment and control their agents. The career structure for commission only sales personnel – particularly those who are self-employed – is often non-existent. All in all, those operating commission only schemes find that money alone is usually insufficient to motivate people to perform at a high level and stay with the company for long.

Quota-based systems

In contrast to straight commission which rewards all sales equally, quota-based systems provide sales personnel with an agreed target to aim for. Quota-based systems provide flexibility for structuring a range of incentives. Companies find this flexibility beneficial as they can adjust the emphasis they place on the promotion of products by the commission and reward system. In itself, the existence of an attractive, reasonable target is likely to motivate and lead to high performance.

Small basic salary with high commission potential

This route provides people with a small degree of basic security and also limits the company's fixed costs. Nonetheless, many of the problems associated with commission only apply equally well to this category of employee.

High basic salary with low commission or bonus

With this situation, companies have to be far more selective in who they employ. It does provide people with security although if the commission is set too low it may not provide much of an incentive.

Salary only

It is hardly surprising, that this is the remuneration system that employees usually prefer and employers like least. It provides security of income but employers have to be far more careful in their selection procedures and usually find that performance is not so high as under commission only conditions.

In recent years, efforts have been made by some of the traditional life offices to change remuneration packages, moving towards more commission and less salary, with the intention of making home service agents more sales conscious. By contrast, some of the more unit linked offices have switched away from remuneration packages which were almost entirely commission based, to include a more significant salary component. In part, the rationale for this move is to encourage more relationship building with clients.

Clearly, each of the main remuneration methods has advantages and drawbacks. Size and method of financial remuneration do influence motivation in terms of job performance and retention levels. They will also vary in their appeal to people according to their needs and aspirations. Whilst not wishing to underplay its importance, financial remuneration alone is unlikely to motivate as will be seen in the subsequent discussion on motivation. Other areas discussed such as: recruiting people suited to the job and providing good quality training and support are also important. In the last couple of years, all financial service organizations have been investing heavily in training and recruitment programmes. Some of the larger offices which traditionally dealt with home service agents are now spending £6m per year to upgrade the quality of the sales force and make them more sales conscious.

Retaining the sales force – motivation and training

High levels of turnover can be reduced if an appropriate candidate for direct selling is recruited in the first instance.

Once salespersons are in post, there are many areas companies must bear in mind if they want to ensure they have a productive sales force. These areas concern: an understanding of sales force motivation; appropriate recognition and reward systems linked to performance monitoring; training and support systems.

Sales force motivation

Within the overall field of motivation research, sales force motivation has attracted a considerable amount of attention. This is because, unlike many other categories of employees, the performance of salespeople is easily measurable and there is a strong link between an individual's work efforts and performance. Moreover, high sales force motivation is thought to lead to high sales performance (Walker *et al.*, 1977). Despite the considerable volume of research in the area of motivation in general and that of sales force motivation in particular, sales managers have found the task of motivating their salespeople to be a difficult one with no simple answers readily available (Doyle and Shapiro, 1980). There are several reasons for this:

1 Poor recruitment and selection techniques can mean that people largely unsuited to direct selling are taken on. Inevitably, it becomes hard to motivate, train and retain people who are not fitted to the type of work.
2 Much of the empirical work on sales force motivation has tended to focus on one conceptual model of motivation – usually that of expectancy theory although others based on needs satisfaction are also popular. Focusing on one model of motivation tends to oversimplify the complexity of human motivation in work settings. Moreover, it tends to overlook the fact that motivation is dynamic and changes across time (Kiely, 1986) and is influenced by career stages (Cron *et al.*, 1988).
3 Concentrating solely on sales force motivation without ensuring that the overall culture and environment within which salespeople operate is appropriate, only addresses part of the picture. Research which has taken a holistic approach has demonstrated that motivation is influenced by far more than perceptions of the job and the fit between individual physical and psychological needs and characteristics of the job. Matters such as perceptions of the organization regarding job support provided, performance monitoring, products and their promotion strategies are all important.
4 Motivation is influenced by circumstances which in many instances are outside of the immediate control of organizations. Matters such as changes in personal circumstances, the availability of alternative jobs and government policies and interest rates can all impinge on motivation.

Organizations in the financial services sector have commonly assumed that what salespeople want most from a job is money. They have applied simple 'rational economic man' models of motivation to the sales force and then been surprised when salespeople have not worked as hard as they possibly can for more money. However, although money may be a major enticement into that type of work, once that need is satisfied other factors may become more important.

There are a variety of studies of sales force motivations using a range of approaches (see, for example, Churchill *et al.*, 1978; Teas, 1981; Tyagi, 1982; Ingram and Bellenger, 1983; Ford *et al.*, 1985; Hackman and Oldham, 1980). For purposes of illustration we will concentrate on one example of these studies; namely, the career stages framework suggested by Cron (1984).

Salespeople, like any other occupational group, pass through distinct career stages. The stage they are at in their career will influence their attitudes towards the job, perceptions of what they need from work and how these needs can best be met. The career stage framework for sales personnel developed by Cron (1984) identifies four distinct career stages: exploration; establishment; maintenance; and disengagement. This can be used to provide a framework for examining what salespeople are likely to look for in their work:

1 At the exploration stage, salespeople are concerned about whether or not they are in the right type of job. Whilst these types of worries are common to new entrants in most occupations, the unique nature of direct selling makes these concerns more pressing. The very high turnover of salespeople in the first few months of their job bears this out. It is at this stage that appropriate training and support from managers is vital. Salespeople at the exploration stage are likely to be least positive about their job situation and be the lowest performers.

   Sales managers have to develop the skills and abilities of their salesforce as well as building confidence. This is not an easy task and sales personnel may be sceptical about the rewards they can achieve from high performance because of their low performance during their brief sales career.

2 At the establishment stage, sales personnel have proved to themselves that they can sell. Their knowledge base has increased which helps them clarify the requirements for effective performance. They now start to want more from their jobs than just money. The task of sales managers in dealing with the needs of sales personnel at this stage in their career is challenging. Sales managers, in conjunction with the reward mechanisms offered by the company, can develop the importance sales personnel place on esteem and achievement needs. Sometimes this is achieved by various recognition procedures or awards such as exotic foreign

travel for the top salespeople each year. Travel incentives are becoming increasingly popular, particularly in the insurance industry, as a means of motivating salespeople. A survey of 1083, commission only life insurance salespeople (Hastings *et al.*, 1988) found travel is a strong motivator and valued more highly than several other types of incentives. Companies who operate such schemes have found that it is not so much winning the actual prize which is important as the 'trophy' value of being recognized throughout the company as one of the top salespeople.

3   At the maintenance stage sales personnel become more committed to the organization and less inclined to leave. If management integrates sales personnel into the organization, they will become more committed. Personnel at this point in their career will have developed work patterns with which they are comfortable and be inclined to want their job and work pattern to remain the same. Sales managers have to ensure that sales personnel at the maintenance stage adapt to changes and keep abreast of new developments and legislation within financial services.

4   Due to the structure of rewards and payment systems for direct sales personnel, the disengagement phase is likely to be relatively short. Sales personnel are likely to minimize the importance of both the monetary and non-monetary rewards found in their work. Lower job performance is associated with disengagement which will have direct repercussions on income. People at this stage present a significant motivational challenge to management. No easy solution can be offered, although the answer may be to avoid the situation arising in the first place. In reality, the situation is normally swiftly resolved by the sales person leaving.

Irrespective of the precise analytical framework used in studying motivation, there are a number of key points which require consideration. Firstly, motivation is a dynamic process. Needs, values, expectations and views of fairness change across time. The career stage of sales personnel will affect what they want and need from work and their perception of their situation. Secondly, the sales manager plays a crucial role in determining and influencing sales force motivation. The level of support and quality of training must be both appropriate to the needs of the individual and his or her career development stage. Thirdly, companies differ in the remuneration method being offered to direct sales personnel. The remuneration method being offered will attract different types of people with different needs.

Training and support

The earlier discussion of sales force remuneration and motivation has emphasized the ways in which training and sales support systems assist retention and improve job performance. Effective training involves both a knowledge and a skills component and an important adjunct to such training is the provision of sales support to staff by management.

A direct sales force in financial services has to be fully familiar with all products and services offered by the company as well as understanding legislative requirements. One of the benefits of the Financial Services Act has been to increase the amount of training received by sales personnel.

The sales force must also understand policies relevant to the selling function. This includes: sales force compensation methods and evaluation; organization of the company and the relationships between functional areas; work organization and reporting mechanisms and procedures; competitors and their products and services.

Most companies are extremely good at conveying the knowledge component of selling to their sales personnel or agents. Selling, though, is a skill which has to be learned, practised and developed. High performing salespeople have learnt and understood the requisite skills and are proficient at putting them into practice. Moreover, they are able to anticipate and plan so they can control sales situations.

Training courses may use a variety of techniques to develop skills training. Talks and discussions can convey the information and knowledge but this must be supplemented by methods such as: interactive video; close-circuit television; case studies; role play and simulation exercises. These techniques let sales trainees practice sales techniques and get feedback which assists learning.

Initial training has to be reinforced by experience gained by real life selling. The role of the sales manager in developing skills and techniques is crucial. By watching and analysing the recruits in action they are in a position to evaluate how situations are dealt with and provide constructive feedback to enhance future performance. The manner in which the sales manager performs these tasks will influence not only the rate of learning but matters such as the self-confidence of the sales person and their likelihood of approaching the sales manager if the need arises. Finally, as discussed earlier, the amount, type and extent of training and support provided by sales managers must be appropriate to each individual case as well as the stage that person is at in their career. It is easy to forget that the established, high performing salesperson also needs support and assistance in updating knowledge and skills.

Conclusion

This chapter has examined some of the major components of direct distribution in financial services. In some respects these methods reflect two extremes. Direct mail and direct response advertising apparently involve minimal contact with consumers while direct selling is closely concerned with building up a strong working relationship between customer and salesperson. In practice, however, they are very much complementary methods of distribution; for standardized, relatively straightforward products, direct mail and direct response advertising are cost effective mechanisms for reaching a target group of consumers. Direct sales force are then able to concentrate on their area of comparative advantage which typically revolves around the distribution of higher value, complex products. Furthermore, there is an important interaction between these two types of direct distribution in that mail shots and adverts can be an effective mechanism for prospecting new customers for the sales force.

CHAPTER 8
Indirect distribution channels in the retailing of financial services
Barry Howcroft

Introduction

The previous chapter examined 'direct' or 'active' distribution channels, which are best exemplified by the tied sales forces of the industrial life offices. This chapter concentrates upon branch networks and certain other emerging distribution systems which are essentially 'indirect' or 'passive', insomuch as they rely upon the customer to take the initiative in purchasing a financial service or product.

Distribution channels are an important means of delivering products and communicating effectively with the market place. In the basic bank markets, which have been traditionally dominated by the London clearing banks and characterized by the collection of retail deposits, the money transmission mechanism and a range of personal lending services, branch networks have fulfilled both these functions with considerable success. As distribution channels, however, branch networks have certain inherent disadvantages, which have become only too apparent with the progressive deregulation of the financial services markets. Alternative distribution channels, particularly those which utilize advanced technology, have partially remedied some of these weaknesses by complementing and supplementing the branch networks. The emergence and very existence of these alternative distribution channels, however, have also introduced some far reaching and potentially challenging strategic implications for financial institutions.

The pre-eminence of the branch is largely due to the difficulties associated with marketing financial services. Branch networks evolved to attract relatively cheap retail deposits through the convenience of branch locations and branch-based payment systems. Traditionally, they have provided a highly effective, though increasingly costly, mechanism for administering, collecting and delivering cash. They have also, simultaneously, facilitated the provision of an extensive range of associated lending and ancillary services.

The relation between the customer and the branch has been referred to as fundamental to the very process of banking (Green, 1982). This exclusivity, however, is only tenable if the conditions which determined the branch networks' historical position continue to apply. The most important of these conditions are that the market continues to respond to it, and that it will remain the basis for existing and emerging patterns of competitive behaviour. The chapter will clearly indicate, however, that the branch networks' exclusive position, even in the basic bank markets, is becoming increasingly less certain, owing to a combination of interrelated factors which are radically changing customer and competitor behaviour in the financial market.

The strategic issues

The optimum mix of distribution channels is an important strategic issue confronting management in financial institutions. The eventual choice will influence both the product range and its impact within the market place. Both these considerations are important determinants of ultimate market share, but an even more important consideration is how the mix of distribution channels affects the basic cost structures of financial institutions and, therefore, their price-competitiveness and profitability.

In deciding upon the mix of distribution channels, financial institutions are effectively determining their ability to operate successfully in the financial markets. The choice is based upon the following considerations:

1 Maintaining a strong market position through attracting and retaining a large, profitable customer base
2 Introducing new distribution channels to counteract the cost benefit characteristics of the branch network
3 Building a distribution channel mix that can respond flexibly to changes in competition and the market place
4 Exploiting fully the benefits inherent in the existing infrastructure.

In deciding upon the mix of distribution channels, the clearing banks probably face the most difficult problem, because their dominant position in the market place is still based primarily upon the branch network. Any change in their strategic distribution system would, therefore appear to necessitate a gradualistic approach in an endeavour to reduce the impact upon the branch structure and the attendant investment in staff and systems (Howcroft and Lavis, 1986).

Another important issue which faces all financial institutions instigating change of this kind is the desirability of maintaining customer franchise during the transitional period. To some extent, this will depend upon the ability of new entrants to gain access to the markets via new distribution channels. Competitive pressures have already increased because of the wider range of distribution channels currently available and because of the customer's increased financial awareness and sophistication.

In addition to competition, technology has become an important arbiter of strategic direction. Not only is it changing the economics of the market place but it is also providing both an opportunity and a challenge to incorporate technology characteristics into product designs. In this way technology-driven distribution channels can focus products and target customers by ensuring that products are sufficiently differentiated from competitors'. Customers can then be locked into products because they are both cost-effective and offer a unique quality of service and information.

Financial institutions are also becoming less capable of determining their strategies solely by reference to internal considerations. Consequently, strategies are increasingly being determined by considerations and options provided by technology, or solely in response to competitive and external market forces. In the process, financial institutions which rely extensively upon branch networks may begin to regard their branches as one of a range of possible delivery systems, rather than the central aspects of their business.

Financial institutions, at whatever stage of their development, need to fulfil certain essential requirements in order to survive. These requirements include the need to occupy the market, the need to acquire new customers, and the need to service existing and emerging customers. The emerging channels of distribution, including home banking, which is potentially the most complete in satisfying all these requirements, have a tendency to emphasize the third category insomuch as they are primarily aimed at providing a range of basic services. The important considerations of market occupation through tangible presence and acquiring new customers through physical location are functions which have been traditionally fulfilled by the branch network.

The fact that branches are prevalent in the basic bank market, and are not readily reduced without incurring loss, combines with the above considerations to suggest that they will almost certainly continue to be an important element in the future distribution channel mix. Branch-orientated financial institutions are, in fact, already attempting to combine the advantages of the branch with those of electronic distribution channels. Implicit in this mix, however, is a definite and deliberate change in the organization of the branch network and its basic function. This change reflects both the need to maintain a cost-effective business and the need to ensure that the branch networks complement, rather than merely replicate, the new and emerging alternative distribution channels.

Arbiters of change

Competition

Branch networks have certainly succeeded in obtaining a high penetration in both the payments system and the savings market. However, the past 20 years of systematic deregulation of the financial system have changed not only the level of competition but also the patterns of competitive behaviour. The Financial Services Act, combined with the government's progressive privatization of pensions and the emergence of the mortgage as the crucial lifetime financial transaction, will compound these changes, and may well place further question marks against the future effectiveness of the branch network in these new and emerging financial markets (Ginarlis, 1988).

The basic problem is that branch networks typical of clearing banks, building societies and estate agents are essentially 'passive', i.e. the emphasis is on the customer to make the effort and visit the office. By contrast, the 'active' sales medium is the tied sales force typical of industrial life offices, unit-linked offices and major retail brokers, which calls for company representatives to visit customers wherever customers find it convenient, e.g. usually at home and outside normal banking hours. Branch networks may be eminently suitable for relatively simple insurance products, such as endowment mortgages or house content policies, but they are certainly less suitable for the more complex life or pension products, which require more detailed information and individual tailoring.

The Securities Investment Board's (SIB) polarization regulations have further complicated the situation by insisting upon the designation of retail salesmen as either company representatives (agents) or independent intermediaries (principals); but, as Table 8.1 indicates, the response has not been uniform. A minority of institutions have independent intermediary status and, therefore, offer a full brokerage service. The majority of clearing banks and building societies, however, have become company representative and, therefore, will only endeavour to sell the insurance products of the companies they

Table 8.1 *Polarization: designation of branches*

Bank/building society	Status	Company represented
Bank		
Barclays	CR	Barclays Life
Lloyds	CR	Black Horse Life
Midland	CR	Midland Life
National Westminster	II	–
Bank of Scotland	CR	Standard Life
Royal Bank of Scotland	II	–
TSB	CR	TSB Life
Yorkshire	II	–
Abbey National	CR	Friends Provident
Building society		
Halifax	CR	Standard Life
Nationwide Anglia	CR	GRE
Alliance & Leicester	CR	Scottish Amicable
Woolwich	CR	Sun Alliance
National & Provincial	CR	National & Provincial Life
Britannia	CR	Britannia Life
Bradford & Bingley	II	–
Cheltenham & Gloucester	CR	Legal & General

CR: Company representative
II: Independent intermediary
Source: Banks and building societies

represent. In the case of Barclays, Lloyds, Midland and TSB, these are associated companies or subsidiaries of the banks in question. This dichotomy in the market is potentially confusing to the average customer, and the bias towards company representatives effectively reduces the outlets for independent insurance companies which desire to remain independent but which do not have their own sales force. This raises the question whether the best interests of the customer are being met under these circumstances.

Electronic technology

In distribution terms there are essentially two types of technology – that which complements a branch's function, e.g. front office terminals, cheque truncation, etc., and that which provides an alternative means of distribution, e.g. ATMs, EFTPOS, plastic cards, home banking, etc. New technology to date has generally supported branch networks by facilitating greater volumes of transaction business. The functional efficiency of branches has, therefore, been markedly improved, but the general availability of this technology has meant that no significant competitive advantage has emerged.

As an alternative distribution channel, however, new and emerging technology is changing the pattern of competitive behaviour. By reducing reliance upon the branch network, technology has significantly reduced the single most important barrier to entry into the basic bank markets. This has enabled credit-card organizations, particularly the non-bank American Express and highly centralized financial service groups, to access the market. Insurance groups, data-processing companies and retailers, similarly, now have the potential to offer a comprehensive range of financial products throughout the UK. Moreover, substantial capitalization, combined with technology, has introduced another competitive threat in the form of large Japanese and American banks with the potential to provide personal and corporate financial services throughout Europe.

The combined net effect of new technology and increased competition has fragmented the market place and eroded the traditional homogeneity of the various financial institutions. As distribution channels based upon technology have the capability to offer specific bundles of services, the traditional interdependence between savings, payment systems and lending products has also started to break down. This has facilitated the emphasis upon market segmentation, and introduced the potential and opportunity to design products which increasingly incorporate reliance upon specific technological distribution channels (Nicholas, 1985).

The development of delivery systems in the UK

Branch networks

The development of large branch networks in the UK is largely a consequence of evolutionary and unplanned growth. The clearing bank mergers in 1968, for instance, saw the formation of a group of four major banks whose networks had grown under the influence of 'functional' competition, insomuch as it restricted price competition but provided a rate of return sufficient to encourage physical expansion. The mergers, however, created overlarge networks which, combined with increased competition, eventually led to a slow contraction in their size. See Table 8.2.

The factors responsible for this contraction derive basically from two sources. The first is that customers are increasingly seeking both greater control and greater convenience in the conduct of their financial affairs. Greater affluence and sophistication have also resulted in enhanced financial awareness, with a resultant decline in the 'endowment' element in bank profits. Essentially, bank customers

Table 8.2 *Branch networks in the UK*

	1983	1988
Girobank	22,301	21,071
National Westminster	3,226	3,086
Barclays	2,912	2,712
Lloyds	2,276	2,189
Midland	2,345	2,090
TSB	1,604	1,546
Royal Bank of Scotland	894	829
Bank of Scotland	559	540
Clydesdale	381	351
Yorkshire	215	247
Co-operative	75	104
Standard Chartered	–	17
Total banks	36,788	34,782
Total building societies*	6,643	6,962

* The number of building societies had declined from 206 in 1983 to 137 by 1987

Source: *Abstract of Banking Statistics*

are seeking higher returns from their savings and are, therefore, less inclined to leave their idle funds in non-interest-earning current accounts. Instead they are increasingly maintaining merely transaction balances with the clearing banks and thereby reducing the ability of the banks to attract cheap money. The second factor relating to a contraction in branch networks derives from the vulnerability of branches to excessive costs. The situation has been exacerbated by the traditional low levels of cost recovery on payment systems and by the emergence of alternative cost-effective technology-driven distribution systems (Hammond, 1981).

Building-society branch networks have in the past been cited as examples to illustrate the deficiencies of clearing bank branches, particularly in terms of style and operating efficiency. The expansion of the societies' networks, shown in Table 8.2, has undoubtedly undermined the clearing banks' competitive advantage of convenience, and has had the almost incidental effect of providing direct price competition. Nevertheless, despite the similarities, not least those afforded by the building societies' pre-1983 cartel, there are fundamental differences in the traditional business conducted by building societies and clearing banks. In essence the traditional building-society function has been more simple and limited in range, compared to the traditional business of the clearing banks. These differences reduce to some extent the validity of a direct comparison between bank and building-society branches. In fact, when the implications of the Building Society Act,

Table 8.3 *Ownership and size of the top ten estate agencies*

Estate Agency	Parent	Mid-1989 outlets	Mid-1986 outlets
1 Royal Life Estates	Royal Insurance	817	256
2 Prudential Property Services	Prudential Corporation	800	92
3 Halifax Property Services	Halifax	643	N/A
4 GA Property Services	General Accident	612	80
5 Black Horse Agencies	Abbey Life (Lloyds)	563	350
6 Hambro Countrywide	Hambros	514	350
7 Nationwide Anglia Estate Agencies	Nationwide Anglia	480	N/A
8 Cornerstone Estate Agencies	Abbey National	434	N/A
9 TSB Property Services	TSB	181	N/A
10 Hamptons	Abaco Investments	160	N/A

Sources: *Chartered Surveyor Weekly* and *Euromonitor Research*

1986, and the Financial Services Act, 1986, are fully realized, building societies too will almost certainly incur problems not entirely dissimilar to those experienced by the clearing banks, particularly those relating to the functional and cost efficiency of branches compared to new and emerging distribution channels (Barnes, 1985).

Estate-agency business, as shown by Table 8.3, has exhibited massive increases in the number of outlets operating in the market. Between 1986 and 1989 the average number of outlets held by the top ten estate agents increased from 123 to 520. This increase was paralleled by an equally impressive change in the diversity of ownership of these outlets, away from the specialist estate agency towards banks, building societies and insurance companies. With approximately 80 per cent of new mortgage business currently being conducted on an endowment rather than a traditional capital repayment basis, these structural changes are to a large extent attributable to the critical link between housing transaction and brokerage income. Despite the collapse of the housing market, which will undoubtedly result in the majority of chains shown in Table 8.3 realizing a loss for 1989, the housing point of sale will, in the absence of any obvious alternatives, remain the focal point for selling insurance products.

The advantages associated with a comprehensive branch network, however, must not be underestimated. Branches still constitute a substantial barrier to competitive entry and remain a most effective distribution channel in the basic bank markets. Information technology has facilitated their importance by making them more cost-effective. Automation of a significant amount of processing, administration and routine customer service has reduced the branches' requirement for traditional bank-clerk manpower, while simultaneously increasing their output capacity. Technology has also reduced the administrative pressures on branches, and provided the opportunity increasingly to regard them as marketing or retailing centres, with the potential to project corporate image.

In the final analysis, however, there remain substantial inherent disadvantages associated with a branch network. They are expensive, and as distribution channels they can justifiably be referred to as 'passive' and 'static' – passive in that the customer needs to be 'induced' (the traditional inducement being the payments mechanism) into them and static in that they are relatively inflexible and difficult to adapt to changing market conditions. In fact, this partly explains why the history of the basic bank markets has been gradual and evolutionary rather than swift and revolutionary. The branch network is also not best suited for distributing the full range of financial services, particularly the more complicated life products, which require a more personalized approach. Non-branch competition in the form of 'active' sales representatives, combined with technology-driven distribution channels, will prove a severe test of branch banking in future.

Against this background some form of branch rationalization has already taken place. 'Hub and Spoke' branching is a system whereby a core branch offers a full service, with satellite branches offering a more limited, sometimes highly automated service. The logistics of the system vary between different banks, but essentially they will be structured around an area office which will have responsibility for between four and fifteen satellite branches. The area office is likely to be referred to as a 'key branch' or 'corporate banking centre', and, in addition to controlling the satellite branches, will have direct responsibility for generating corporate business and other predesignated key accounts. The satellite branches themselves will concentrate upon personal banking services or banking for small businesses, and may even be given general, support, counter or agency branch status, depending upon their primary function. Implicit in this system is the removal of the processing function to a centralized department. Opinion, however, remains divided upon this latter point, as some form of in-branch processing may be necessary to maintain the traditional banker–customer relationship at branch level (Doyle *et al.*, 1979).

Technology

The need to make branches more cost and functionally efficient has

Table 8.4   *Installed cash dispensers and ATMs*

	1983 No.	1988 No.
National Westminster	1,304	2,445
Lloyds	1,535	2,068
TSB	445	1,795
Barclays	683	1,777
Midland	703	1,581
Royal Bank of Scotland	469	613
Bank of Scotland	203	311
Clydesdale	194	291
Yorkshire	92	203
Girobank	–	182
Co-operative	–	60
Total banks	5,628	11,326
Link	–	1,300
Matrix	–	660
Halifax Building Society	–	886
Total building societies*	112	2,846*

* Includes Abbey National
Sources: *Banking World* (various) and *Financial Times Survey: Plastic Cards*, 15
   September 1988

resulted in the wide-scale introduction of Automatic Teller Machines
(see Table 8.4). This development has not only mitigated the decline in
branch numbers but also made 24-hour branch banking a reality. In
addition to cash dispensing services, ATMs provide balance enquiries
statements, chequebook request services and, in some instances,
deposit collection facilities. Marketing messages can also be transmitted on to the ATM screens (Choraphas, 1988).

The move towards ATM-sharing agreements has largely been
caused by the desire to reduce both variable and fixed costs, and to
spread the risks associated with the new technology. The actual
company groupings typical of Matrix and Link, for example, have
largely been based upon technological compatibility rather than any
other consideration, but they do, nevertheless, raise the possibility of
future power-groupings. The possibility constitutes another reason
why financial institutions should attempt to establish distinctive
market positions, and so endeavour to safeguard corporate identity
and market share. The inextricable linkage between cooperation and
competition will, at least in the medium term, serve to safeguard the
future of branch networks, because, unlike cooperative ventures, the
branches will inalienably define and identify the individual bank and,
therefore, project corporate image.

EFTPOS (Electronic Funds Transfer at Point of Sale) is essentially a payment system that may also be described as a distribution channel, which works on the same principles as ATM-sharing. The joint development of an EFTPOS network has the potential to create a barrier to the entry of other groups, and thereby maintain the market position of individual institutions in the same way that the payment systems oligopoly did. Accordingly, a report commissioned by the Bankers' Clearing House to review the organization, membership and control of the entire British clearing system made specific recommendations regarding the implementation and control of EFTPOS. The position to date is such that to gain full settlement membership of EFTPOS an institution, or group of institutions, must be:

1 Ready and able to comply with technical and operational requirements
2 Able to establish settlement facilities at the Bank of England
3 Willing to pay a fair share of operating costs
4 Willing to pay a fair entry price (purchase of EFTPOS UK Ltd shares)
5 Able to meet minimum 0.5 per cent volume criteria (or show evidence of ability to do this within first year of membership).

The only prudential regulation relating to members of EFTPOS UK Ltd appears to come from their ability to establish settlement facilities at the Bank of England. Clearly the Bank of England will be the final arbiter on this point, but it will presumably wish to ensure that only 'appropriately regulated' institutions gain membership.

The introduction of EFTPOS is a major initiative in using technology to control the growth in overheads; paradoxically, although it is an adjunct to branch banking and dependent upon an established customer franchise, it nevertheless weakens both the role of the branch and the banker–customer relationship. EFTPOS, therefore, may be perceived as the most significant technological step to date away from the branch-banking concept, and may ultimately be responsible for a further significant rationalization in the branch network. A counter argument, however, could be postulated on the grounds that EFTPOS may actually strengthen the need to have highly visible 'retail' outlets whose primary function is to sell financial services rather than provide payment services. This will compensate for the possible breakdown in the personal relationship between the banks and their customers when operating a full EFTPOS service, but will raise the most difficult problem of how to attract customers into branches which do not have money-transmission facilities.

The advantages of EFTPOS to retailers and customers are ambiguous, and, despite the frequently vaunted view concerning its potential to curtail rising costs, the advantages to banking institutions remain similarly debatable. Its introduction will almost certainly disrupt the existing pattern of conducting business at not inconsiderable cost to both financial institutions and retailers. It will not overtly build and foster customer franchises, and will possibly undermine the existence of branded credit cards and the economic and functional validity of the branch network. In this respect, EFTPOS encapsulates the major strategic dilemmas posed by new technology in the traditional banking markets.

Home banking has even farther-reaching implications as a new distribution channel, because it relies even less than ATMs and EFTPOS upon an established customer franchise and marketing base. It is also not dependent upon co-operative schemes with other financial institutions, although it will require the intermediation of a communications company to provide the interactive communications networks. The technology is now readily available in the form of videotext systems based upon either telephone lines using packet switching techniques, or cable television systems utilizing their ability to carry several hundred channels simultaneously. Much will depend upon the demand for these technologies by the general public in determining the future success of home banking. The success of financial institutions in developing software packages capable of delivering an appropriate product mix, with a high degree of interactivity between customer and institution, will also be critical in determining future long-term success.

For established banks and building societies the objectives behind the introduction of home banking on a national scale will, if it ever occurs, be essentially twofold: firstly, as a strategy to defend market position against non-traditional competitors who may seize upon the opportunity provided by relatively low entry costs to access the basic bank markets; and, secondly, as yet another opportunity to introduce a more explicit pricing strategy based upon fee income and, therefore, attempt to mitigate to some extent the increasingly volatile endowment income business.

Other distribution channels

The existence of highly efficient postal and telephone services in the United Kingdom has enabled highly centralized operations, such as plastic cards, money market funds, cash management accounts, etc., to attract substantial volumes of business despite having no captive customer base or retail branch network. This has enabled non-branch financial institutions with completely different cost structures to compete against institutions with branch networks, by underpricing them and offering relatively high levels of service and convenience. Although the threat is marginal, it is nevertheless sufficiently great to disrupt the economics of branch banking based upon competition between industry groups with similar cost structures.

Financial institutions which rely heavily upon branch networks can also utilize the postal and telephone-based distribution channels. They have large customer franchises, with a commensurate store of information concerning their financial behaviour, which places them in a good position to exploit direct-mail and telephone-selling techniques.

Despite the inherent changes in such an approach, it does potentially offer a highly cost-effective method of developing customer relationships and increasing sales. The importance of this distribution channel within the basic bank markets will almost certainly increase as direct contact between the customer base and the branch network decreases (Donnelly, 1976).

Conclusions

Distribution channelling represents a central issue in the future development of the financial services industry. Already the effects of electronic technology, deregulation, increased competition and heightened customer awareness have had a significant impact upon the delivery of financial products and services. In the basic bank markets, branch networks have already been modified by number, organization and function, but they will probably remain an important distribution channel in these markets. They will, nevertheless, increasingly be complemented and supplemented by new and emerging distribution systems. In the long term, the effects should produce financial institutions that are far more efficient and competitive, but in the process some of the fundamental aspects of their business may change. Home banking, for instance, will almost certainly provide a most substantive threat to the branch networks in the basic bank markets and introduce a fundamental change in the traditional banker–customer relationship. The traditional 'tied' sales forces of the life companies will constitute a similar threat to the branch network in the emerging private investment markets, especially with the more complicated products, which ideally need a more personalized service. In the final analysis, these and other considerations alluded to in the chapter will almost certainly undermine the branch networks' dominant position. The networks' importance in determining both organizational structure and competitive behaviour will, therefore, be reduced. Branches will, however, continue to form an important distribution channel, which, together with new and emerging distribution channels, will have to be managed in an endeavour to optimize performance. Indeed, the actual management of this mix of distribution channels will be of increasing importance in determining future competitiveness in the financial services market.

CHAPTER 9
Bank marketing
Barbara Lewis

Introduction

Banks were traditionally in the 'business of banking', namely borrowing from one market and lending to another. However, as seen in Chapter 1, since the early 1970s their orientation has become, and will continue to be, the 'business of financial services', with a much wider focus in relation to consumer/market needs and consequent marketing strategies.

The UK banking system is dominated by the Big Four – Barclays, National Westminster, Midland and Lloyds (Table 9.1). After a lengthy period of stability in the structure of the industry, following notable mergers in the 1960s, further restructuring became more in evidence in the late 1980s. The TSB Group underwent substantial reorganization and stock market flotation. The Clydesdale Bank was sold by the Midland Bank to the National Australian Bank. Williams' and Glyn's Bank, which had long been a part of the Royal Bank of Scotland while maintaining its separate identity in England, became fully incorporated into the Scottish bank's corporate identity. In a further strategic development, reflecting some major non-UK banks' desires to extend their cross-border activities for the reasons outlined in Chapter 1, the Yorkshire Bank was acquired by National Australian Bank, which fought off competing bids from Deutsche Bank and BNP. These developments have important implications for further diversification by banks beyond the extensive amount which has already taken place, with varying degrees of success, as the development in profits between 1983 and 1988 shown in Table 9.1 indicates. By extension, there are also implications for marketing strategies.

In this chapter, the focus is the marketing strategies and activities of the major UK banks in the provision of personal financial services, i.e. with respect to retail markets. The setting of marketing objectives and the design of marketing strategies are elements within the marketing planning process (see Figure 9.1) whereby a bank will carry out, on an iterative basis, an audit of the company, its markets and environment; determine strengths and weaknesses, opportunities and threats; set

Table 9.1 *Assets and profits of UK banks (£m)*

	1983		1988	
	Assets	Pre-tax profit	Assets	Pre-tax profit
Barclays	57,976	485	104,645	1,391
National Westminster	59,880	519	98,642	1,407
Midland	52,613	225	55,729	693
Lloyds	38,432	419	51,834	952
Standard Chartered	28,917	268	23,692	313
TSB	9,185	150	22,516	420
Royal Bank of Scotland	11,077	96	21,660	309
Bank of Scotland	5,361	50	11,005	131
Clydesdale	2,254	18	3,561	30
Yorkshire	1,330	37	3,185	100
Co-operative	1,064	8	2,228	23
Girobank	904	18	1,865	24

Source: *Abstract of Banking Statistics*, May 1989

objectives; develop strategies and tactics; and implement, evaluate and control the total marketing programme.

Initial attention is given, briefly, to aspects of the marketing audit, in particular the changing environment. This is followed by a review of the strategic considerations relating to market segments and elements of the marketing mix, presentation of product/market mix strategies and discussion of the opportunities for growth within the banking sector.

The marketing audit

The basis of the market audit is to review and analyse all the business conditions affecting a bank and its operations.

Environmental analysis

The major elements in the changing environment of the clearing banks which impact on all elements of their marketing strategies are the following.

Economic elements

Inflation, interest rates and employment levels are the most important. Demand for financial services is usually derived from the demand for other products and services which are affected by economic conditions.

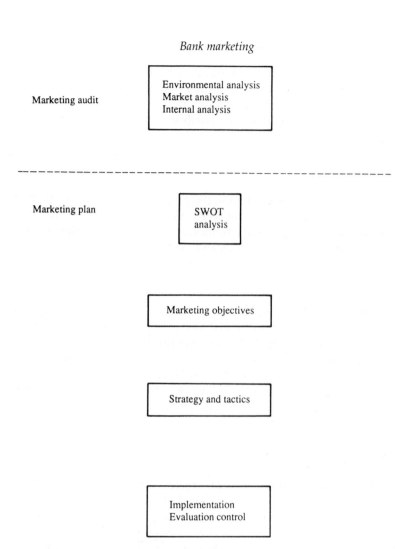

Figure 9.1 *The marketing planning process*

Demographics

The changing age distribution of the population and increasing education levels affect people's financial service needs.

Social and cultural factors

Changing lifestyles and public opinion have a number of effects, e.g. traditional values with respect to thrift and the stigma of credit are disappearing, with the emergence of a credit culture and resultant attitudes and behaviour with regard to spending, and the use of a wide range of credit and other financial services. Further, consumer attitudes with respect to technologically based bank services continue to become more favourable, and consumers are more discerning with respect to expectations of service quality and the quality of service actually received.

Technological developments

These developments are evident in the operations *and* management of banks, in their products, delivery systems and also in their communications/promotional methods, and enhance the banks' abilities to manage their products and customers.

Legal/political

Government continues to play a major role, via legislation, in several dimensions. New patterns of consumer behaviour are encouraged in terms of home-ownership, share-ownership, pension-planning, taxation, etc. Further, as seen in Chapter 1, deregulatory legislation in the form of the Banking Act and the Building Societies Act has been designed to remove competitive barriers and create open and free markets, although this has been accompanied by regulatory supervision (the Financial Services Act).

Competition

The new legislative environment creates both opportunities and threats for the banks in terms of the level of competition from existing bank competitors, new bank competitors (e.g. overseas banks – what will happen after 1992?), and new market entrants; the last include building societies, retailers and other present and potential providers of financial services, e.g. American Express, estate agents, accountants and solicitors.

The building societies are developing growth and competitive strategies in a number of ways (see Chapter 10), in particular with respect to their branching and product policies. Retailers have few barriers to entry into financial services, and can take advantage of their store networks and technological capabilities as an alternative to the traditional branch. A number of retailers will eventually offer a wide range of financial services, and one can pose the question whether or not companies like Marks and Spencer will follow the Sears Roebuck example and move beyond credit cards and loans, into insurance, mortgages and other financial services. To do so would enable them to focus on long-term relationships with households and to meet their changing financial service needs over time; their strategies might be to offer innovative products/services on the basis of superior value/ quality, and to provide excellent customer service.

Competitor analysis will include not only identification of key organizations/sectors but also their position and coverage in the market, and their image.

Market analysis

The concerns of market analysis are to monitor trends relating to size, market share, competitive position and growth potential; to investigate customer profiles, needs and market segments; and to consider influences on the consumer decision-process in relation to buying financial services.

Internal analysis

In conjunction with environmental and market analysis, a bank needs to audit its internal resources to include its people, production capacity, financial/investment capabilities, and management expertise, together with its product range, branch network and delivery systems. As a result, the bank should be able to identify its internal strengths and weaknesses and match its strengths to the opportunities in the environment and market, convert its weaknesses to strengths, avoid environmental-marketing threats, and move on towards marketing planning, i.e. setting objectives and marketing strategies.

Marketing strategy

Instrumental to the marketing-planning process, a bank needs to set objectives with respect to products, markets and performance, it also needs to develop strategies relating to markets, and the various elements of the marketing mix, to include product, price, place, promotion and also people, i.e. all employees within the bank.

Market segments

Consideration of present and potential market segments for the bank cannot be separated from strategic issues relating to elements of the marketing mix. Nevertheless, there are a number of issues which relate to bases and approaches to segmentation.

Banks segment their markets on several bases, e.g. demographic, geographic, life-cycle, psychographic, cognitive and behavioural. In so doing, they aim to identify and respond to the particular needs, motives and expected benefits of customer groups. Examples of traditional demographic segments are:

1   Students: prime needs for deposit and overdraft facilities, cash/ ATM cards
2   Working women: financial independence and, if 'single', buyers of a wide range of financial services
3   Self-employed: targets for loans, insurance, pension plans, tax advice
4   High net worth individuals: targets for Gold cards, investment management services, large mortgages and loans
5   Professionals (e.g. doctors, accountants, solicitors): high net worth customers with additional potential as small business clients

Beyond demographics, the banks increasingly consider consumer lifestyles to include interests, opinions, attitudes and behaviour, when designing segmentation strategies. They are interested in:

1   The image of/attitude towards banks and competitor institutions
2   Attitudes towards saving, credit and borrowing
3   Financial services behaviour: saving/spending/credit, bank accounts/products/usage/loyalty factors
4   Benefits required: convenience, security, service, professionalism, price, speed, technological sophistication
5   Knowledge and expertise with respect to financial services
6   Willingness to buy new financial services/innovativeness/perceptions of risk
7   Price-sensitivity: willingness to compare interest rates and charges
8   Media habits

Knowledge about consumer attitudes, behaviour and needs will allow banks to develop and enhance relationships with present customers, and to consider the costs and benefits of new-product and market development.

Product decisions

The product offerings of the UK banks include:

1 Current accounts: chequebooks, standing orders, direct debits, bank giros, electronic funds transfer
2 Savings: deposit account, bonus saving, money market deposits
3 Loans: overdraft, house, car, home improvements, etc.
4 Card services: cheque card/cash/ATM, credit-card operations
5 Advisory services: wills, trusts, executorships, tax planning, investment advice, money management etc.
6 Financial service: pensions, personal equity plans, insurance products, etc.
7 Other: e.g. travel and foreign services

Increasingly, the banks are being driven by a combination of internal and external forces to develop and offer new products and services. The internal pressures relate to growth opportunities, and the need for increased earnings and market shares; and the external factors are competition from banks and non-banks offering banking and financial services, possible future entrants to the market, and technological advances. In particular, new products are needed to attract customers from untapped markets, to cross-sell to existing customers, to attract accounts from competitors, to sell to competitors' customers (independently of the core product), and to reduce the costs of service provision.

One may ask what is a 'new' or innovatory financial service product. Generally, one might suggest that innovative products are fundamentally new services based on new technology, a sizeable investment, considerable risk and significant market potential and rewards, e.g. the first ATMs and bank credit cards, home banking and EFTPOS. However, in banking, innovation is not likely to lead to any significant amount of product differentiation, owing to the lack of protection by patents and copyrights for the innovating organization, i.e. it is easy for competitors to copy new ideas.

At present, most of what is new in financial services comes either in the form of product/service development (e.g. new facilities of ATMs, banking by mail, credit-card insurance), or new product lines for particular banks, in services which are new to the bank but not the market. In the latter case the bank enters a market in which other companies already compete, such as insurance, trust and travel services, and competes with insurance companies, accounting firms and travel agents.

As an integral element of product range decision-making, banks may carry out a product portfolio analysis in which products/services are classified as high, medium or low in respect of market attractiveness and competitive strength (see Table 9.2). Competitive strength comprises components such as market share, size, customer loyalty,

Table 9.2 *Product analysis*

| | Market attractiveness | | |
Competitive strength	High	Medium	Low
High			
Medium			x
Low		x	x

technology, personnel, image, and management capabilities; and market attractiveness has components of market size, market growth, extent and type of competition, cross-selling potential, ease of customer switching, etc. As a consequence some products will emerge as having greater potential than others, and marketing resources and management effort will be allocated accordingly.

Pricing

The UK banks have not, until recently, viewed price as a major element of marketing strategy, because of government regulation with respect to price, the fact that banks tend to operate as an oligopoly, and because the services offered are not standard. However, pricing is becoming more important as a result of deregulation, increasing competition and decreasing consumer loyalty to particular banks.

Pricing for banks takes a number of forms:

1 Charge levels for different types of transaction, e.g. debits, cheque clearance, standing orders
2 Charge rates for overdrafts, loans
3 Fees for services, fixed or on a commission basis
4 Interest rates, on current/deposit/savings accounts
5 'Free' banking

In setting their fees, charges and interest rates, the banks are influenced (and to some extent controlled) by the government/Bank of England/legislation, competitor activities, cost structures, demand factors, benefit/value to the customer of particular financial services, and their pricing objectives (e.g. profit maximization, market-share leadership, return on investment).

In relation to current accounts, the banks have been trying to maximize profits regardless of underlying costs (market-rate pricing), and have been reluctant to pay interest on current accounts until competitive factors have forced them to. Additionally, consumers are largely ignorant with respect to prevailing interest rates and the impact of notional interest on their current account balances, and consequently there is little price-sensitivity with respect to personal financial services.

Current bank emphases with respect to pricing relate to free banking/market penetration pricing, flexible pricing policies and relationship pricing. Free banking services are traditionally offered to students, and free advisory services may be offered to them and to established or potential customers; management needs to ask which products/services might be offered at no charge in order to attract and keep customers. New services may be offered at prices less than cost (accepted as very difficult to measure and allocate in banking) in order to build competitive advantage and market share, say with the first home-banking trials. Price 'discrimination' in the form of flexible pricing is evident in relation both to customers, i.e. varying prices for the same service or different packages at the same price for students *vis-à-vis* other customers, and place, e.g. ATM transactions may cost less than counter service.

Lastly, relationship pricing is becoming increasingly relevant as customer relationships become more complex. It will be possible and necessary to improve profits from client relationships by cross-selling high margin services, and at the same time offering relationship-building services at a low margin or at a loss.

Distribution systems

Strategic decisions relating to the delivery of financial services concern the bank branch network and the increasing opportunities for the remote provision of financial services, via ATMs, EFTPOS and home banking, brought about by rapid and continuing technological advancements.

The full service bank branch has been the conventional means of distributing banking and financial services. It has been effective for collecting and delivering cash and deposits, making loans and providing a range of services. The history of the very extensive full-service branch network is well-documented, and has provided banks with a great deal of presence/visibility on the high street and customers with locational convenience. There have not, until recently, been any significant moves by the banks towards either rationalization of branches or towards limited service branches.

However, the rationale for an extensive network of full-service branches is no longer justifiable, in the light of increasing costs, alternative distribution/transaction systems, changing consumer expectations with respect to convenience and availability, and competitive elements. The trends for the next decade and into the third millenium, which may be seen to have advantages and disadvantages to both the banks and their customers, are:

1   Branch closures
2   Limited service branches
3   Specialist branches

There are now as many ATMs as bank branches, and the trend is towards having them in remote locations (supermarkets, stores, airports, railway stations, etc.) and for companies to have their 'own' ATM linked to all banks. This latter trend is possible as a result of the growth in shared ATM networks. At the time of writing there are two networks serving the seven main clearing banks in the UK, and a third network linking all the top building societies and five other major banks; and there are also links between the banks and ACCESS/VISA. The pressure for shared networks has come both from consumers and from retailers, so that all the customers of the latter can access cash from one machine on their premises.

Electronic Funds Transfer at Point-of-Sale (EFTPOS)

'Smart Cards' were invented as recently as 1975, and may be used as either ATM cards or for electronic funds transfer at point of sale. The forces driving EFTPOS have been social (customer demand), competitive and technological. In the last few years a number of experiments have been going on in various shopping centres/petrol stations throughout the UK, involving banks and retail outlets. The main advantages and disadvantages of direct debit at the point of sale may be summarized as follows:
1   Fully automated branches, with few staff – the appeal perhaps limited to younger/higher educated people.
2   Remote banking (via ATMs, EFTPOS, home banking).
3   The 'financial supermarket', whereby a very wide range of financial services are offered in one 'retail' outlet as a result of mergers/ acquisitions between providers of financial services. At present, most consumers do not fully understand or appreciate the concept, but the opportunity is there and the banks may move in this direction.

Following various experiments and trials, EFTPOS UK Limited was set up to develop a national system, including the Bank of England, ten high-street banks and three building societies, but NOT the retailers. The retail consortium represents 90 per cent of UK retail outlets with a commitment to EFTPOS. EFTPOS UK began operation in August 1989, with 500 retailers agreeing to participate in various cities and 800 terminals lined up for use, to try out a set of proposed national standards. In parallel with this cooperation, the banks are also competing to offer retailers their own schemes, e.g. four banks presently operate the SWITCH system and have issued 6 million SWITCH cards and have 2000 terminals in operation (1989). The EFTPOS UK national scheme will handle the debit cards offered by the SWITCH group, and also VISA and ACCESS cards.

The success of EFTPOS in the UK will depend on customer acceptance, and also on the resolving of differences of opinion between retailers and banks with respect to management of the system and who will pay for the software and hardware developments. The success of the SWITCH and VISA systems, although apparently less sophisticated than the fully integrated EFTPOS system, has led to EFTPOS streamlining its various operating systems and accepting a downgraded role as a clearing system through which existing debit cards will operate. The growth of these debit-card payment systems has been given a boost by the changes taking place in the credit-card market, particularly with respect to annual charges for credit cards and the possibility of retailers being able to charge a higher price to credit-card users than to cash and debit card-users.

ATMS

ATMS, along with EFTPOS and home banking, may be considered to be a 'product' development or, perhaps more appropriately, an innovation in the delivery of financial services. ATMs have progressed from being merely cash dispensers to provide facilities for deposits, balance reporting and inter-account transactions. Consumer reactions to ATMs are well-researched, with perceptions of service improvements as a result of automated facilities generally outweighing criticisms. The most advantageous features of ATMs are 24-hour availability, time saving/convenience, avoidance of queues and the perception that bank staff have more time to deal with counter customers (Table 9.3). The features which attract criticism are computer breakdown/out-of-order/lack of cash, lack of certain facilities, personal safety when withdrawing cash, the possibility/liability of unauthorized use, mistakes, lack of privacy, impersonal nature (i.e. preference for counter service) and *queues*. Some of these criticisms are real and others merely perceived deficiencies; either way, they are of concern to the banks and in the long term will be reduced through further technological developments, improved security and advertising and promotion.

Table 9.3 *ATMs – pros and cons*

	Advantages	*Disadvantages*
Banks	Reduces paperwork/cheques	Competitive threats
	Reduces costs	Installation costs
	Extends banking base via new accounts	Running costs
		Security
	Provides a wider range of ATM-style operations	System fraud
Retailers	Increased customer service	Competitive threats
	Competitive edge with respect to technology	Installation costs
		Running costs
	Reduced time at the checkout	Customer privacy
	Reduced cheque handling/ cash security	Customers without bank accounts
	Store account credited more quickly	Poor customer relations (resulting from non-authorization)
Customers	Security	Too easy to overspend
	Time-saving	Instant debiting
	Convenience	Possible technical error
	No need to visit a bank	Loss by fraud
	Fewer cash payments	Lack of privacy
	Simplicity	Cost passed on to consumer
	Cheaper than cheques	Monitoring of buying behaviour

Home banking

A further area of technological advancement in service delivery the banks are giving strategic attention to is the provision of home banking facilities. The first commercial in-home banking system in the UK was launched by a building society in 1983, and was operated via British Telecom's Prestel videotex system as the standard interface, offering a two-way communication system to any subscriber. However, this and other early systems using a microcomputer or other terminals linked by 'phone or videotex had limited appeal and success, owing to the high cost and the narrow range of services available. To some extent the rush to technology may have preceded the search for market needs and consumer acceptance.

The UK is well behind France, where a number of home-banking systems participate in a national videotex network, MINITEL, operated by the French posts and telecoms industry, which provide the basic equipment – a screen and a keyboard attachment for the telephone – free to subscribers. Further, two-thirds of European banks now offer home-banking systems, which provide account interrogation, payment of bills, inter-account transactions, loan generation and other banking facilities. Consequently, the UK banks would seem to be at a competitive disadvantage *vis-à-vis* the European banks – a potential threat for 1992! However, vital technological and strategic initiatives are taking place (including market trials), encompassing both screen-based videotex and also voice-response systems whereby customers may talk to the banks' computers using only their telephone (with customers possibly having their voices pre-recorded and registered).

The trends in the delivery of financial services are towards the separation of production and distribution/consumption, increased networks between providers (e.g. with respect to ATMS), and linkages between banks and other companies providing financial services.

Promotion

The objectives of banks' promotion are several: to build image and reputation, to differentiate each from its competitors, to generate interest and knowledge, to attract new customers, and to generate customer loyalty. To achieve these objectives the banks develop promotional strategies and tactics which utilize the usual mix of advertising, sales promotion, public relations and personal selling, with the number of methods becoming increasingly important and evident.

Advertising

Bank advertising is carried out in many print and broadcast media, each with its own strengths and weaknesses, costs and benefits. Target audiences include financial service customers and also employees – reached by means of in-house magazines and training materials. Of special interest now and into the future is direct marketing or direct response marketing.

The main contributor to the growth of direct marketing is the development of computer technology and databases of consumers and potential consumers, which allows prospects to be identified accurately. Computers, for example, have the capability to store data, such as in-house bases containing customer profiles and services used, and produce mailing lists. Key characteristics of direct marketing are its selectivity with respect to segments, versatility (e.g. it provides unlimited space for offers), ability to generate leads, testability (of an approach or appeal with a clearly defined target segment), immediate and quantifiable feedback, and ease of control.

The channels used for direct marketing are both print and inter-active media. For example, direct mail advertising may be sent out with a customer's statement, and may be a personal communication (including a letter from the bank or branch) which is not competing at the time with other advertising/promotion. Limited use has been made, so far, of reply cards and envelopes, as customers are expected to be pro-active in getting in touch with the bank. Further, the banks have by no means developed the potential of inter-active media such as the telephone, mainly used as an inbound device to respond to enquiries and complaints, and the emerging new technology on inter-active television. But the situation will no doubt change significantly in the coming years, as banks begin to realize, more fully, the strategic implications of direct marketing.

Sales promotions

These comprise mainly short-term incentives, often used in conjunc-tion with advertising campaigns, and include, for example, free banking for students to generate accounts, free home banking to create awareness and generate publicity and consumer reaction, free cheque-book and statement holders, and gifts to children and students. Additionally, more recent activities include promotions among employees, to encourage and as rewards for achievement and quality service.

Public relations

PR strategy among both internal and external publics is planned to publicize a bank and its services, so as to enhance and maintain favourable images. Most activities have high credibility and include:

1 Articles in magazines and journals
2 Press releases, annual reports, editorial comments
3 Talks to schools/community groups/prospective employees
4 Participation in Institute of Bankers' affairs
5 Charitable donations
6 Fund-raising with a charity
7 Sponsorship of the arts/sport/events on a national and local basis

In relation to sponsorship strategies, as with direct marketing, the banks are to some extent followers, as compared with organizations in other product and service sectors (e.g. fast-moving consumer goods, motor cars). In consideration of sponsorship schemes, the banks wish to emphasize their social responsibility and their desire to provide assistance. However, at the same time they will want the bank to be presented favourably with respect to its target markets, and to use the sponsorship as a platform to promote the bank and its services, and will be anxious to see a 'return on their investment'.

Personal selling

This has only recently become evident with regard to personal financial services. Attitudes towards selling, among the banks were well-researched and documented in the 1970s and were largely negative – indeed, many managers equated selling with marketing. However, the present emphasis within banking is increasingly to change the corporate culture so that not only are ALL employees market-oriented, i.e. everyone will have some influence on sales of the bank's products/services, but also that customer-contact personnel are sales-oriented and can take advantage of situations and opportunities in order to cross-sell services.

Indeed, the banks are participating in relationship selling, whereby customers are viewed as clients, and the emphasis is to retain, not just acquire, clients. Relationship selling may be defined as the attraction, maintenance and enhancement of client relationships. This is vital in an environment of decreasing customer loyalty, easy movement of accounts, a declining branch network, and access to bank services via plastic card and telephone. The rationale behind relationship banking is to transform single-service users into multi-service clients, and indifferent customers into loyal clients. Key ingredients for success are:

1 Market segmentation and discovery of client needs
2 Identification of a core service around which to build relationships
3 Incentives for clients, e.g. relationship pricing – 'free' investment advice/service if more than a certain amount of money is kept on deposit
4 Account representatives, i.e. the liaison between the bank and the client, to include customer advisors in the branches and tele-sales staff
5 Training for relationship managers and other bank employees with respect to sales skills, either in-house or from outside consultants

People

Turning to a fifth, additional, element of the marketing mix, PEOPLE, the banks may be seen to participate in a number of strategic initiatives which focus on the role of employees in the delivery of financial services, and subsequent consumer satisfactions and dissatisfactions. The banks' focus on employees is sometimes referred to as 'internal marketing' whereby employees are viewed as internal customers and jobs as internal products. Strategically, success internally affects success externally and so the needs and wants of internal customers with respect to pay and associated benefits and their working environment, including interpersonal relationship, need to be satisfied before those of external customers.

A characteristic of most of the banks' service provision is simultaneous production and consumption, the majority of which necessitates interpersonal interactions between employees and customers. Thus, the banks' personnel are inevitably instrumental in the creation of quality in the service product, hence the phrase 'customer care'. Indeed, quality is a major contributory element to the effectiveness of service provision, and banks now regard customer care/quality as a key variable in strategic planning – and quality is seen as a means to achieve differential advantage and increase market share.

So the banks are developing and implementing customer care/ quality programmes, with a prerequisite for success being the total commitment of the organization from top management downward, with effective leadership driving a customer-oriented culture throughout the company. The banks consider their programmes to be a high priority, with high expenditures, and view them as a long-term investment. They see the benefits in terms of improved customer service, which leads to retention of existing customers and increased loyalty, attraction of new customers, and also improved staff morale and loyalty (see Smith and Lewis, 1989).

The programmes encompass activities related to staff attitudes and behaviour. They are, therefore, concerned with staff training, and may be one component of a total quality programme designed to enhance all aspects of service to the customer, to include improvements in technology, retail design, systems and procedures.

Further, the banks include all employees (management and staff, front-office and backroom personnel), and programme objectives relate to:

1 Emphasizing the increasing need for high levels of service and the importance of the customer

2   Training staff with the skills and knowledge required to deal with customers effectively
3   Motivating staff through encouragement and reward
4   Developing a new style of leadership and management.

The implementation of quality programmes (incorporating special 'events', workshops, quality circles and in-house training) is already leading to some cultural changes, such as a more open management style and an environment where all work together with shared goals and values, and improvement in terms of internal communications and staff relationships. The payoff is in terms of a true market-orientation, a better understanding of customer need, improved service quality and increased customer satisfaction. However, at the end of the day, excellent levels of customer service or total quality may be described as a 'striving rather than an achieving process', and as a philosophy which needs to be ingrained into a bank's culture.

Growth and competitive strategies

A final element of discussion with regard to the banks' strategies relates to their growth and competitiveness, which may be considered in terms of their product/market mix (see Figure 9.2), from which the other elements of the marketing mix follow. The main growth strategies are via market penetration, market development, product development and diversification (see Ansoff, 1965, and the discussion in Chapter 3).

		Products/services	
		Present	*New*
Markets	*Present*	Market penetration	Product development
	New	Market development	Diversification

Figure 9.2   *Product/market mix*

Market penetration

The focus of this strategy is to increase sales of present products/ services in present markets, by means of increased and/or more effective positioning and targeting, delivery and promotional activities. Various penetration objectives and strategies prevail, as follows.

Selling present services to more customers

Within the framework of such present customer segments as students, high net worth individuals, and self-employed, the banks may wish to attract a higher share of the market, which may be achieved from:

1   New residents in an area, who may be 'persuaded' to switch banks and who may be targets for a wide range of services
2   New bank users (e.g. students or weekly cash-paid workers) – typically for current accounts
3   Individuals who decide to become self-employed and need tax advice/planning, pension plans etc.
4   Competitors, in respect of any or all present markets or products.

When communicating with potential customers in these categories, banks will emphasize a competitive advantage or superiority over other banks and financial services providers with respect to products, price and delivery systems, and may include promotional gifts (to students and young people).

Selling more service to present customers

This means trying to develop relationships with existing customers in order to cross-sell other services to them – promoting savings accounts to people with bank mortgages, investment/pensions plans/PEPs to professional customers. This is perhaps the most important growth strategy for banks now and into the future, and to achieve success they need to be efficient and effective with respect to:

1   Segmenting present markets and determining customers' needs for further services. Advertising and promotion, including direct mail and telephone selling in order to reach customers
2   Personal selling, in the branch and/or via 'account representatives', which has implications for continuing sales training for all customer-contact employees.

Encouraging increased product/service usage

There is only a limited analogy here with traditional product-based industries. However, customers may increase their savings/deposit levels if terms are sufficiently attractive, or, if they are satisfied with a particular service – say investment advice or share dealing – they may become repeat customers.

Discouraging account-switching

A further means of increasing market shares is to maintain customer loyalty at a higher level than that of competitors, thus reducing customer dissatisfaction and switching to other organizations. This may be achieved by giving appropriate attention to customer service and service quality – by developing systems and training personnel to provide high levels of service quality and by establishing procedures to deal with customer problems and complaints, thus expediting 'recovery'.

Market development

Here the banks are concerned with developing sales of their present products/services in new markets. This is perhaps a difficult route for UK banks all of which have wide market coverage already with respect to personal financial services, but examples include:

1 New segments within broadly defined existing markets, e.g. the targeting of working women, in particular those who have not previously been potential customers for mortgages/loans/investment advice etc.
2 New markets based on geographical factors. There are a number of opportunities with regard to international market expansion following the abolition of exchange controls, and there will be more with the introduction of 'open' European markets from 1992. Additionally, some of the UK banks are already pursuing growth in North America, partly via merger with and acquisition of US banks.

Product development

The objectives of product development are to introduce and develop sales of new products/services in present markets. This is most evident in all the UK banks, primarily from a combination of legislative, technological and competitive change. It is doubtful whether or not the banks would have envisaged, 20 years ago, the amount of change which would occur in their environment and the consequent need to develop and introduce new products/services in order to remain competitive and to grow.

Product development may be, as already highlighted, a modification of existing banking products (say interest on current accounts), advancements in delivery systems (say home banking and remote ATMs), or expansion into financial services (say life assurance, tax services, financial advice, and travel-related services).

Diversification

The fourth type of growth strategy, diversification, refers to attempts to grow by simultaneously focusing on new services and new markets. A bank could aim to pursue 'newness' outside the mainstream of its present business, e.g. by offering an integrated house-buying service to include conveyancing and estate agency, or agency business activities by linking with pension or insurance brokers, stockbrokers, etc.

In addition to the various growth strategies banks might also consider 'competitive' strategies, in the extent to which they wish to be one of the following:

1   A market leader: with an emphasis on market share, economies of scale, a strong distribution network, etc.
2   A market challenger: also with an emphasis on market share but together with aggressive pricing, delivery and promotional tactics
3   A market follower: attempting to maintain or build a market share and profitability, and focusing on cautious marketing tactics
4   A market nicher: focusing on niches with respect to products and markets, i.e. NOT trying to offer all financial services to all markets

At present, the UK banks, operating in UK markets, would all claim to be market leaders or, at worst, market challengers. However, with regard to European and other overseas business opportunities, they may have to be content, at least in the short term, with being either market followers or market nichers.

Conclusions

Finally, returning to the marketing planning framework, it is necessary to comment on the need for the effective implementation, evaluation and control of the banks' marketing strategies. To achieve success, the banks need an appropriate marketing organization, with leaders who are able to provide a true marketing orientation throughout their companies. Further, they have to set standards for performance with respect to all aspects of their marketing activities, to include sales and profitability; efficiency of systems and operations, e.g. automated facilities; the impact of advertising and promotion; customer satisfaction and service quality; and staff performance. Additionally, the banks must establish methods to evaluate their performance in the market place: and instrumental to the process of evaluation and control is the increasingly vital role played by marketing research and marketing information systems. Once their actual performance has been evaluated against standards and expectations, the banks will be able to modify objectives and redesign strategies and participate in a continuous marketing audit and planning process.

CHAPTER 10
Building society marketing
Don Cowell

Introduction

The UK personal financial services sector has experienced major change in recent years. Once a highly fragmented market, the traditional boundaries between financial institutions have now become blurred. In response to more intensive competition, advancing technology and greater consumer sophistication, financial institutions have expanded into areas once the traditional preserve of competitors. In recent years building societies have broadened their activities to include unsecured loans (e.g. Woolwich), overdrafts (e.g. Nationwide Anglia), credit cards (e.g. Halifax Visa), and travellers' cheques (e.g. Alliance & Leicester), activities traditionally associated with financial institutions such as banks and insurance companies. As shown in detail in Chapter 1, diversification opportunities for building societies were relatively limited until 1986 and the enactment of the new Building Societies Act. This provided them with powers to engage in a wide range of new activities essentially covering all personal financial services, investment, banking and housing. Within two years the Act was reformed, extending the powers of societies in the areas of investment and insurance services, trusteeship, executorship and land services.

As a direct result of the new legislation, and its subsequent reform, societies were able to revise their strategies with greater freedom. However, while the legislation provided societies with greater opportunities, the new, highly competitive environment in which they now operated also posed considerable threats. Building societies had little previous experience of the market conditions they now faced. Previous competition had been between societies and controlled by the Building Society Association. In addition, consumers had been relatively unsophisticated and comparatively loyal. In response, building-society strategies were supply-driven (by cost and technology) rather than demand-driven (by consumer needs). Such strategies were inappropriate to the new situation they faced (Watkins and Wright, 1986; Wright *et al.*, 1986).

The major environmental changes which had such an impact upon

178

building societies have been coupled with moves to adopt and implement the marketing concept. An essentially conservative and traditional set of institutions has become much more market-driven. Recent empirical evidence suggests that financial services organizations in general have shifted from the operations-centred and finance-dominated emphasis common a few years ago to a more market-driven approach (Hooley and Mann, 1988). Indeed, growing experience of strategic marketing and of marketing-mix tools has moved a number of the major players in the building society industry rapidly up the marketing learning curve. Some have achieved considerable marketing sophistication in a short space of time.

Competitive strategies and building societies

All strategies are long term, though they require continuous reworking in response to environmental changes. Building societies, like any other organizations, must monitor these changes and select appropriate strategies to meet the challenges of the new market. Within the strategic management literature a variety of strategic options exist. According to some management models, though, there are only three generic strategies to follow (Saunders, 1989; Porter, 1985; Ennew and Wright, 1990b). These strategies, of 'differentiation', 'focus' and 'cost leadership', have been outlined in Chapter 3 and may be applied to building societies as follows.

Differentiation

A differentiation strategy is based on consumer-perceived unique or superior distinguishing features – perhaps through the range of services available, the image created or the quality of service. Effective differentiation strategies can increase customer loyalty and reduce price-sensitivity and the risk of substitution.

Differentiation poses a unique challenge for building societies, as they are service organizations. The intangible nature of services means that the features of services can be replicated very quickly by competitors. To ensure success, the means of differentiation must have a real effect on customers' choice of building society and be difficult to replicate. Societies basing strategies on differentiation need to be creative and innovative to stay ahead of competitors.

In the early 1970s many societies attempted to differentiate themselves by television advertising, e.g. 'We're with the Woolwich' and 'Get the Abbey Habit'. Such advertisements increased awareness of societies, but failed to create meaningful differences. More recently, the Bradford and Bingley and the Halifax building societies have successfully pursued a strategy of differentiation, the former creating an image of the traditional society and the latter highlighting its size as the largest society.

The findings of recent research suggest that a differentiation strategy is particularly applicable to the medium-sized societies (Robson, 1989; Ennew and Wright, 1990b). Associations of size provide large and small societies with distinct images. However, the images of medium-sized societies are less clearly defined. In addition, medium-sized societies are sometimes too small to convert to plc status and thus diversify into all areas of personal finance, and too large to become niche players, i.e. focus on one market segment. Differentiation thus offers them a particularly appropriate strategy.

Differentiation, however, can only be classed as a successful strategy when the means of differentiation corresponds with actual consumer wants and needs. The attributes which have a real effect on consumer choice of building society – the determinant attributes – must take into account both the importance of the attribute and the individual's ability to differentiate between societies on the basis of that attribute. Societies must address this area if they are to pursue a differentiation policy successfully. It is known that suitable attributes for differentiation in service businesses are often those connected with staff and service. For example, societies can attempt to improve the quality of their service, the personalization of their service or the helpfulness of staff. Indeed many societies are investing considerable effort in training (e.g. Woolwich, Eastbourne) and in customer care (e.g. National and Provincial).

Previous research has established that image is 'learnt', and each exposure (e.g. visit to the society or advertisement) reinforces the image held, making it more vivid. Attempts to change a society's image dramatically can result in consumer confusion, as it may undermine the collective basis upon which the image is formed. Societies should take care to assess their current image before selecting a means of differentiation. In recent research, the National and Provincial Building Society was perceived by consumers to have a good service, while the Alliance & Leicester had the most up-to-date products; such images could be strengthened and used to differentiate these societies even further (Robson, 1989).

New legislation has provided societies with the ability to exploit actual differences between them. The polarization rule (Financial Services Act, 1986) allows societies (and banks) to differentiate themselves according to whether they are or are not tied agents. For example, few societies have retained their independent status with respect to insurance companies. Among the top twenty societies, few remain independent (see Chapters 2 and 8 for further details). Independent status thus represents a means of differentiation, which has been exploited by the Bradford and Bingley Building Society as it publicly voiced disapproval in response to the removal of the consumers' freedom of choice.

The Building Societies Act also provides societies with a means of differentiation by enabling certain societies to convert to plc status, thus becoming a new type of financial institution. This option is, however, only available to the larger societies who meet the specified asset requirements. To date the Abbey National is the only society to pursue this option, although others have received substantial publicity as they consider whether or not to convert. While differentiation will be achieved for those societies who are among the first to convert, little recognition may be given to those subsequently converting.

Focus

A focus strategy offers a product/service which meets the needs of a well-defined group of customers. Such groups, or segments, are sometimes too small or specialized to attract large competitors. While this strategy is commonly associated with small organizations, larger building societies can adopt a focus strategy by pursuing several segments.

Previously, societies segmented the consumer market by geography, targeting the local areas in which they operated. For example, the Regency and West of England Building Society conducted a series of campaigns to encourage people residing in the southern and western parts of England to identify the society as 'their' society, and thus build customer loyalty. More recently some societies have attempted to segment the market by means of other factors. Halifax, for example, used age: Little Xtra account for children, and Quest for teenagers. The focus strategy, however, remains relatively under-developed.

Research suggests that consumers can be segmented in a number of ways by means of demographics and savings behaviour (Robson, 1989). An attractive segment for societies to target is high net worth individuals. Consumers receiving high net incomes prefer a society which is modern and bank-like, with quicker decisions and shorter waiting times than those acceptable to respondents in receipt of smaller incomes. Hence, attributes of flexibility, understanding, speed of decision and safety can be particularly appealing to this group.

Studies in the US also found that high net worth individuals choose their financial institutions on the basis of 'ego-enhancement', i.e. according to the use of names, personal attention, access to the managers, etc. Research conducted by the Leeds Building Society identified speed as an important factor in choice behaviour for mortgages in the 'Yuppie' segment.

It could be concluded from these findings that a society wishing to target high net worth individuals should focus upon the speed and quality of service offered to them. The smaller societies are perhaps already suitably positioned to target this segment. Associations of size suggest that small societies provide a more personal service. In addition, a number of societies, such as the Chelsea and the Regency and West of England, are perceived as 'up-market' societies, and thus may have the image of exclusiveness acceptable to those looking for ego-enhancement.

Another attractive segment of the consumer market is the older members of society, the 50 plus age group. This group has considerable disposable income, resulting from paid mortgages and the absence of dependent children. In addition, it is this group which is most likely to benefit from substantial inheritances, particularly through house-price rises.

A number of smaller regional societies already have a high proportion of consumers aged 50 years plus, owing to their location in traditional retirement areas, e.g. the Wessex Building Society. Such societies could use these characteristics to their advantage. By maintaining a traditional image, and by providing additional services specific to this group (say advice on wills and inheritance), the societies can develop their share of this market.

Cost leadership

A cost-leadership strategy is based on lowest costs and hence greatest profit margins. It should not be confused with low price. There are numerous ways in which a society can attempt to achieve cost reduction, the major options being diversification, merger and rationalization, which are now considered.

Diversification

Diversified organizations achieve cost reductions by spreading the fixed costs of operating over a larger number of units. Diversification can take a number of forms. At its simplest, it may comprise the introduction of new products in areas related to the base activity. Alternatively, it may consist of diversifying into product markets in which the society has no previous experience. A diversification strategy may encompass both these aspects, and may be accompanied by a departure from existing areas.

To date, a substantial proportion of societies have diversified to varying degrees. Most have introduced new products into areas related to the base activity, e.g. home contents insurance (Bristol and West, Portman, Leeds Permanent), while others have entered new markets, e.g. travel and car insurance (Britannia, Leamington Spa). Societies will continue to diversify both within related and non-related areas, as the majority have now obtained their members' permission to do so.

The choice of a diversification strategy is not, however, available to all societies. While the larger, national societies have sufficient assets to allow them to become major providers of personal financial services, the smaller societies are confined by the 1986 Building Societies Act to areas with minimal risk association.

The appropriateness of a diversification strategy to individual building societies can be considered from two aspects: expected cost reduction and consumer response.

While economic theory suggests that diversification generally results in *cost reduction*, this association may not occur in all industries. For example, building societies currently operate in areas of low risk, requiring little provision for bad debts. The majority of the new areas available to societies, e.g. unsecured loans, are comparatively high risk. Entrance into these areas requires increased expenditure on staffing and provision for bad debts. Costs can be particularly high during the introduction of the new services; specialized and skilled staff are required to supervise the new areas of operations and current staff require training. While these costs will reduce as the society gains experience in producing the service, all costs would offset any economies of scale.

In addition, potential benefits associated with the entrance into new areas may be minimal, due to over-capacity. All financial institutions are currently evaluating the markets of their competitors, markets from which they were previously prohibited entry. Some of these markets are generally mature markets and the prospects of growth are limited. The entrance of new players into the mortgage market is a prime example of over-capacity. Many new providers have gained market share by accepting lower returns. New players currently find it both expensive to stay and expensive to withdraw from this market. The current account market is an example. Interest-bearing current accounts were offered both by societies to gain market share and by banks to defend their market. While such accounts may have cross-selling opportunities, their cost makes them an unattractive alternative to the traditional building-society savings account.

Consumer response to the pursuit by societies of a diversification strategy appears to be unfavourable. For example, the Building Society Members' Association has campaigned to retain housing, rather than banking, as the main concern of societies. In addition, several surveys have repeatedly identified the resistance of the consumer to use services from those financial institutions with which they are not traditionally associated.

Current research would also appear not to support building-society diversification. Consumers are found to possess a low level of knowledge and awareness of financial institutions and their services; they are still learning about personal finance and often find the subject difficult. The introduction of a variety of new services by the societies can result in consumer confusion.

Experience in the US appears to support this view. One saving and loan association introducing twelve different cheque accounts failed to attract consumer support. Rather than calculate the optimum choice, consumers simply chose a different institution.

Research suggests that the response of UK consumers to building-society diversification is largely determined by the type of diversification pursued. Diversification in related areas adds to the specialist nature of societies and thus enhances their image, e.g. societies could offer a complete housing package, with estate-agency services, conveyancing, mortgage, anti-gazumping insurance, home contents and structure insurance and unsecured loans for home improvements. But diversification into new and different areas alters the very nature of societies. For example, societies wishing to extend their portfolios to include products traditionally associated with the clearing banks, e.g. cash cards, chequebooks, etc., could attract a more bank-like image.

Clearly, adoption of a diversification strategy is appropriate to only a very small number of societies, and even then must be implemented with great care. Individual societies need to consider their current image and adopt a diversification strategy which takes account of current consumer perceptions. For example, the Alliance & Leicester and Nationwide Anglia are currently perceived as modern, bank-like societies, with a wide range of services. A diversification strategy may therefore be appropriate for those societies, provided adequate consideration is given to the quality of staff and service.

Mergers

The building-society industry has been characterized by mergers (transfer of engagements) throughout its development. Since 1900 the number of societies has fallen from 2286 to just over 100 today (1990), a trend which is expected to continue (Table 10.1).

Table 10.1 *Building society trends*

Year	No of societies	Total assets at current prices (£m)
1890	2,795	N/A
1900	2,286	60
1910	1,723	76
1920	1,271	87
1930	1,026	371
1940	952	756
1950	819	1,256
1960	726	3,166
1970	481	10,819
1975	382	24,204
1980	273	53,793
1981	253	61,815
1982	227	73,033
1983	206	85,869
1984	190	102,688
1985	167	121,000
1986	151	140,603
1987	138	160,097
1988	130	188,844
1989*	115	N/A

* Includes Abbey National, provisional figures
Source: *Housing Finance*, Various issues

While economic theory suggests that up to a certain point an increase in size results in economies of scale, there exists some doubt as to whether or not building-society mergers actually achieve economies of scale (Barnes, 1985; see also Watkins and Wright, 1986, for a review of surveys), which is also in line with studies of industry generally (see Mueller, 1988). Assuming that societies can achieve some economies of scale, what are the likely responses of consumers to continued mergers? The effects of merger on the image of the participant societies can be viewed from two perspectives – increase in size and change in identity.

The perceived size of a society is an important attribute. The word *size* has many associations: for example, a large society is associated with financial soundness, a wide range of services, better chance of obtaining a mortgage, efficiency and preferential interest rates. A small society is associated with a limited range of services, but a more personal service. It is the medium-sized societies whose images are least defined. While the growth of medium and large societies could have a positive effect on image resulting from the associations of size, the growth of smaller societies, via merger, could damage consumer perceptions of their personal service.

As for change in identity, in the event of a merger either one or both

185

participating societies adopts a new identity. Three options are available to societies following merger:

1   Retention of one name – the name of one of the participating societies (usually the larger) is retained. For example, following the mergers of the Paddington with the West of England and the Property Owners with the Woolwich, the names of the second societies in each case – the larger ones – were retained.
2   Combination of names – the names of both participating societies are retained. This usually occurs where societies of an equal or similar size merge. For example, following the merger of the Alliance and Leicester building societies and the Nationwide and Anglia building societies, combinations of the names were used. While a new name is created, the identities of each society are retained. Societies passing through several mergers are, however, unable to continue this practice.
3   Creation of a new name – new names are usually adopted when societies have merged several times. The Britannia Building Society, for example, was originally the Leek and Moorlands Building Society, and merged with several other building societies in its time, including the Westbourne Park.

The response of consumers to building-society mergers will largely depend upon the nature of the merger. Research suggests that new (and hence unfamiliar) names are associated with a new society, despite the participating societies having been in existence for many years. For example, the Nationwide Anglia merger brought together two old societies, the Anglia (established 1848) and the Nationwide (established 1884). Knowledge of a society and familiarity with its name are important attributes, indicative of stability and security. A newly merged society has to invest heavily in promotion to increase name awareness, which can offset initial economies of scale.

An alternative strategy for societies wishing to achieve economies of scale would be to enter joint ventures with other societies and/or financial institutions. For example, societies joined together to form the LINK and MATRIX ATM networks. Reciprocal use of the machines allowed them to provide their consumers with a near national network, the cost of which most individual societies would have been unable to meet.

Rationalization

This focuses upon cost reduction either by improving branch

productivity and product mix or by deleting unprofitable products or branches.

For example, branch productivity may be improved by reducing branch costs and increasing consumer 'sales', i.e. the level of consumer transactions. In a service organization staffing usually accounts for a higher proportion of costs, and is, therefore, a prime area for cost reduction. The number or quality of staff may be lowered to raise the profit-to-cost ratio. Reduction in the number of staff could lead to longer waiting times, both within societies for counter service, and at a managerial level in decision-making. Speed in both these areas is important to consumers. Consumers prefer a society with a short waiting time and quick decisions. A number of societies are currently perceived by consumers to be deficient in these areas, suggesting a need to increase staffing levels and/or invest in training.

Branch productivity may also be improved by closing unprofitable branches. Research suggests that branch location is more important than absolute numbers of branches. Branches with high operating costs to profits should therefore be relocated in areas more convenient to the consumer, thus increasing consumer flow through branches. Research is, of course, required at local branch level to determine which locations are perceived by the consumer to be convenient.

It is suggested that building societies may build their success through the use of the above strategies. However, leading societies are not necessarily differentiators, focused or cost leaders. They may be cost leaders and differentiators (e.g. Cheltenham and Gloucester). Some of the smaller societies owe their success to combining differentiation with a clear focus, say on well-defined customer groups. What is of fundamental importance for marketing effectiveness is that societies build marketing programmes around effective competitive strategies and tactics and not only upon markets. The ability of a society to evaluate its weaknesses and strengths compared with the competition, and to choose an appropriate core strategy, has become of major importance to market success in the current highly competitive climate.

Building society marketing mix

The marketing mix for a building society service is, in practice, little different from that for a product. What differences do exist arise from:

1   The general distinctions between services and products, which include such features as intangibility of services, heterogeneity of

service quality and perishability, and the complexities these features sometimes pose for building societies.

2   The growing recognition among building-society marketers of the importance, in what are often undifferentiated product markets, of such features as customer care and service, branch atmosphere, smooth operational and transaction performance and image.

The planning of an efficient and effective marketing mix is facilitated through marketing research. The building societies have become major users of market research in recent years, contributing to the expansion of financial services research expenditure, both in-house and among the Association of Market Survey Organisation's members. The aim of a building society's marketing mix is to create a differential advantage to make the society and its services better than those of its competitors, so that a particular group of customers (the target market) prefers its services. Differential advantage may occur fortuitously. It is, however, much more likely to occur when it is based on an effective marketing strategy and the detailed planning and implementation of marketing programmes to meet the needs of the society's target market customers. A society's differential advantage may result from one or more parts of its marketing programme, including service quality, interest rates, branch ambience, ease of transaction processing, location, and psychological benefits created through skilful promotion.

The marketing mix consists of the principal variables with which building-society marketing managers are concerned in their attempts to manage demand for their services. Defined as 'the mixture of controllable marketing variables that the firm uses to pursue the sought level of sales in the target market' (Kotler, 1986), the process of marketing-mix formulation and balancing is unique to each society and service. An appropriate framework which provides a guide for building societies is:

(a) Services (i.e. products)
(b) Price
(c) Promotion
(d) Place

Services

Building society customers derive satisfaction and benefits from the services they are offered and use (e.g. high interest accounts; financial advice). The decisions, therefore, that are associated with the planning, development and offering of a society's range of services are central to its success. Marketing concepts such as the product life-cycle, systematic new service development and deletion procedures, service concept testing, blueprinting and design, branding, after-sale customer-care procedures and processes, which are common in product markets, are of just as much validity to building societies. The characteristics of the services offered (e.g. intangibility, heterogeneity, perishability) may, though, require adaptation and refinement of conventional marketing ideas in building-society contexts. For example, services cannot be patented, and it is thus difficult to prevent competitors from copying new types of accounts, say for children, or new kinds of mortgage arrangements (e.g. based on PEPs). On the other hand, service product warranties can be important in marketing certain kinds of accounts, such as those which guarantee a high rate of interest for a fixed period of time or which guarantee a rate of interest above normal rates for a fixed period of time (e.g. Bristol and West Vantage Bond). Expanding the number of features associated with a service is also a common practice (e.g. Town and Country developments to its interest-bearing chequebook account). So too is adding additional service product lines – Alliance & Leicester Capital Choice and West Bromwich budget account – or linking services with other organizations and schemes – Norwich and Peterborough link with BUPA.

There is evidence that some societies are taking a much more systematic and rigorous approach to the profitability and contribution of their services. For example, a number of societies have dropped their share-dealing services and have rationalized their children's savings accounts (e.g. Cheltenham and Gloucester). Equally new service possibilities are being considered (e.g. Halifax and Unit Trusts) or launched (e.g. Cheshire Building Society and estate agency).

There have been considerable innovations amongst building-society services in recent years and this process is likely to continue. However, there is also evidence to suggest that some societies have rushed into introducing new services without thinking through the implications on other elements of the marketing mix (e.g. staff training) as well as upon the range of services on offer. One outline set of questions societies can use in their planning and integration of this element of the marketing mix is:

1 What benefits will the customer derive from this service?
   * How clear are we that these benefits are needed?
2 What is the service formula?
   * What is the bundle of elements of the service, both functional and psychological, tangible and intangible?

3   What service levels are required?
    * What quality and quantity of service need to be associated with it?
4   What delivery system is needed to ensure successful service operation and marketing?
    * How clear are we about the linkages between the service features and its delivery, including systems and staff?

Central to the success of building-society service policies is continuing focus on the benefits the customer derives from them, and whether the services offered are desired and relevant. In addition, the service range and its development must be part of a marketing and institutional strategy. There is no doubt that the range of services offered by building societies will expand dramatically as they search for new opportunities in the UK and in Europe. While mortgages will remain the core business for some societies, the sheer number of players in the market will mean that alternative services will need to be introduced if some of the societies are to survive. Large societies, through their branch and estate-agent networks, are likely to offer a wider range of financial services, including insurance broking and in some cases banking. In addition, Europe will provide a major opportunity for some institutions in the traditional mortgage markets. Service innovation will be a major feature of the societies' portfolios in the 1990s.

Price

The notion of 'price' in a building-society environment can take a number of forms. It is concerned, for example, with 'interest' rates that may apply to a mortgage, with a 'fee' that may be payable for a house survey, with a 'premium' that may be due on an insurance policy, or with a 'charge' that may be levied on a particular kind of account. Though the terms used to describe building-society prices may be different, the traditional forces influencing price – costs, competition, demand and customers' perceptions of value – are similar.

An integrated marketing strategy implies that the various elements of the marketing mix – including price – are formulated and implemented in the light of the objectives underlying that strategy. For building societies the pricing decision must take account of a number of factors, including:

1   How the 'price' set will influence the customers' perception of the service in relation to other competitive sources (i.e. perceptual position). In the current highly competitive mortgage market,

interest-rate differences of only a few percentage points are of considerable significance.

2   The building society's views of where the service is in its 'product life-cycle'. A new service, like a low-cost mortgage aimed at young couples, may be very competitively priced to gain market share and obtain maximum penetration. Alternatively, unusually high percentage mortgages could be charged to high earning couples to 'skim' the market. The effectiveness of either policy would be determined by the elasticity of demand, i.e. the responsiveness of demand to price changes. In some building-society markets, such as deposit accounts, there is much depositor inertia. However, customers are growing in sophistication and are increasingly prepared to shop around for the cheapest loan or switch deposits for a higher interest rate elsewhere. Societies cannot assume continuing customer inertia to switch accounts in the future.

3   The competitive situation is currently a major influence. Usually 'price ranges' operate in even the most competitive markets. Some societies, because of their reputation, may have more room for manoeuvre than others in a particular market and may be price 'makers' as opposed to price 'takers'. Nevertheless, there is rarely scope to be positioned very differently from market norms on price. This single factor of competition, is a major influence on the price discretion available to building-society marketing managers. Even so, the variations in interest rates on 'short notice' accounts reflect the opportunities available for setting different 'prices' across different values of deposits through the interest rates offered.

4   Government policies, like interest-rate policies, also influence building-society prices. However, they more often influence the general level of prices rather than the discretionary range or bank around which a particular price may be set.

5   Finally, many of the tactical price techniques used in other markets are relevant to some kinds of building-society services. They include 'differential pricing', 'discount pricing', 'guaranteed pricing' and 'loss leader pricing'. Recent special offers on mortgage rates by various building societies, targeted at different customer groups, reflect the use of some of these tactical price techniques.

Thus price is an important element in marketing-mix strategies of building societies in their competition for business.

Promotion

The aim of a building-society's promotional efforts is to communicate with its customers, employees and other relevant audiences. The main goals of promotion are to inform, to persuade and remind audiences about the society and its services. An informative promotion might, for example, advise customers of interest-rate changes; a persuasive promotion might, for example, try to encourage non-users to open an account or take out a mortgage; while a reminder promotion might seek to maintain a society's position and presence in the market through, say, major sponsorship of a sporting event. There are a large number of promotional tools available to the building-society marketer. Astutely used, whether singly or in carefully integrated combinations, these tools constitute a powerful set of instruments for communication and influence. The key consideration is to ensure that specific communication campaigns are designed for particular marketing situations to achieve the desired emphasis and impact.

Some building societies have shown a readiness to experiment with many of the available tools. Examples of some of the direct promotional tools currently used include the following.

Press advertising

Press advertising is an important medium for all societies, large and small. It attracts much of all building-society advertising appropriations. The large number of national, regional and local publications available, together with the array of specialist publications on offer in the UK, provide wide opportunities for coverage and flexibility. All societies advertise in the national and financial press, with their expenditures tending to reflect asset size, from the Halifax and Nationwide Anglia at one extreme to the smaller Mornington and Walthamstow societies at the other.

TV advertising

Television advertising is more expensive than press advertising (as much due to the costs of production as to media costs) and national TV campaigns tend to be undertaken mainly by the larger societies. However, satellite broadcasting, coupled with the single European market after 1992, could have a dramatic impact on the costs of existing TV advertising through opening up new opportunities for innovative societies.

Cinema advertising

Cinema advertising, whilst constituting a very small proportion of total advertising, is nevertheless a most potent medium for reaching cinemagoers, who tend generally to be young adults. Low-cost starter mortgages and regular savings schemes can often be targeted at particular market segments through this medium. Radio advertising, too, is useful in reaching certain target groups.

Exhibitions

Exhibitions provide opportunities to widen the exposure of a building-society's services to existing and new customers.

Public relations

PR activities are undertaken increasingly by building societies. They have included help with community projects (e.g. restoring older properties); special· events for young people, the elderly or the disabled; providing educational opportunities (e.g. through prizes and grants); and sponsorship of the arts and cultural events. Such activities provide a potent way of enhancing corporate image and involvement within the community and with worthwhile causes.

Point of sale

Point-of-sale materials in the form of brochures and leaflets are used by nearly all building societies. Such materials can perform a range of functions (e.g. cross-sell services) and raise awareness of levels of services available. In recent years, greater attention has been devoted to coordinating the design of such material as part of an integrated total promotional effort.

Personal selling

Personal selling and the role of counter-service staff are increasingly recognized by the societies as most persuasive forms of promotion. Great importance is now attached to customer-focused staff training, staff appearance, staff availability, 'internal' marketing and customer care in general. Some societies have made major investments in these areas, as it is recognized that the relationship between staff and customer can be a major determining influence upon patronage decisions.

Other promotion methods

Other, less direct methods of promotion which building societies seek to develop and harness include 'image', standards of service, logos and the use of brand names. These are seen as valuable means of differentiation in markets where the distinctions between one core service and another are minimal.

There have been major changes in the promotional efforts of building societies in the last few years. The effect of competition has been a strong influence upon the greater sophistication of promotional tools now employed.

Place

The place element of the marketing mix, concerned with how to make services available and accessible to customers, has always been of importance to building societies, although in the past attention was mostly focused upon building up branch and agency networks in convenient locations to serve customer needs. Such policies have been justified by consumer surveys of building-society customers, which reveal the importance of location and accessibility in society choice and patronage. Branch expansion (e.g. Town and Country) and agency expansion (e.g. Gresham) remain important strategies for some societies.

However, societies have begun to take a critical look at the profitability of their branch and agency systems, and some societies have closed branches (Nationwide Anglia) or dropped agencies (Alliance & Leicester). In addition, major refurbishment programmes and branch redesign have been put into operation (Leeds; Norwich and Peterborough) to improve both the image projected and facilities available to customers. The societies are learning from other high street retailers, and have recognized the importance of 'atmosphere' and 'ambience' in branch design and their contribution to the creation of a distinctive 'personality'. It is likely that this trend will continue in the 1990s.

Of particular interest in recent years has been the adoption by a number of the major societies of 'alternative channels' to permit service access and service use. New technology in the form of automated telling machines (ATMs) and automatic cash dispensers has been increasingly applied in the industry. In addition, mailed services have been developed to overcome restricted branch presence in certain locations (e.g. Cheltenham and Gloucester) and direct mailing itself is growing in use as a method of selling and distributing services. One building society (Nottingham) was an early experimenter with 'computer-based home banking', which is certain to expand in use in the 1990s in the UK.

Nevertheless, the branch – its location, design and operation – is likely to remain a key element in the marketing-mix programmes of many building societies. A significant recent trend has been the application of operations-management tools and techniques to the management of branch services, in conjunction with marketing tools and techniques. The main roles of the operations manager, the efficient and effective management of resources, and the provision of customer service, are often more complex in service operations, because of variations in customer needs, conflicts between different kinds of customer needs, problems of specifying and delivering service 'quality', and the role of the customer in service operations. Customer service in building society operations increasingly demands motivating the customer to play a role in service delivery (e.g. queuing systems, ATMs). The effectiveness of a building-society's delivery systems provides a potentially powerful means of differentiation in the more competitive climate in the sector.

Conclusions

Building societies will continue the development and use of appropriate marketing tools during the 1990s, both for offensive and defensive reasons. Rationalization through merger, together with likely further changes in the status of societies, will mean that there are likely to be around 50 or 60 societies left by the mid-1990s. Many smaller societies will have disappeared. There is no reason, though, why some of the smaller societies will not still be around, provided they can focus their marketing efforts on distinctive regions or services; effect alternative organizational arrangements to maintain independence through some form of federation; and, most importantly, offer valued services and care to their customers.

While there is likely to be more diversity between societies in terms of their range of services, methods of operation and managerial sophistication, the underlying principles of marketing apply. In essence, customers seek solutions to their problems and expect services to fulfil their needs and provide the benefits they seek. If customers do not receive what they want from a particular society, then the changed competitive environment gives them opportunities to take their business elsewhere.

CHAPTER 11
Insurance marketing
Trevor Watkins

Introduction

This chapter examines the contribution marketing can make within the insurance industry. The first section outlines the main features of the sector, in terms of product types, marketing approaches, characteristics of consumers and changes in the structure of insurance companies. This section is followed in turn by demand analysis, and the elements of the marketing mix as applied to the insurance industry. The marketing mix is analysed in the context of different stages in the product life-cycle.

Trends in the insurance industry

The insurance industry provides a range of services. It is common within the industry to split services into life and non-life types. Life services are essentially concerned with elements of protection and saving built around life insurance, including term and endowment insurance, life assurance and pensions products. The last have grown in importance since the implementation of the Social Security Act, 1986, enabled the provision of pensions products to be liberalized in the sense that private sector providers have been able to compete for a wider range of market segments. Non-life insurance covers accident, motor household insurance on the personal side, and marine, aviation and many types of business insurance on the business side.

An alternative way of viewing the wide range of insurance products on offer is from the customer-benefits perspective. Most financial institutions make promises to pay their customers a sum of money in the future, in many cases, if an unpredictable (from an individual's perspective) event occurs. Long-term insurance (life and pensions products) include an element of saving for the customer. Reading insurance company advertisements could lead on to the simplistic conclusion that pure protection products (e.g. motor insurance, term insurance) are sold on price, and that 'saving' products are sold on rate of return promises. However, many other marketing appeals are made, such as:

1 Corporate image advertising to emphasize that the company will be around to meet its promises in the future and is 'respectable', 'trustworthy' and 'secure'.
2 New product development and product rejuvenation. Although the basic customer appeals are 'saving' and 'protection', many companies try to compete by new product features rather than on price appeals.
3 New distribution channels offering more convenience or more advice to customers. The role of the professional independent financial intermediary has already been discussed in Chapter 7.
4 Other promotional appeals, such as sponsorships.

Thus, a range of marketing appeals has been developed in response to competitive pressures which, as we have seen from earlier chapters, have developed since the industry was deregulated.

The current state of the industry in the UK for life and general

Table 11.1 *Life assurance: demographics (by class, age and TV region)*

	Population	Whole life	Term	Any endowment	Investment bonds
AB	17	15	21	21	38
C1	22	19	23	24	31
C2	30	32	31	33	20
DE	32	34	25	21	10
18–20	7	2	4	4	1
21–24	9	4	8	9	6
25–34	19	16	19	28	10
35–44	16	18	25	24	19
45–54	15	18	19	18	23
55–64	15	19	16	13	27
65+	19	23	7	5	14
London	20	21	17	20	18
TVS	9	9	9	11	12
Anglia	7	6	8	6	8
HTV	7	6	7	8	7
TSW	4	3	5	3	4
Central	17	15	15	17	14
Granada	11	11	13	9	16
Yorkshire	11	12	14	9	8
Tyne Tees	6	7	5	7	7
Scotland	10	12	8	9	10
Male	48	51	57	52	65
Female	52	49	43	48	35

Source: Whitmore (1988)

Table 11.2   *General insurance: demographics*
(by class, age and TV region)

	Home contents	House structure	Medical	Motor
All adults	71	57	13	50
AB	84	80	29	72
C1	76	66	14	56
C2	73	60	11	55
DE	58	35	5	30
18–20	29	20	9	33
21–24	46	37	10	46
25–34	71	62	14	57
35–44	81	71	18	64
45–54	81	69	17	60
55–64	81	62	13	51
65+	73	48	6	30
London	69	56	18	51
TVS	77	65	19	59
Anglia	72	57	14	54
HTV	73	65	10	58
TSW	74	63	11	59
Central	69	57	12	52
Granada	68	58	11	49
Yorkshire	72	59	11	47
Tyne Tees	73	56	8	42
Scotland	69	38	5	30
Male	71	59	15	61
Female	71	55	11	40

Source: Whitmore (1988)

insurance is illustrated in Tables 11.1 and 11.2 respectively. Just over 60 per cent of the population of the UK owns some form of life assurance, 71 per cent of the population is covered by home contents insurance, 57 per cent by house structure insurance, 50 per cent by motor insurance and 13 per cent by medical insurance (Whitmore, 1988). While life- assurance ownership is evenly distributed by social group, it is skewed towards older people (35+). The general insurance categories noted above are more likely to be owned by AB social groups and by the 25+ age groups. One reason for the even distribution of life-insurance ownership by social class is that ownership is measured by volume not value. Small value industrial branch policies, common amongst C2DE social groups, give a high count in these groups when measured by volume.

One of the implications of these figures is that, with the exception of medical insurance, it can be arranged that, when measured by volume, penetration of these personal insurance products is approaching a maximum level. Sales opportunities could be argued to be limited to new household formations and to cross-selling products to existing

customers. MacKay (1988) has illustrated the implications of demographic trends for the UK with a stable population at just under 60m
projected until well into the twenty-first century, but with the number
of households growing as their average size declines.

Reflecting the basic dichotomy in product types, insurance
companies may specialize in supplying general or long-term products,
or, less frequently, be composite companies, providing the full range.
Little more than half the authorized insurance companies in the UK are
active in carrying out insurance business (Table 11.3). The majority of
active companies deal with general business only, with around 100
conducting life-insurance business and the balance selling both types
of product. Through the 1980s the total number of active insurance
companies declined, partly as a result of merger. Notable mergers in
the late 1980s included Phoenix and Sun Alliance, Trident Life and
Imperial Life, and Eagle Star and Hambro Life. Target Life was
acquired in 1987 by TSB. Target Life, which sold to high net worth
clients via independent intermediaries, complemented TSB Life's
direct-sales-force approach to lower net worth customers, but there are
clear marketing advantages to retaining separate identities.

Changes in the sector are also taking place through joint ventures.
Approaching fifty insurance companies now own unit-trust management companies, which enables unit trusts to be sold through existing
distribution channels and entry into the linked-life market to be
effected through a group's own unit trusts. As noted in Chapter 1,
following its decision to adopt tied status under the polarization rules

Table 11.3 *Insurance groups*

Year-end	Total authorized[1]	Net active[2] total	Composites[3]	General[4] business only	Long-term[4] business only
1982	849	446	47	304	95
1987	838	477	52	311	114
1988	838	438	50	287	101

Notes:

1 As reported in DTI's *Insurance: Annual Report*.

2 Authorized total less inactive companies, specialists, and subsidiaries of
groups where a group has several subsidiaries engaged in insurance,
which produces the net figure of active independent insurance outlets.

3 When a group consists of a composite insurance company plus one or
more other long-term and/or general insurers, it has been counted as one
composite company.

4 When a group consists of two or more companies authorized to write
only long-term (or general) insurances, it has been counted once only in
the appropriate category. When a group consists of two or more
companies authorized to write both types of insurance, it has been
counted twice, once in each of the two categories.

Source: R. L. Carter, *et al.*, *Insurance Industry Statistics*, various issues

of the Financial Services Act, the Midland Bank formed a joint new company with Commercial Union Insurance Company, as it did not already have its own life subsidiary.

The extent of acquisition and joint-venture activity in the insurance sector has also already been referred to in Chapter 1. Since the mid-1970s, foreign entry into the UK market has increasingly been by acquisition rather than through the establishment of a branch office. In 1987, of the 166 composites and life-only companies active in the UK, 37 were foreign controlled, 104 were British controlled and 25 were foreign companies' UK branches. For the 142 companies carrying out these classes of business in 1982, the corresponding figures were 40, 78 and 24, respectively. About one quarter of foreign-owned companies are subsidiaries of European Community companies (Carter *et al.*, 1986).

Demand analysis

The two basic questions to be answered from an insurance company's marketing point of view are the following. Why do people buy insurance? How do consumers choose which company (and, if appropriate, intermediary) to buy from? Some of the main economic and other factors influencing a consumer's demand for insurance are discussed below, but a further examination of corporate-insurance purchases can be obtained in Main (1982).

At the macro-economic level there are a number of indicators which are important influences on the total market size. For personal insurances these include the level of disposable income, the saving ratio for different income levels, employment levels, the rate of inflation, expenditure levels on various goods and services, levels of home-ownership and indebtedness, car-ownership, holiday expenditure, etc. For corporate customers relevant macro-economic indicators include the level of business activity, the number of new business registrations and the values of net capital stock.

At the micro-economic level the competition for personal savings forms a major economic influence on the demand for life insurance. The determination of the total amount that will be spent from the consumer's budget on insurance will be influenced in part by the level of that income but also by competing demands for the funds by other forms of personal savings (for example, building-society accounts, bank-deposit accounts, National Savings and shares).

The purchase of an insurance contract is influenced by many variables, not all economic, including:

1 *Compulsory insurance requirements*, both statutory and contractual.
2 *Fiscal*, which are often important in both long-term insurance for individuals and non-life insurance for corporations.
3 *Perceptions of risk and attitudes to insurance.* There is a substantial body of evidence that people do not rank their perceived risk in the 'statistical' order of riskiness and that these perceptions of risk have an important impact on their willingness to purchase insurance. A notable feature is the disinclination of many people to insure against low-probability disasters.
4 *Previous experience of losses* and of the purchase of insurance.
5 *Family life-cycle.* Market research agencies tend to segment many consumer markets by family life-cycle characteristics, tempered by income and occupation influences.

The measurement of lifestyle (known as psychographics) often uses other psychological subdivisions of these basic categories (aggressive–submissive, independent–dependent, etc.). See, for example, Cornell and Bond (1988).

6 *Sociological factors*, e.g. cultural and sub-cultural influences, family and work-group influences, social class, and reference group influences, can all affect household purchasing of insurance. Because corporate purchasing decisions are made by individuals or committees, these types of influence are carried over into the organizational environment and influence purchasing behaviour.

Other qualitative aspects of demand have been discussed in Chapter 2, and have an effect on the demand for insurance products.

The marketing mix for insurance companies

The types of marketing activities which make up the marketing mix of insurance companies depend at least in part on the particular features of the industry. Each element will now be considered in turn.

Pricing

Pricing is a complex variable in insurance. While in life assurance the price or premium paid is linked inextricably to the level of protection and/or savings provided, general insurance prices (e.g. for motor insurance) are much more closely related to the decision to purchase. Compared with other types of products and services, insurance products are much more difficult for consumers to compare on price or value for money. Customized versions of products drawing from a wide range of options make price comparisons difficult and even meaningless. Thus, price competition, common with many types of goods, is much less common in insurance, and product proliferation enables suppliers to avoid direct price comparisons. Price features in the marketing mix of insurance companies in two ways:

1   As a 'technical' component, in that actuarial tables, which provide the basic cost component of price, are likely to be similar for different suppliers offering similar types of product. Some trade journals publish 'striped down' price comparisons of benchmark insurance services, e.g. cost for £1000 protection for defined categories of consumers, but these are not very likely to be accessible to members of the general public. Equally, investment performance tables for life and pensions products are published by journals such as *Planned Savings,* which enables potential investors to compare suppliers on past performance. However, extrapolation of these results can be difficult. It could be argued that it is better advice to purchase a product which has performed badly in the recent past because the management is likely to be 'shaken up' and have everything to prove in the next period.

2   As a promotion offer of the 'first monthly premium free' type commonly used in direct response advertising and direct mail offers as a hook for new buyers. These offers feature a price saving as an appeal but do not necessarily make price comparisons any easier.

Life insurance is particularly prone to difficulties in price comparisons, as the products are customized, in that buyers have to fill in a questionnaire (the proposal form) which aims to assess the degree of risk offered. The increasing risk of AIDS is a new factor which exacerbates the problem. In addition, the investment element of the life policy cannot be predicted easily in advance. Past performance, as noted above, may not be the best guide to future performance.

Price as an element of the marketing mix plays a unique role in insurance companies, especially life-insurance companies.

Distribution

Distribution plays a complex and idiosyncratic part in the marketing mix of insurance companies. Direct selling, through company-owned retail outlets or the traditional 'home-service' ('the man from the Pru') or the self-employed sales consultant, have taken a significant proportion of insurance sales for a long time. The FSA polarization rule has led more insurance companies to set up direct sales forces. Insurance is sold at the client's home or workplace in a significant proportion of cases, unlike many other industries. The issues which affect this distribution route, as explored in greater depth in Chapter 7, are very important to insurance companies. Much effort is expended on recruitment selection training and motivation of the sales force.

Indirect selling through independent intermediaries such as brokers gives insurance companies a two-stage selling process. The 'into the pipeline' role is served by inspectors, who liaise between the company and intermediaries, and the 'out of the pipeline' role is provided by the sales force of the intermediaries. The role of the inspector is usually technical, offering help on complex or marginal cases and the 'selling' aspect of a 'soft' rather than 'hard' type.

Other forms of distribution, such as direct mail, direct response advertising and telephone selling, have been growing in importance in recent years as insurance companies have responded to the changing environment by seeking a multi-channelling distribution strategy. These changes have been traumatic. Many insurance companies were traditionally 'broker only' and had built up a strong loyalty with their intermediaries. In the marketing-led moves into new distribuution channels which followed the introduction of the FSA in 1986, the insurance companies feared conflict with existing, well-established channels. Initially, as explained in Chapter 1, a body known as CAMIFA (Campaign for Independent Financial Advice) was launched, funded by the manager 'broker only' companies and backing the independent intermediary route through a TV and press advertising campaign. Since 1986, CAMIFA has lessened in importance, and companies led by Equity and Law have left the broker-only route to market and hence CAMIFA, and have set up other routes, notably direct-sales teams. The independent intermediary route is most important for the more complex insurance products (group pension schemes, marine and aviation insurance, for example) which require more comprehensive knowledge and training. For more straightforward products (endowment policies and term assurance for individuals, for example) other routes have been opened up.

Thus, distribution has been a major marketing battleground in the insurance industry in the last few years, and insurance companies have assiduously courted building societies (as joint venture 'tied' agents) and estate-agency chains to try to gain competitive advantage in the distribution chain.

Advertising and promotion

Advertising and promotion are important because insurance companies have traditionally been 'invisible'. Customer awareness levels have been well below those associated with the major banks and building societies. As will be seen below, insurance companies have belatedly tried to rectify this situation by heavy spending on media advertising and on sponsorship. In contrast to many consumer-goods and services companies, there has been no attempt to utilize a long-term advertising strategy so as to develop company and brand image. Advertising has been treated as a knee-jerk response to competitive pressure rather than as a long-term investment in brand and company image. It will take some time for this impression to be rectified, and these elements of the marketing mix are clearly important in the current competitive environment.

Product policy

Products have tended to be treated from an actuarial rather than a demand perspective in insurance. Unlike many consumer-goods and service industries, there has been little attempt until recently to develop branding. Successful brand-image creation can be a valuable competitive advantage, and insurance, and indeed financial service companies generally, are only belatedly turning their attention to brands. The Midland Bank's innovative branding of Vector, Orchard, Meridian and First Direct led the way. In insurance, Choices pensions from Guardian Royal Insurance exemplify a trend which may develop in the 1990s.

Competition through new-product development and profit proliferation is treated later in the chapter, when we look at the product life-cycle, but was a significant marketing activity for insurance companies in the late 1980s. Companies have sought to open up new market segments (as discussed in Chapter 2) by providing new versions of products aimed at specifically targeted sectors of the market.

Service quality

Service quality is also of increasing concern as customer awareness and buyer sophistication grows. In the search for new business, existing clients can easily be overlooked. However, as competition continues to intensify, companies have developed cross-selling strategies which

204

attempt to sell more products to existing clients. In insurance terms, this can mean increasing the level of cover in a life-insurance product, covering more members of the family or adding related policies to the initial sale. Effective cross-selling relies on building up long-term relationships with clients, and stresses the importance of service quality. Insurance companies are beginning to train staff in servicing, and to deal with customer queries in a positive way, so as to try and open up new sales possibilities through customer satisfaction and referrals.

Marketing planning

The five major elements of the insurance company's marketing mix, outlined above, need to be combined together into a unified whole. The art of marketing lies in combining the elements to gain positive synergy, so that the whole is greater than the sum of the parts. Thus, a policy aimed at high net worth individuals would need to be sold through 'up-market' channels, using up-market promotion and packaging, with a high level of service quality. Each element should fit neatly together and so produce an image and an impact which are appealing and easily understood by the prospective customer.

This section has introduced the major elements of the marketing mix for insurance companies and stressed those of growing importance. The following section applies some of the major marketing concepts to the insurance industry. They will be discussed within the framework of the product life-cycle, which was introduced in Chapter 3.

The product life-cycle

The development phase

As has been discussed in detail elsewhere (Davison *et al.*, 1989), insurance companies make relatively little use of market research in the development of new products. The main reasons relate to, first, the costs associated with developing and operationalizing the market-research function. Equally important is the time taken in research. The insurance companies perceive copying competitors' (successful) products as a major source of new product ideas, and market research is commonly seen as a delaying factor which helps competitors by allowing for their development. Unlike manufacturing industry, where production capacity for a new product may take many months to build and implement, the insurance industry has merely to define the product from an actuarial perspective. Commonly this is a much shorter process. In addition, pressure from senior directors or other important influencers may be such that the product will be launched anyway, and market research is seen as redundant in these circumstances. The pressure to launch personal equity plans (PEPs) came from the Chancellor of the Exchequer rather than the market place or any effective market research.

Additional reasons why the use of market research has been limited include a lack of interest by consumers and a lack of marketing sophistication. Consumers are characterized as being unwilling to discuss insurance products in any meaningful way in market research, owing to their lack of interest or lack of knowledge. These factors, if true, make market research more difficult and costly to carry out and less valuable to insurance companies. Furthermore, as has been shown in Chapter 2, few financial services organizations have market-research departments. The value of market research in this scenario is less likely to be perceived.

Where market research is used in the process of developing new products, it has tended to be concerned with:

1 Research to test proposed advertising material on small groups drawn from the target audience
2 The purchase of syndicated research such as the NOP FRS (see Chapter 2)
3 The purchase of 'off the shelf' reports on particular market sectors, e.g. Mintel, Euromonitor.

The development phase of NPD in the insurance industry can be characterized as usually being short, concerned with ironing out the actuarial small print, evaluating competitor action and reaction, and training the sales force. This important prerequisite is often carried out by a 'roadshow' approach, where a central training team visits each region in turn to introduce the new product to regional sales staff. At this stage, there is also a significant amount of effort devoted to establishing the administrative procedures for the new product and organizing the relevant computer systems. Much of the launch training referred to above is concerned with administrative processes and which forms to fill in. Increasingly, where computer links exist, these procedures do have an important IT dimension.

An interesting and controversial trend is the use of brands in insurance. Choices, a pensions product from Guardian Royal Insurance, introduced in 1988, exemplified one of the first big attempts to use TV advertising to launch a new insurance brand. The most usual approach has been to rely on the name of the insurance company to sell the product. Relying on the brand name, a novel approach in insurance, follows a similar trend for bank products led by Midland Bank with branded accounts (Vector, Orchard and First Direct, for example).

The introduction phase

The launch of a new insurance product is now likely to include TV advertising. Mass-media advertising by insurance companies has been increasing rapidly for the sector as a whole but inconsistently for specific companies. These trends are shown in Tables 11.4 and 11.5.

Table 11.4 *Advertising trends by insurance companies*

Date	Total (000s)	TV (%)	Press (%)
1970	2,852	3.2	96.8
1975	4,273	18.9	81.1
1980	12,494	28.6	71.4
1981	18,089	27.0	73.0
1982	24,411	33.8	66.2
1983	35,223	31.7	68.3
1984	37,962	25.9	74.1
1985	49,111	33.0	67.0
1986	62,896	38.0	62.0
1987	67,315	–	–
1988	96,346	52.0	47.0
1989*	87,877	50.0	49.0

* Third-quarter figures
Source: MEAL

Table 11.5 *Main media advertising expenditure by selected insurance companies, 1983–9 (000s)*

Company	1983	1984	1985	1986	1987	1988	1989*
General Accident	–	111	2979	4661	541	5552	4790
Commercial Union	2014	1992	2225	3161	4454	52151	4518
GRE	1099	686	422	229	103	8520	8516
Legal & General	2030	2057	3198	246	4463	4736	4330
Norwich Union	1030	1589	2001	3430	4980	5466	4794
Pearl	448	630	564	106	1974	1446	1801
Prudential	1111	1149	811	5794	2875	5880	6544
Royal	1583	952	1400	956	4995	2610	2257
Sun Alliance	4770	6014	5717	10138	9046	6401	12882

* Third-quarter figure
Source: MEAL

Insurance companies have traditionally been very poor at corporate image creation. When Prudential created its new 'Prudence' image, it spent at least £5m on the introductory campaign alone. A glance at the MEAL figures for insurance and assurance advertising shows the growth in the 1980s. There is evidence of both a rapid growth and a trend to TV from press advertising, despite the restrictions imposed by the FSA. The spending by individual companies has been fragmented but is increasing across the sector. Although, much of this expenditure is company image building, some of the companies have moved on to product-specific advertising (e.g. the Choices campaign) on TV. Much of the Sun Alliance spending is direct-response press advertising.

The coordination of the launch specifically with the training of sales staff and the introduction of administrative procedures requires careful planning, as in any industry. Given the nature of the insurance industry, it is very difficult to make a 'splash' and to create an impact with a new product launch. Rather, it is a slow process. As the sales force revisits clients or visits potential clients, the new policy will be introduced (if it can be shown under the FSA to meet clients' needs after a factfind). Direct mail or direct response advertising may also be used to bring the new product to customers' attention in a more targeted way. As it is not common to use a test market, companies will often have no clear advance idea of which sub-set of customers will be most responsive to the new product.

If not already alerted, competitors will closely monitor the perceived success of the product. For existing insurance companies there are generally low barriers to entry making the launch of copy products likely sooner rather than later. Barriers may exist:

1 Where special technical, sales or marketing staff are needed to launch the product
2 When the product imposes substantial technical or technological requirements (e.g. a new computer system or new software procedures
3 When large marketing expense levels need to be incurred (e.g. for an expensive advertising campaign to launch the new product)
4 (For international competitors) where regulatory requirements need to be met to enter a particular national market.

The growth stage

During the growth stage, sales increase at their most rapid rate and the product becomes established. In insurance this stage has a prerequisite that the sales force (tied or intermediaries) becomes convinced of the

208

value of the product, particularly its sales potential (and hence commission-earnings potential). Having gained practical experience in selling the product by this stage, the members of the sales force should have honed their sales pitch to the level at which they have become highly effective and efficient at the sales presentation.

Customers who are 'followers' rather than 'leaders' buy the product during the growth stage. Thus, sales force members can refer to others who have bought the product within the sales presentation, thus encouraging the 'followers' to buy.

Importantly, as the distribution of the product becomes established, the members of the sales force become more effective at selling the product. More independent intermediaries are likely to recognize the potential of the product, and to make increased sales efforts. The product thus becomes better known within the distribution channel, and sales staff are better able to sell it and are more likely to have been trained to sell it. Sales training plays an important role in both the introduction and the growth stages. For a company with a large sales force, this training process may take some time.

The distribution training and motivation of sales staff are important prerequisites to sales growth. As noted under the introduction phase above, product-copying is endemic in the insurance industry, and it is likely that new brands from competitors will appear. Promotion policy is likely to switch towards emphasizing differences from other brands rather than continuing to emphasize the benefits of the product *per se*. In other words, the advertising message switches from 'buy life insurance' to 'buy OUR life insurance'.

Competitors' brands may include major (or minor) product improvements. To some extent, this depends on how successful the first brand into the market was at getting the right blend of product features and characteristics. Comprehensive brands searching for their own unique proposition will strive to eradicate what are considered to be weaknesses in the format of the innovative brand. The first brand into the market has the advantage of gaining most publicity, and having a longer time to become established. Later brands may be perceived as inferior copies and find more difficulty in becoming established. Product improvements and new product features become an important form of competition within the growth phase, as competitors strive to find the ideal product formulation.

Price may well decline during the growth phase, sometimes by economies of scale as sales grow, but more likely from competitive pressure. Price may be used for promotional reasons and also to gain more distribution outlets by offering better margins. It is likely that over-supply is a feature at this stage, and that the sum of the sales targets for the competing products is much higher than actual sales achieved. Price can thus be seen as one form of competition, although in insurance the price variation is much less straightforward than with other products and services because of customization and the range of options often available.

Finally, increasing competitive pressure at this stage is likely to push marketing effort into selective demand cultivation through market segments, with the creation of own-niche markets which insurance companies can try to dominate. A good example is the use of affinity-group marketing, whereby specific groups are offered special offers. Thus Teachers Assurance has specialized in life insurance for those in the teaching profession; it has formed bonds with the National Union of Teachers and trains staff to understand the intricacies of the Teachers Superannuation Scheme. Thus, a highly specialist professional service can be offered to this particular niche market, often by means of sales staff recruited from the teaching profession.

The mature stage

Most insurance products are in the mature phase of the life-cycle and most marketing activities for the products in this stage centre on one or more of the following areas:

New distribution channels

Traditionally, insurance products were sold through brokers (or other independent financial intermediaries) or by company representatives. More recently new channels have opened up, including direct sales forces (e.g. Abbey Life, Allied Dunbar), estate agencies (usually subsidiaries of insurance companies such as Prudential, Royal, General Accident), building societies through tied arrangements (Halifax/Standard Life, Abbey National/Friends Provident), direct-response advertising and direct mail. Tables 11.6 to 11.8 show the impact of these changes recently for three classes of insurance.

Let us first consider *life assurance*. The channels of distribution have changed in recent years as the importance of insurance-company representatives from industrial companies has declined. However, representatives still account for 48 per cent of all outstanding policies and 36 per cent of those taken out in the last year (Table 11.6). The highest growth has come from building societies, banks, brokers and estate agents, largely due to the increasing importance of mortgage-related business.

Second, let us consider *home contents*. Table 11.8 shows that building societies showed a very rapid growth in their market share of the

Table 11.6 *How life assurance is obtained*

	All covered	Covered by policy taken out in last year
Insurance company office	8	8
Insurance company rep	48	36
Insurance broker/consultant	11	17
Building society	23	34
Bank	6	10
Local authority	1	1
Employer	4	5
Family/friends	11	11
Estate agent	2	6
Accountant/solicitor	2	3
Other	3	5

Source: Whitmore (1988).

Table 11.7 *House structure insurance: how it is initially arranged*

	All covered	Covered by policy taken out in last year
Insurance company office	8	5
Insurance company rep	12	8
Insurance broker/consultant	8	7
Building society	41	54
Bank	5	9
Local authority	3	1
Employer	2	1
Family/friends	4	3
Accountant/solicitor	2	1
Estate agents	1	2
Other	3	3

Source: Whitmore (1988).

distribution of home-contents insurance in the 1987–8 period, which has continued subsequently. This gain has been largely at the expense of direct distribution via insurance-company representatives. The banks also doubled their market share in the 12-month period, though from a lower base. This change is particularly important because of the polarization requirements of the FSA. As most leading building societies have now tied in with insurance companies, the distribution can be expected to become concentrated, with building societies continuing to take a significant market share. The changes show the success of the building societies in marketing home-contents insurance alongside mortgages as a package deal.

Third, as regards *house-structure insurance*, Table 11.7 shows a very

Table 11.8   *Home contents insurance: how it is initially arranged*

	All covered	Covered by policy taken out in last year
Insurance company office	13	11
Insurance company rep	34	23
Insurance broker/consultant	12	11
Building society	10	19
Bank	4	8
Local authority	2	3
Employer	2	2
Family/friends	9	11
Accountant/solicitor	1	*
Other	3	6

* Negligible
Source: Whitmore (1988).

similar pattern to that in Table 11.7, although the building societies had already dominated the distribution of this type of insurance product. The banks also made a significant gain, again from a small base. The decline of the direct distribution channel from insurance companies to householders is even more marked for this type of insurance.

Product rejuvenation

Adding new features to established products so as to create more customer interest, and to aid differentiation from rival products, sums up project-rejuvenation. A good example is motor insurance. Price has been shown to be *the* major influence on purchase. New features are one way of adding value to the product, and can then be used to justify a higher premium. Dyer (1988) gives recent examples of this phenomenon.

Special promotional offers

Although the Financial Services Act restricts the incentives which can be used to promote life-insurance products through the SIB rulebook, offers such as free gifts and 'first premium free' are being used for some insurance products, particularly in direct response advertising and direct mail, where such offers are used to create customer interest. The general marketing principle that such special offers can easily become product demeaning and easily copied is valid. Unlike the case with many consumer products, however, the customer, once having purchased an insurance product, particularly a life insurance product, is less likely to switch to another company, at least in the short term. With many consumer goods it has been found that customers who switch suppliers because of special offers are easily won back when their original supplier runs an equivalent offer later. This pattern is unlikely to occur with insurance products, and hence such offers may have more long-term potency than is usually the case.

Sponsorship

A frequent marketing criticism of insurance companies is that they are anonymous monoliths. The companies have, as has been shown in Table 11.4, been spending money on media advertising to try to overcome this deficiency, which is shown by poor showings in prompted and unprompted awareness tests. Many insurance companies have turned to sponsorship to help create some awareness and to demonstrate good corporate citizenship. Both these factors can be seen as prerequisites to purchase. A good example is the sponsorship of the Royal Shakespeare Company by Royal Insurance, described by Kallaway (1988).

Telephone marketing

Although telephone marketing is really another distribution channel, it is treated separately here because, at least in the UK, unlike the US, it is novel in insurance distribution. To date it is used to back up mail to try to increase rates of return, e.g. for renewal of motor insurance a phone call may jog the memory of the purchaser or may be used to give a competitive quote. A further use is to seek appointments for specialist salespersons to call in person. The use of the telephone in insurance marketing is expected to grow rapidly. Some interesting recent examples of campaigns are provided by Garland (1988).

Packaging

Packaging has become a particularly important part of the marketing activities of insurance companies using direct marketing methods. The design of direct mail appeals needs careful thought if they are to have maximum impact (Martin, 1988). The design of sales aids for use by the sales force (or that of intermediaries) is also important if the company's product is to stand out from competitors. Customer communications need to be carefully packaged also. A strategic requirement is that the company image or logo should be carried through all written communications material to maximize impact. An obvious example is that when Prudential launched its 'Prudence' image, its move into estate agency enabled it to reinforce the image by using 'For Sale' boards outside the many properties it handled throughout the country. The advertising effect of this marketing activity was estimated by one Prudential executive as being worth £1.5 million of media advertising in the first year. The same logo was carried through into the house description sheets and other written communications throughout the Prudential group (Llewellyn, 1988).

Other customer communications

In the race to attract new business, it is easy to forget the need to keep existing customers satisfied and to develop cross-sell opportunities, i.e. sell more products to existing clients. Customer communications can facilitate this marketing activity. Renewal notices, bonus statements and statements of account are regular customer communications which can be used as means of introducing new products or features to existing clients. A customer magazine sent to the client base can be another useful marketing aid. *Dimensions*, a magazine issued by the National Westminster Bank is a good example of the potential of positive customer communications.

Sales incentives

The use of sales incentives has been developed to a fine art by some insurance companies which run direct commission-only sales forces (see Hastings *et al.*, 1988). Incentives range from small gifts for meeting short-term targets or quotas to long-term incentives – up to 2 years for a major, usually travel-based, incentive. These incentives are carefully constructed to try to motivate sales staff to increase their sales over time so as to qualify for the rewards. In a similar vein these organizations run clubs – the 'Chairman's Club' or similar – whose membership depends on sales achievements. Many insurance companies suffer from 'comfort zone' problems, in which some sales staff achieve a level of sales which offers them an acceptable level of income, but then are not motivated to make further sales. Incentives can be one method of motivating staff in this zone. Motivation theory was developed in detail in Chapter 7. Sales incentives in the insurance sector were discussed in detail by Hills (1988). It is interesting to note that the ethos in the insurance sector is to generate further sales by motivating the seller not the buyer.

Market segmentation

In the earlier part of this chapter and in Chapter 2, the attraction of particular market segments was highlighted. One way of developing marketing activity during the mature stage of the product life-cycle is to identify attractive new market segmentors for an existing product. New product features, new packaging or other marketing activities may need to be used to present the product effectively to the new sector but potentially can develop the market for the existing product. The segmentation may be by age, purchase reason, family life-cycle stage, geographical or other relevant factor. The product range should then reflect the different needs to each segment served.

The decline stage

A particular feature of the insurance sector is its longevity. Life-insurance products have a life measured in decades. It is particularly difficult to withdraw products from the market. What seems to happen in practice is that products which are in decline are simply not promoted. It is possible that attempts to persuade existing clients to switch to new types of policy are made, but if these attempts are not successful, the policy continues to be administered passively.

Thus, insurance companies commonly have a high array of products on their books which are not actively marketed but are not withdrawn from the portfolio. There are hidden costs in this approach. The administrative costs, the costs of computing and of training staff may not be attributed to a product's indirect costs, but nevertheless exist and need to be considered. There is a cost of management time also in having to deal with declining products. Nor are such products likely to be popular within the organization. An ambitious product manager with a name to make will not usually wish to be associated with declining products.

These problems are exacerbated for industrial branch products, where, by law, the premiums have, at the customer's request, to be collected at the client's home in cash. For long-established policies the premium may be a few pence per week. Clearly, the inefficiencies are immense.

There are potential benefits to be had from declining products. For ordinary branch business paid by regular standing order or direct debit, the collection costs are likely to be minimal, and without marketing costs the product can be very efficient in generating inflows of cash. Effective investment performance by the insurance company can generate higher return levels for the client (and for the shareholder if the company is not a mutual). Good performance can lead to increased business from the client. Even for industrial branch products, the regular contact with clients to collect premiums often leads to the building of a trusting, long-term client relationship. Such a relationship can lead to successful cross-selling when the insurance-company representative translates customer needs, as they arise, into product offerings from the company's range. Thus, established relationships with clients are a valuable asset to insurance companies and their sales forces. The relationships can be developed through some of the devices already noted, particularly careful customer communications, which can develop a sense of belonging in long-established clients.

The premise that individuals are either net savers or net borrowers implies that an insurance company with a wide range of products can develop the concept of lifetime care for its clients, offering a different combination of products at each life-cycle stage, including products for:

1   Dependent (living in the family home, under 25)
2   Pre-family (established separate household, no children, mainly under 35)
3   Family (under 65, with children in the home)
4   Late (adults, children left home or childless and 35 or over)

Although a more refined set of stages can be developed, the four listed above illustrate the point.

Within this 'broad sweep' strategy, a decline-stage product could be kept in the product range to avoid a gap in the range. It can be argued that the profitability of the range rather than each individual product should be the strategic guideline in this context.

Conclusions

This chapter has attempted to identify the specific marketing features of the insurance sector. It has examined some of the features of demand for insurance and the current trends in the sector. Following from this analysis of demand-side influences, the use of marketing activities as a part of competitive strategy has been attempted. The approach taken has been to discuss these marketing activities through the medium of the product life-cycle concept, broadened to include a wide range of possible marketing activities.

CHAPTER 12
The marketing of unit and investment trusts
Paul Draper

Introduction

Unit and investment trusts are collective investment vehicles for pooling subscribers' contributions and investing them in a variety of transferable assets such as ordinary shares and bonds. They are run by investment managers, who use their knowledge and experience to select individual securities which are aggregated to form portfolios that meet predetermined objectives and criteria. These portfolios are then sold to the public and offer investors three main services: portfolio diversification and the reduction of unsystematic risk, portfolio management in the form of specialist investment knowledge and administrative services, and financial intermediation by creating a new financial asset which may be more easily marketable than the underlying securities in the portfolio.

These services provide the basis around which the marketing manager must work. Existing and potential investors must be convinced of the expertise and skill of the portfolio manager, and persuaded to save rather than spend, to invest through a financial intermediary in preference to investing directly, to choose risky securities and not fixed-interest deposits, to select unit or investment trusts instead of life assurance or increased pension contributions, and finally to identify the appropriate investment manager and objective. The marketing manager must identify strategies and target promotion efforts that will reach investors at each of these crucial decision stages, and must do so within constraints on expenditure in an atmosphere of vigorous competition and increasing regulatory activity.

This chapter sets out the environment in which the marketing manager must operate. The first part explores the nature of unit and investment trusts, paying particular attention to their structure and organization, the creation and valuation of their securities, product differentiation, and performance comparisons. The second part examines the market for unit and investment trusts with emphasis on the impact of regulation on marketing decisions. The third part considers some of the opportunities that exist for expanding the sales of investment products; it explores three areas of interest – increasing the variety of securities available, improving channels of distribution so as to make the managers' investment products easier to acquire, and possible alterations to the investment packages on offer with a view to making them more flexible and useful to investors.

The nature of unit and investment trusts

Structure and organization

Investment and unit trusts offer the same services to investors. The number of investment trusts has been declining for at least three decades, and in the 1980s fell by some 20 per cent (Table 12.1). Total assets have continued to increase. The value of investment trusts' shares has also declined sharply as a proportion of total stock market value. In contrast, both the number and value of unit trusts have developed rapidly since the mid-1960s. In the 1980s, the value of funds increased almost tenfold and the number of unit trusts almost trebled (Table 12.2).

The legal form of the two investment vehicles, however, is quite different, and may result in differences in value, marketing, advertising and distribution. Investment trusts are companies regulated by the Companies Acts, with their business activity that of investing in the securities of other companies. The object of investment trusts is to raise capital from investors by the issue of their own ordinary shares and invest the proceeds, together with any capital they may have raised from the issue of fixed-interest securities such as debentures or loan

Table 12.1 *Investment trust statistics, 1981–7*

	No.[1]	Total assets (£m)	Market value of shares (£m)	Inv. trusts' value as % of total market
1981	202	9,335	6,123.2	6.2
1982	191	10,506	7,322.3	6.0
1983	184	13,888	9,670.0	6.2
1984	164	15,998	10,991.1	5.4
1985	166	19,236	12,264.6	5.0
1986	156	21,722	15,806.4	4.9
1987	162	19,500	13,934.2	3.7

1 AITC members
Source: AITC

Table 12.2 *Unit trust statistics, 1981–89*

Period	Value of funds (£m)	Gross sales (£m)	Repurchases (£m)	Net investment	Unitholder accounts (m)	Number of trusts
1981	5,902	955.6	428.0	527.6	1.79	529
1982	7,768	1,157.5	567.2	590.3	1.80	553
1983	11,689	2,459.8	960.2	1,499.6	2.04	630
1984	15,099	2,918.2	1,476.7	1,441.5	2.20	687
1985	20,308	4,487.7	1,949.1	2,538.6	2.55	806
1986	32,131	8,716.7	3,482.1	5,234.6	3.41	964
1987	36,330	14,545.1	8,214.3	6,330.8	5.05	1,137
1988	41,574	7,675.7	5,880.4	1,795.3	4.89	1,255
1989 Q1	49,224	2,629.8	1,597.6	10,322.2	4.80	1,265
1989 Q2	53,226	2,404.3	1,744.6	659.7	4.83	1,302

Source: Unit Trust Association

stock in the securities, both equity and debt, of other enterprises. Some constraints exist on the extent and the scope of their investments, the precise terms depending on the company's memorandum and articles of association, but in general they are free to invest in a wider range of assets than unit trusts, and historically have had strong overseas links as well as a variety of specialisms, including the provision of venture capital. Possibly the most important constraints on their activities arise from the desire of most investment trusts to secure 'Approved' status, which carries with it significant tax benefits but requires the trusts to meet a number of conditions with regard to the size and spread of their holding and distribution of dividends.[1]

Investment trusts are taxed like other companies, and are, therefore, in a position to issue fixed-interest debt, the interest on which is deducted from profits before the calculation and payment of tax. The existence of debt allows the trusts to gear up their activities by borrowing and to invest the proceeds in equities. Provided the return on equities is greater than the cost of borrowing, the investment trust benefits. The ability to borrow is not, in general, available to unit trusts, and potentially enables investment trusts to offer investors a wider spectrum of risk-return investment products, since increases in gearing provide a simple means of increasing the risk and hence the return on a trust.

In contrast to the company structure of investment trusts, unit trusts are legal trusts governed by a trust deed. The trust deed is an agreement between the trustees and the managers of the fund which covers the main aspects of the running of the trust, sets out the rights and responsibilities of all concerned and includes the maximum charges that can be levied, provisions for new members, the pricing of new units, and the investment aims of the trust, including restrictions on the proportions of equity held in any one company and on the proportion of the portfolio invested in any asset. Investment management is in the hands of the managers of the fund, but the trustees issue and redeem unit-trust certificates and handle the cash and securities. The role of the trustees, often a major bank, is to ensure that the trust is managed within the terms of the trust deed, and so protect the owners of the unit trust from fraud and malpractice.[2]

The creation and valuation of securities

The portfolio of securities owned by a unit trust is divided into a number of equal portions called units which are held by investors (unitholders). Each unit represents a specific proportion of the portfolio and has a value that is exactly tied to the value of the underlying assets in the portfolio. In purchasing a unit, a unitholder is purchasing an exact entitlement to part of the portfolio, and, as such, must bear all the costs associated with creating that portfolio, including brokerage fees and taxes. If the value of the portfolio rises, then so also will the price of the unit. If the value of the portfolio falls, then the price of a unit will fall. This correspondence between asset values and unit prices is an important factor in the sale of units, since investors can be confident that a rise in the share prices of the underlying investments will be reflected in the price of the units. Units can be bought or sold at any time, as the managers of the unit trust will buy back or create units to meet demand. If necessary, units bought back can be destroyed by selling assets from the underlying portfolio. In practice, however, most trusts have been expanding and the bought-back units are simply sold to new unitholders. If demand for units is greater than the supply of bought-back units, the manager simply creates new units, which must be of equal value to the existing units. There is an infinitely elastic supply curve; the manager will always be ready to create units so long as there is a demand for them. The unit-trust manager has no control over price as such. The price of units is a direct function of the value of the trust's assets. Managers cannot promote sales by reducing prices and must look for other ways of competing and promoting sales. By reducing their own charges, unit trust managers can and do offer small discounts to investors but the extent of such discounts is typically small.

The capital of an investment trust is fixed and can only be increased with the approval of the shareholders. The return on its equity arises from the investments of the trust. The value of these investments goes up or down, as does the value of the investment trust's own ordinary shares, but there is no one-to-one relationship between the change in value of its assets and the change in value of its own shares. The value of an investment trust's own ordinary shares depends on the forces of supply and demand, which in turn reflect relative risks and yields and the abilities of the managers to secure above-average returns. At times, generally infrequent, the value of the investment trust's own shares may exceed the net value of its assets. The abilities of its investment managers to secure above-average returns may be recognized, so that its shares are in demand and trade at a premium. More commonly, however, the net value of the investment trusts assets exceed the value of its ordinary shares, and the equity trades at a discount. Figure 12.1 provides an illustration of the size of the discount on investment trusts over the last 30 years. It has been persistent, often large, and an important factor affecting the freedom of action of investment-trust managers.

Growth of an investment trust occurs either by the increase in value of its own assets or by the issue of new shares to new and existing investors. Increases in asset value have been a notable feature of the share market in recent years, but such growth is restricted, since it fails to provide access to the pool of new consumer savings in the economy. To tap this pool the investment trust must issue new shares, but this is severely hindered by the existence of the discount. There is no incentive to subscribe for new investment-trust shares if their price falls once trading begins. For this reason new issues of investment-trust shares have been small and restricted, in general, to the creation of trusts with specialist objectives and managerial skills.

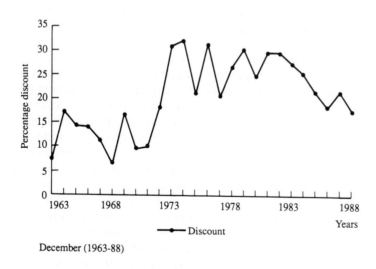

December (1963-88)

Figure 12.1 *Average discount*

The small number of new issues contrasts sharply with the unit-trust market, where new units can and have been created in massive amounts. Indeed, the situation is worse than this suggests. The existence of a discount implies that the value of the investment trust's assets is greater than the value of its own equity. There is a strong incentive to buy investment-trust equity and to liquidate or break up the trusts so as to secure the underlying investment values. The result has been a stream of takeovers, liquidations and other similar events aimed at releasing these assets (Draper, 1989). Until the discount is eliminated or at least greatly reduced,[3] there is an incentive to break up an investment trust, and the concern of management will be more with its defensive position than with expanding the market and promoting their particular type of investment products. Marketing is of crucial importance in attacking and reducing the discount so as to enable trusts to expand once more.

Product differentiation and promotion

Unit trusts make extensive use of advertising to sell their products. In the early years of the industry it was common to advertise in the national press, inviting subscriptions. In recent years the importance of block offers[4] and off-the-page sales has declined, but unit trusts continue to advertise heavily to reinforce brand loyalty and product differentiation. Sales are usually made through financial intermediaries, particularly insurance brokers, as well as through accountants, solicitors, stockbrokers and other financial advisers. Direct mail and sales representatives also play their part, so that unit trusts can be bought through a broad spectrum of financial service firms.[5]

Investment trusts are also marketed through financial intermediaries, but the inability of the managers to buy and sell securities in the trusts they manage and the need to acquire the investment-trust equity through the stock market makes investment less easy and precludes off-the-page selling. Investment trusts are marketed much less aggressively than unit trusts, and for many years they undertook little promotional activity. The problem, as the industry perceived it, was the Prevention of Fraud (Investments) Act (now the Financial Services Act), which prohibited a company from promoting its own shares. More recently, the prohibition has been interpreted less strictly, so that investment trusts have engaged in more promotional activity than previously. The ability of unit trusts to advertise extensively remains, however, an important advantage for them over investment trusts, and has resulted in a level of consumer awareness

Table 12.3 *Portfolio and product differentiation*

Investment trusts	Unit trusts
International general	International growth
International capital growth	International income
International income growth	UK growth
UK general	UK general
UK capital growth	UK equity income
UK income growth	Mixed income
N. America	Gilt and FI growth
Far East, incl. Japan	Gilt and FI income
Far East, excl. Japan	N. America
Japan	Japan
Australasia	Australia
Europe	Europe
Financial and property	Investment trust units
Commodity and energy	Financial and property
Technology	Commodity and energy
Smaller companies	Managed
Venture capital	
Split capital trust	

Sources: *Unit Trust Yearbook, Investment Trust Index*

and knowledge of unit trusts that far surpasses that for investment trusts.

In recent years the Association of Investment Trusts (AITC) has devoted considerable effort to marketing the industry as a whole, but its activities are necessarily limited. A recent survey by London Weekend Television of London investors found that only 14 per cent of their total sample had not heard of unit trusts but 32 per cent had not heard of investment trusts (6 per cent and 19 per cent respectively of those with over £10,000 of savings). More worrying perhaps for the investment trusts was that, of savers with over £10,000, 44 per cent claimed to know a considerable amount about unit trusts but only 27 per cent to have a similar knowledge of investment trusts. In the past the better-off private investors were the main market for investment-trust shares.

As part of their marketing campaigns, unit and investment trusts compete by differentiating their investment portfolio. They offer investors a wide range of alternative investment objectives in the hope of exciting a potential investor's interest. Table 12.3 provides a summary of the main investment objectives offered by each. The variety is extensive and even then obscures some of the more unusual objectives, such as investment in precious metals or investment in small country funds. Increased specialization and greater product differentiation have been pronounced features of recent years, although investment-trust groups have found it less easy than unit trusts to start new trusts and to fill gaps in their marketing profile. The incentive for further differentiation of portfolios is the prospect of increased sales, but the discovery of new, previously uncatered for objectives and the launch of a successful new fund are not without problems. Products in the financial sector are easily replicated, so that it is easy for competitors to copy successful products.

In addition to increasing their appeal to investors by specialization, both unit and investment trusts employ a wide variety and range of marketing schemes to achieve wider sales. The unit-trust movement pioneered repackaging techniques that enabled unit trusts to appeal to a wider market. Of particular significance was the sale of unit trusts with life assurance.[6] By linking unit trusts to life assurance the unit-trust management companies were able to tap a new market and benefit from favourable tax treatment, since, before 1984, tax relief was granted on premiums, so boosting the investment input from the policyholder. Insurance linking was much slower to arrive in the investment-trust industry, although a number of schemes now exist.

Other schemes that exist for both unit and investment trusts include personal pensions, personal equity plans (PEPs) and regular savings schemes. The aim of the schemes is to use the investment portfolios of unit and investment trusts as the savings element of any plan that requires regular savings contributions. PEPs, for example, offer tax advantages to encourage personal-sector investment in UK shares, and are ideally suited to being linked to unit and investment trusts.

Remuneration and profitability

Unit-trust managers are rewarded by the levy of two different charges on unitholders: an initial charge and an annual management fee. The initial charge is normally around 5 per cent and is included in the price payable to the managers on purchase. It is used to meet the advertising and promotional costs of the unit trust, including the payment of commission to independent intermediaries. Newman (1984) notes that advertising expenditure as a proportion of sales has been falling, although it fluctuates markedly and will tend to be higher when stock markets are bouyant. The maximum rate of commission currently agreed by the majority of firms in the industry is 3 per cent. By altering the initial charge the managers can alter their competitive position and strategy. In the short run, high initial charges will fund high promotional expenditures. In the long run, they are likely to affect performance adversely.

The annual charge is usually levied half-yearly, and amounts to around 1 per cent of the total value of the fund, although it can for some specialist trusts be very much higher. A few gilt funds have lower charges because commissions on gilts are lower, but generally, specialist funds are characterized by higher charges. The charge is deducted from the income earned by the unit trust, and is intended to reward the managers for their expertise. As with the initial charge, alteration of the annual charge provides the managers with some control over value. A number of other small charges, such as trustee fees, may also be levied on the fund.

Unlike unit trusts, investment trusts generally impose no initial fee on purchase of their shares, since purchasing through the stock market provides no mechanism for such a fee, although commission and taxes are payable. The requirement to purchase through the stock market reduces the appeal to many intermediaries of promoting investment trusts, since the commission from such sales is small. Although no initial fee is payable, annual management charges are levied. These charges may either represent the actual costs incurred or represent a charge based on the fee payable to the investment-management group that undertakes the investment for the company. The annual management charges are generally considerably lower than for unit trusts.

Performance comparisons

Performance comparisons are a source of interest to investors and an important tool in the marketing of portfolios. However, the abilities of the portfolio manager to influence the performance of a trust is much less than is commonly accepted. Some gloss can be added by appropriate comparisons, although, as seen in Chapter 1, the life-assurance regulatory body makes specific provision for information disclosure with respect to the performance of investments and requires comparisons to be fair, so that the possibilities for massaging performance figures are strictly limited.

Portfolio performance is the sum of the change in price of the portfolio over a period, the capital gains, and the dividends received on securities over the same period. The dividend element is generally stable and small, (although it may be a significant element of total return over an extended period) but, in contrast, changes in price are largely unpredictable and may be swiftly reversed. Share prices are a result of competitive pressures. At any moment the share price of a company is based on all available information, since any information that investors can use to improve their predictions of future share prices is immediately acted upon. The result is that a firm's share price reflects what is currently known about the company and the environment in which it operates. Changes in price come about only when new information reaches the market, and since the arrival of new information is likely to be unpredictable, share prices also move in an unpredictable fashion.[7] Consequently, changes in share values can be sudden and dramatic. By chance, some investors will earn very large profits from these changes but it is unlikely that they can earn such profits with any degree of consistency.

A variety of empirical tests including analysing the buy and sell recommendations of investments analysts, financial journalists and market tipsters have all suggested that it is impossible to make abnormally large returns consistently. Such a conclusion has implications for the management of investment portfolios, since if share price changes are unpredictable, portfolio performance must also be unpredictable. Information arriving at the market that is favourable for the securities in which the fund is invested will result in good investment performance for the fund, whereas the arrival of information that is less auspicious will result in poor performance. In the long run the chance factors will largely balance out and the investment funds will earn the return for the risk they assume, no more and no less.

Once we accept that consistent superior investment performance is difficult to achieve, it becomes apparent that there is an asymmetry in investment performance. On average, investment portfolios will secure the return for the risk they assume, but this return will be reduced by management costs, so that the lower the management costs, the better the funds' performance. Evidence for this position is provided by numerous empirical studies of portfolio performance (see, for example Guy, 1978 or Lyall, 1983) and, more persuasively perhaps for practitioners, by the move of many large, informed investors into index funds, which follow a passive strategy of imitating the market index and keeping management costs low. There is, however, no evidence to suggest that the majority of investors either know or believe in such concepts, and it appears true that many investors are apparently insensitive to changes in management charges.

The market for unit and investment trusts

Competition

Unit and investment trusts do not operate in isolation. They must sell to investors who have the choice of a wide spectrum of financial products, as well as the option of additional consumption. It is convenient to assume that individuals make decisions on how much to save and then decide on the distribution between alternative investments, but in reality the decision process is certainly more complex. Attractive investment products may be able both to increase the trust's share of the total market for savings and to increase the size of that market.

The very term market is ambiguous. We portray the trusts as competing against the entire spectrum of financial assets from bank and building-society fixed-interest deposits through pensions, life assurance and the direct purchase of equity and debt and even property. In reality, by no means all savings are free to move. Many are contractual, particularly pensions and existing life-assurance policies, while individuals may have preferences for property or safe fixed-interest deposits that are almost immovable. However, it is clear that at the margin investors do switch between products and that investors can be persuaded to invest in one product rather than another.

Little is known about how investors make such decisions. Financial theory presents the choice as one of risk and return. Investors wishing for low risk should invest in fixed-interest deposits and those wanting more risk should invest in equities, but while such trade-offs may be an appropriate guide to action for the informed investors utilizing the stock market, it is difficult to believe that it is a useful guide for the less sophisticated consumer. Indeed, the relative unpopularity of the investment trust over the unit trust, despite lower charges, cannot be explained by poorer performance, and suggests that advertising and information, ease and convenience of purchasing, availability of 'advice' and sales effort and innovation are all important determinants of sales. In short, sales of financial products respond to marketing efforts, and despite a wide spectrum of alternatives, investors can be persuaded to choose particular products. The market for financial products is not entirely free, however. Regulatory agencies supervise most aspects of the market and impose considerable constraints on the activities of the companies. The details of the regulatory framework were set out in Chapter 1, and the relevant parts for unit and investment trusts are referred to in what follows.

Impact of regulation on marketing

The regulatory framework administered by the Securities and Investment Board (SIB) has imposed considerable costs on both unit and investment trusts (see Chiplin and Wright, 1990). The regulators' rulebooks have forced changes in investment practice, particularly with regard to the marketing of investments. Two issues stand out as having particularly important consequences for unit and investment trusts: the disclosure of life-assurance commissions, which effectively put life assurance on the same footing as other collective investments, and the requirement of advisers to provide 'best advice'.

The nature of life-assurance business, with the issue of policies which are frequently for 10 years or more and require annual payments throughout their life, means that the costs of selling a policy are incurred at the beginning of its life, whereas the revenues to the company flow in over an extended period of years. The result is that the initial premiums received from the policies are swallowed up in expenses and do not go into the investment fund. Fearing perhaps that new policyholders will be deterred by the size of the expenses, the insurance companies have been reluctant to disclose the size of commission and other initial costs. After much argument, the life offices have been forced to reveal the effect of expenses on the yield of a policy. From 1 April 1990 it was possible to compare the expenses of with-profits life assurance with unit-linked life policies, and indeed with unit and investment trusts. Over the longer term there may be moves to reduce expenses by the use of fee-based advisers, where commissions are not paid to intermediaries but instead a fee is charged to clients for advice, so that advisers are not persuaded to sell particular products as a result of the commissions offered. The rules of LAUTRO explicitly preclude companies structuring the remuneration of company sales staff in such a way as to influence the tied representative to recommend particular products. Sales staff are expected to sell the type of product most suited to the client.

The result of disclosure is to make the costs of alternative investments more transparent. In so far as many life policies have heavier expenses than unit or investment trusts, there could be significant shifts in consumer choice from life policies to unit and investment trusts. The benefits from disclosure to the investment and unit trusts should not be overemphasized, however. It is of interest that, despite the disclosure of commission and publication of unit-trust charges, which have doubled since controls were lifted, unit-trust sales have gone from strength to strength. Higher charges do not appear to have deterred investors.

Best advice is a cardinal principle of the regulatory authorities but its meaning is not as clear-cut as might be hoped. The regulatory framework has as one of its major tenets the concept of polarization. Intermediaries who advise on investments must either be fully independent or the 'tied' representative of just one company. The requirements for each are different. All salesmen of investment products are required to give the client best advice on the type of investment best suited to his needs. For the tied representative this will be the appropriate product from the company's range, and in the absence of any suitable product from within the company's own range, tied salesmen must refrain from recommending any. For independent intermediaries the requirements are more stringent, and they must believe that no other 'investment of which the member is or ought reasonably to be aware' would be likely to better meet the client's needs. This requirement has been interpreted by many industry observers to mean that independent intermediaries should have knowledge of other investment products than life assurance and unit trusts. To ignore the merits of investment trusts, for example, in making recommendations would be in breach of the independent intermediary's duty. The requirement for best advice will affect independent intermediaries and salesmen's recommendations. The marketing manager must be aware of the implications of the current regulatory system and any changes in regulation for their sales strategies (Kane, 1980).

New directions in product differentiation and distribution

The problem for the marketing manager is to determine how unit and investment trusts can be made more attractive to both existing and new investors. What improvements must be made to the products and the marketing and distribution channels to make them more easily saleable? Three areas for improvement are of particular interest; increasing the choices open to investors: improving the channels of distribution and making easier the sale and administration of funds, and extending the usefulness of the investment product to give investors greater flexibility. The possibilities of increased advertising, the choice between media and the benefits of direct sales over intermediaries are not explored here, since these are essentially empirical matters which require market research and estimation of marginal costs and benefits, so that advertising and promotion expenditure can be directed to equate marginal returns. Instead, it is assumed that investment trusts will extend their advertising in so far as they are allowed, and examine ways in which the products of both unit and investment trusts can be made more saleable.

Wider product choice

Increasing the choice open to those who invest in unit and investment trusts is, in part, simply a continuation of existing trends. As investing becomes easier and cheaper, with an ever-increasing range of alternative financial products, the trusts must continually ask what they can do that investors cannot easily do for themselves. Increased specialization, both geographic, with a greater variety of one country funds, and by industry, with a wider range of industries and assets, is an obvious area of development, although progress may be limited by the availability of expertise and market liquidity on the supply side, and investor sophistication on the demand side.

Geographic and industry sector specializations are simply two of many possible methods of differentiating trusts. Other alternatives include differentiating funds by risk and by management strategy. The advent of new financial instruments, particularly options and futures, has opened up the possibility of portfolio insurance strategies which can be used to determine the risk and return of a fund in advance. By suitable use of futures the minimum performance of a fund can be set and the fund's performance guaranteed. It is possible to offer investors a range of risk and minimum returns over a period with far greater certainty than is possible by using all equity portfolios. Such funds could enable the trusts to tap new market segments and attract investors away from other savings media, such as building-society and bank deposit accounts at one end of the risk spectrum and high-risk activities such as high leveraged funds at the other end.

Portfolio insurance strategies imply a disciplined approach to fund management. At present, investors purchase fund management with little differentiation between management styles apart from that conveyed by brand and management names, which may imply respectability, caution or even excitement. A further area of opportunity lies in exploring much more carefully the role and nature of fund management, and differentiating products by exploiting differences in management. Active and passive management are popular terms in the investment industry, but these two alternatives do not adequately encompass the range of styles and possibilities. Active managers vary from the rule-based ones who may, in the extreme, follow the recommendations of a computer programme to those who invest on the basis of the most recent 'hot' tips. Passive management styles may be reflected in index funds, low turnover or long-term buy and hold and cost-minimization strategies. Theoretical support for passive management styles is manifest in the earlier discussion of portfolio performance and, given the emphasis on reducing costs, could lead to the emergence of the 'plain vanilla' investment or unit trust with no initial fee and low annual management fees. Such an approach, however, may lack appeal since it restricts the investment managers' opportunities to charge premium fees for their services.

The index fund is another possible marketing response, appealing to the sophisticated investor who recognizes the difficulty of securing above average performance. Further possibilities include targeting particular groups of investors, who may either be uninformed, or informed and believing that by specialized investing they can secure additional returns. Targeting the uninformed has been a popular method of promoting sales in the past, using as justification the past performance of a trust and offering the opportunity of untold wealth and riches. However, if best advice is to be meaningful, one would expect advisers in the future to be more aware of the evidence on performance and to be under a duty to look less favourably on high-cost general funds.[8]

The targeting of investors interested in specialized funds is more acceptable. By their nature specialized funds are either aimed at exploiting some perceived anomaly, such as investing in small firms, or represent funds that are deliberately imperfectly diversified. Investing in particular industries is one example of such specialization; investing in particular countries is another. Such specialist funds allow investors to follow their own hunches and preferences by forming a portfolio which itself consists of specialist trusts investing in particular countries, sectors or securities. International diversification has been shown to reduce portfolio risk below that available by investing in UK equities alone, but changes in exchange rates can introduce an additional risk particularly for shorter time horizons. Progress in providing more specialized portfolios has been held back in part by regulatory and taxation problems, or by a wait-and-see attitude as other managers experiment, but possibilities include immunized (Elton and Gruber, 1987) and fixed duration portfolios, as well as portfolios that specialize in particular financial instruments searching for mispriced and other attractive securities.

The discussion so far has centred on the possibilities of providing more specialized investment portfolios for investors. Investment trusts also have the opportunity of providing specialized securities more directly through the direct issue of equity, debt or hybrid securities in the investment-trust company. Warrants are now a common feature of the capital structure of investment trusts, but other securities on offer include zero coupon and stepped preference shares, split capital and income shares and in one case the issue of equity index loan stock, which represents a pure index fund free of dealing and management costs. Such securities provide a range of risk and repayment provisions and enable investors to construct portfolios that meet their requirements better.

Improved channels of distribution

Increasing the choice open to investors makes unit and investment trusts more attractive to new customers and may attract further savers into the industry. Improved choice may not, however, be sufficient. It is also necessary to improve the distribution of funds. There are two areas of particular concern – the purchase procedures and the methods of alerting consumers to the benefits of the trusts. The purchase of unit trusts is already a simple procedure, and transactions can take place with the minimum of delay. The same is not always true of investment trusts, which, as stock-exchange securities, cannot be bought directly from the managers but must be acquired in the market. Once learned, the procedure is no more difficult than for unit trusts, but to the new investor may appear cumbersome and off-putting. Efforts to simplify the purchase of investment trusts are in progress. Three of the largest investment-trust management groups have introduced schemes to sell investment-trust shares through intermediaries such as insurance brokers, accountants and solicitors, and offer commissions much like the unit trusts. Many of the trusts have also introduced savings schemes which allow for cheap and easy purchase of investment-trust shares. Such schemes have brought the purchase of investment trusts more in line with the procedures for unit trusts, but there still remain areas of improvement.

A more fundamental problem is the method by which consumers can learn of the benefits of the trusts and be encouraged to invest. Traditionally investment trusts have relied on stockbrokers and press comment. The result has been slow growth and a lack of knowledge of the trusts outside the traditional stock-market investors. Unit trusts have appealed to a wider public, with the use of extensive advertising, financial intermediaries and direct marketing and sales. Expansion of sales through building societies and banks is a possibility, although there is the essential difficulty that equity savings may be at the expense of their fixed-interest deposits. What is required is a greater expansion of sales, using other purchase and sale mechanisms, such as credit cards, bill payment and retail sales. There is no reason to believe that investments cannot be sold along with other household items, although regulatory requirements for cooling-off periods, knowing your client and best advice may restrict some of the possibilities. The move by Marks & Spencer into selling unit trusts shows the possibilities of using the retail-payment network for sales, but as yet progress is slow. Regular accumulation of savings followed by periodic investment in units or shares, or loans for investment followed by periodic repayment, are ideally suited to existing retail-sales payment mechanisms, and, properly promoted, could lead to a considerable expansion of sales.

Improved product flexibility and usefulness

The linking of unit and investment trusts to life assurance, personal pensions and PEP schemes has already been noted, but we must also ask whether there are any other financial services investors might like which could be linked to unit or investment trusts. Wilcox and Rosen (1988) for example provide a list of consumer needs which should be addressed in the development and promotion of financial services. A number of authors have identified the key characteristics of financial products as including money transmission and payment, savings and investment, insurance, lending, and information and advice; and have suggested that the ability to evolve products which embody more of these characteristics is a useful and profitable institutional strategy, since it provides customers with increased flexibility and enables the financial institution to sell clients a wider range of services. The ability to borrow is possibly the main financial service that is lacking from the majority of unit- and investment-trust packages on offer, and some thought could be given to facilities which allow individuals to borrow against their accumulated units or shares at lower interest rate to reflect the security, or even to borrow to invest in units or shares. Such an approach highlights a life-cycle approach to investment, recognizing that individuals' requirements vary over the years, so that borrowing is heavier and saving smaller for families with young children than it is for the family shortly before retirement. Completely integrated financial planning is unlikely, given the uncertainty in employment and income that faces most individuals, but for specific and targeted groups, e.g. middle-class professionals, realistic forecasts of borrowing and saving may be possible. Carefully targeted marketing, together with new-product innovations that extend the range and variety of the savings/investment packages, could provide a useful extension of the market.

Conclusions

Kotler (1988) argues that for service organizations their marketing mix consists of five Ps – product, price, place, promotion, people. Unit and investment trusts exercise little control over price and, except through direct sales, little over people. Their problem is, within the existing regulatory and institutional constraints, to differentiate their products, and, depending on the particular trust – whether it is specialized or general, independent or part of a large group – to choose a segment of the market to which it can most appeal and by suitable promotion in the appropriate place attract investors. The services they provide are far from unique and for the most part easily reproducible. There is competition from other products and institutions, and the difficulty is to identify new market opportunities and target potential investors more accurately. Extensive advertising is unlikely to be successful in cost-benefit terms. Unit and investment trusts need to develop marketing strategies that build on their strengths and appeal more widely. A wider choice of products, a more extensive distribution network and more flexible products are all possible areas for building a competitive advantage.

Notes

1   Unlike a unit trust it is not necessary for a UK-based investment trust to secure approved status. However, such status is fiscally advantageous, so that most trusts endeavour to secure and retain this status.
2   Our comments here relate to Authorized Unit Trusts, trusts that have been vetted by the Department of Trade and Industry (DTI) and can be offered for sale to the general public. Offshore funds are funds run from tax havens and are not subject to UK tax and regulation.

Under the EEC UCITS (Undertaking in Collective Investments in Transferable Securities) directive all funds authorized in member states will be recognized in the UK and can be marketed in the same way as unit trusts.
3   Since there are costs associated with liquidating a trust, the liquidation value of a trust is less than the net asset value of a trust.
4   The offer of a large number of units for sale to the public.
5   Unit-trust managers are owned by a wide range of financial intermediaries, including banks, insurance companies, investment trusts and independents. Consequently they are sold in a variety of financial outlets and through the direct marketing efforts of insurance and other financial companies.
6   Life assurance is an investment portfolio with insurance added in. It is very similar to investment in a unit- or investment-trust portfolio plus the purchase of term assurance. The portfolios are not identical, however, since life assurance adds bonuses to the underlying policy on a year by year basis. These bonuses become part of the policy and must be paid. The effect is to guarantee that part of the capital gains on the investment fund will be paid even if the market subsequently collapses. In effect, life assurance reduces risk.
7   This is known as the efficient market hypothesis. Share prices impound all publicly available information. Although controversy surrounds some points of detail concerning the hypothesis, there is little disagreement about its central propositions. Empirical evidence has revealed a few investment opportunities that appear to contradict the hypothesis and offer above average returns for the risk assumed but in the main there is little evidence to suggest that it is not a good description of stock markets. Studies of the reaction of the stock market to new information consistently show that it reacts rapidly once the information becomes publicly available.

There are many books that set out the concepts of the efficient market hypothesis and review some of the evidence but there are few that provide a comprehensive up-to-date survey. Elton and Gruber (1987) provide a good introduction to the topic. An excellent, if somewhat technical, survey of the meaning of efficiency and assessment of the evidence is provided by Ball (1988).

8 The efficient market hypothesis is now accepted by many major institutions and investors in the city. In the absence of a new paradigm it can only be a matter of time (or legal action?) before its implications are reflected in best advice.

References

Ansoff, I. (1965). *Corporate Strategy*. New York: McGraw Hill.

Baggozzi, R. P. (1978). 'Sales performance and satisfaction as functions of individual differences, interpersonal and situational factors', *Journal of Marketing Research*, vol. 15, November, pp. 517–31.

Ball, R. (1988). 'What do we know about stock market efficiency'. Paper presented to NATO Advanced Research Workshop, Sesimbra, Portugal.

Bank of England (1989). 'The Single European Market: Survey of Financial Institutions. *Bank of England*.

Barnes, P. A. (1985). 'UK building societies – a study of the gains from merger', *Journal of Business Finance and Accounting*, vol. 12(1).

Barksdale, H. C. and Harris, C. E. (1982). 'Portfolio analysis and the product life cycle,' *Long Range Planning*, vol. 15(6), pp. 74–83.

Binks, M. R., Ennew, C. T. and Reed, G. V. (1989). 'The differentiation of bank services to small firms', *International Journal of Bank Marketing*, vol. 7(4) pp. 10–16.

Black, S., Gattorna, J., Kennedy, S., et al. (1985). *Handbook of Marketing and Selling Bank Services*, Bradford: MCB University Press.

Booz, Allen and Hamilton (1982). *New Products Management for the 1980s* New York: Booz, Allen and Hamilton Inc.

BSG (1989a). 'Special report on corporate image', *Building Societies Gazette*, June, pp. 44–66.

BSG (1989b). 'Selling insurance – the direct approach', *Building Societies Gazette*, October, pp. 58–9.

BSG (1989c). 'The age of marketing', *Building Societies Gazette*, November, pp. 64–5.

Carey, T. P. A. (1989). 'Strategy formulation by banks', *International Journal of Bank Marketing*, vol. 7(3).

Carter, R. L., Chiplin, B. and Lewis, M. K. (1986). *Personal Financial Markets*. Oxford: Philip Allan.

Carter R. L., and Diacon, S. R. (1989). *Insurance Industry Statistics 1990*. London: Croner.

Central Statistical Office (1988). *Social Trends 18*, London: HMSO.

Channon, D. F. (1986). *Bank Strategic Management and Marketing*, New York: John Wiley.

Channon, D. F. (1988). *Global Banking Strategy*. New York: Wiley and Sons.

Cheese, J., Day, A. and Wills, G. (1988). 'Handbook of Marketing and Selling Bank Services', *International Journal of Bank Marketing* vol. 6(3).

Chiplin, B. (1986). 'Information technology and personal financial services'. In *Personal Financial Markets* (Carter R. L. *et al.* eds).

236

Chiplin, B. and Wright, M. (1987). The Logic of Mergers: The Competitive Market for Corporate Control in Theory and Practice. IEA Hobart Paper no. 107.

Chiplin, B. and Wright, M. (1989). '1992 and the European market for corporate control', *Kiny Journal*.

Chiplin, B. and Wright, M. (1990) 'The situation and outlook for funds and portfolio management institutions in the UK'. In *The Future of Mutual Funds* (Preda S. and Rozi R. eds.) Milan: Newfin, Bocconi.

Choraphas, D. N. (1988). *Electronic Funds Transfer*. Guildford: Butterworths.

Churchill, G. A., Ford, N. M. and Walker, O. C. (1974). 'Measuring job satisfaction of industrial salesmen', *Journal of Marketing*, vol. 11, August, pp. 254–60.

Churchill, G. A., Ford, N. M. and Walker, O. C. (1979). 'Personal characteristics of salespeople and the attractiveness of alternative rewards', *Journal of Business Research*, vol. 7, April, pp. 25–49.

Clarke, P. D., Edward, P. M., Gardner, E. F. *et al.* (1988). 'The genesis of strategic marketing control in British retail banking', *International Journal of Bank Marketing*, vol. 6(2), pp. 5–19.

Cockburn, P. (1989). 'Taking a cautious view of the single market', *Financial Times*, 6 November.

Cornell, R. and Bond, S. (1988). 'Developments in demographic research'. In *Insurance Marketing* (Dyer N. and Watkins T. (eds.) London: Kluwer.

Cowell, D. (1984). *The Marketing of Services*. Oxford: Heinemann.

Cron, W. L. (1984). 'Industrial salesperson development: a career stages perspective', *Journal of Marketing*, vol. 48, fall, pp. 41–52.

Cron, W. L., Dubinsky, A. J. and Michaels, R. E. (1988). 'The influence of career stages on the components of salespersons motivation', *Journal of Marketing*, vol. 52, January, pp. 78–92.

Davies, T. (1989). 'Bleak year for fund managers', *Planned Savings*, June, pp. 22–3.

Davis, E, and Smales, C. (1989). 'The integration of European financial services'. In 1992: Myths and Realities, Centre for Business Strategy (Davis, E. *et al.* (eds).

Davison, H., Watkins, T. and Wright, M. (1989). 'Developing new personal financial products – some evidence of the role of market research', *International Journal of Bank Marketing*, vol. 7(1) pp. 8–15.

Donnelly, J. H. (1976). 'Marketing intermediaries in channels of distribution for services', *Journal of Marketing*, vol. 40(1), pp. 55–7.

Donnelly, J. H., Berry, L. L. and Thompson, T. W. (1985). *Marketing Financial Services*. Illinois: Dow Jones-Irwin.

Doyle, P. H., Fenwick, I. and Savage, G. P. (1979). 'Management planning and control in multi-branch banking', *Journal of Operational Research Society*, vol. 30, pp. 105–11.

Doyle, S. X. and Shapiro, B. P. (1980). 'What counts most in motivating your salesforce?', *Harvard Business Review*, May–June, pp. 133–40.

Draper, P. (1989). *The Investment Trust Industry*. Aldershot: Avebury.

Dyer, N. and Watkins, T. (eds) (1988). *Insurance Marketing*, 2nd edn, London: Kluwer.

Dyer, N. (1988). 'The changing market place: product development – general business'. In *Insurance Marketing* (Dyer N. and Watkins T. eds). London: Kluwer.

Elton, E. J. and Gruber, M. J. (1987). *Modern Portfolio Theory and Investment Analysis*, 3rd edn. New York: Wiley.

Engel, J. E., Blackwell, R. D. and Miniard, P. W. (1990). *Consumer Behaviour*, 6th edn. Dryden Press.

Ennew, C. T. and Wright, M. (1990a). 'Retail banks and organisational change: evidence from the UK', *International Journal of Bank Marketing*, vol. 8. In press.

Ennew, C. T. and Wright, M. (1990b). 'Building societies in transition: strategy in a new market environment', *Managerial Finance*. In press.

Ennew, C. T., Watkins, T. and Wright, M. (1989), 'Personal financial services: marketing strategy determination', *International Journal of Bank Marketing*, vol. 7(5), pp. 3–8.

Ford, N. M., Walker, O. C. and Churchill, G. A. (1985). 'Differences in the attractiveness of alternative rewards: additional evidence', *Journal of Business Research*, vol. 13, April, pp. 123–8.

Garland, C. (1988). 'Telephone marketing in financial services'. In *Insurance Marketing* (Dyer N. and Watkins T. eds). London: Kluwer.

George, W. R. and Myers, T. A. (1981). 'Life underwriters' perceptions of differences in selling goods and services', *CLU Journal*, April pp. 44–9.

Ginarlis, J. (1988). *The Savings War Competition Between the High Street Banks, Building Societies and Life Assurance Companies*, Kluwer/Banque Paribas Capital Markets.

Green, C. F. (1982). 'The future of the bank customer relationship', *Journal of the Institute of Bankers*, vol. 103, August, pp. 114–16.

Guy, J. R. F. (1978). 'The performance of the British investment trust industry', *Journal of Finance*, vol. 33(2), pp. 443–55.

Hackman, J. R. and Oldham, G. R. (1980). *Work Redesign*. Reading, Mass.: Addison-Wesley.

Hall, M. J. B. (1989). *Handbook of Banking Regulation and Supervision*, Cambridge: Woodhead-Faulkner.

Hammond, C. (1981) 'Running a profitable branch network', *Bankers Magazine*, vol. 225, July, pp. 15–16.

Hastings, B., Kiely, J. and Watkins, T. (1988). 'Sales force motivation using travel incentives: some empirical evidence', *Journal of Personal Selling and Sales Management*, vol. 8(2), pp. 43–51.

Hills, A. (1988). 'Marketing support: incentives'. In Insurance Marketing (Dyer N. and Watkins T. eds). London: Kluwer.

Hooley, G. J. and Mann, S. J. (1988). 'The adoption of marketing by financial institutions in the UK', *Service Industries Journal*, vol. 8(4), pp. 488–500.

Howcroft, J. B. and Lavis, J. (1986). 'A strategic perspective on delivery systems in UK retail banking', *Service Industries Journal* vol. 6(2), pp. 144–58.

Howcroft, J. B. and Lavis, J. (1987). 'Image in retail banking', *International Journal of Bank Marketing*, vol. 4(4), pp. 3–13.

Howcroft, J. B. and Lavis, J. (1989) 'Pricing in retail banking', *International Journal of Bank Marketing*, vol. 4(4), pp. 3–13.

Jain, A. K., Pinson, C. and Malhotra, N. K. (1987). 'Customer loyalty as a construct in the marketing of bank services', *International Journal of Bank Marketing*, vol. 5(3), pp. 49–72.

Johne, A. F. and Harborne, P. (1985). 'How large commercial banks manage product innovation', *International Journal of Bank Marketing*, vol. 3(1).

Jolson, M. A., Dubinsky, J. A. and Anderson, R. E. (1987). 'Correlates and determinants of salesforce tenure: an exploratory study', *Journal of Personal Selling and Sales Management*, vol. 7 November, pp. 9–27.

Jones, C. S. (1985). 'An empirical study of the role of management accounting systems following takeover or merger', *Accounting Organizations and Society*, vol. 10, pp. 177–200.

Kallaway, B. (1988). 'Marketing support: sponsorship'. In *Insurance Marketing* (Dyer N. and Watkins T. eds). London: Kluwer.

Kane, E. J. (1980). 'Accelerating inflation, regulation and banking innovation', *Issues in Bank Regulation*, Summer, pp. 7–14.

Kiely, J. (1986). 'The dynamics of job satisfaction – a longitudinal study', *Personnel Review*, vol. 15(4), pp. 7–13.

Killough, J. (1978). 'Improved payoffs from transnational advertising', *Harvard Business Review*, July/August, pp. 102–110.

Kotler, P. (1988). *Marketing Management: Analysis, Planning and Control*. New Jersey: Prentice Hall.

Kotler, P. (1986). *Principles of Marketing.* New Jersey: Prentice Hall.

Laroche, M., Rosenblatt, J. A. and Manning, T. (1986). 'Services used and factors considered important in selecting a bank: an investigation across diverse demographic segments', *International Journal of Bank Marketing*, vol. 4(1), pp. 35–55.

Levitt, T. (1960). 'Marketing Myopia', *Harvard Business Review* July/August, p. 26.

Levitt, T. (1980). 'Marketing success through differentiation – of anything', *Harvard Business Review*, January/February.

Lewis, B. R. (1984). 'Marketing bank services', *Service Industries Journal*, vol. 4(3).

Lewis, B. R. (1989). 'Customer care in service organisations', *Marketing Intelligence and Planning*, vol. 7(5/6), pp. 18–22.

Lewis, M. K. (1986). 'Financial services in the US'. In *Personal Financial Markets* (Carter R. L. *et al.* eds). Oxford: Philip Allan.

Lewis, M. K. and Wright, M. (1986). 'Banking and deposit services'. In *Personal Financial Markets* (Carter R. L. *et al.* eds). Oxford: Philip Allan.

Lyall, K. (1983). 'Investment trust companies, 1971–80'. Unpublished PhD thesis, University of Edinburgh.

Llewellyn, B. (1988). 'Product design: packaging'. In *Insurance Marketing* (Dyer N. and Watkins T. eds). London: Kluwer.

Marketing (1987). 'Money talks', *Marketing*. Special report, pp. 39–49.

Marketing (1989). 'Financial marketing', *Marketing*. Special report, pp. 33–41.

Marsh, J. R. (1988). *Managing Financial Services Marketing*. London: Pitman.

MacKay, B. (1988). 'Who is there?'. In *Insurance Marketing* (Dyer N. and Watkins T. eds). London: Kluwer.

Main, B. G. M. (1982). 'Business insurance and large widely held corporations', *Geneva Papers*, 7, 24, pp. 237–47.

Martin, A. (1988). 'Direct marketing: direct response'. In *Insurance Marketing* (Dyer N. and Watkins T. eds). London: Kluwer.

McIver, C. and Naylor, G. (1986). *Marketing Financial Services*. London: Chartered Institute of Bankers.

Meidan, A. (1984). *Bank Marketing Management*. Basingstoke: Macmillan.

Miles, R. H. and Perreault, R. (1976). 'Organisational role conflict: its antecedents and consequences', *Organisational Behaviour and Human Performance*, vol. 17, October, pp. 19–44.

Mitchell, J. W. and Sparks, L. (1988). 'Technology and bank marketing systems', *Journal of Marketing Management*, vol. 4(1), pp. 50–61.

Monopolies and Mergers Commission (1989). *Credit Card Services: A report on the supply of credit cards in the UK*, Cmnd 718. London: HMSO.

Morello, G. (1988). 'The image of Dutch banks', *International Journal of Bank Marketing*, vol. 6(2), pp. 38–47.

Morgan, N. A. (1989). 'Developing information strategies in the UK financial services sector', *Marketing Intelligence and Planning* vol. 7(7/8), pp. 24–8.

Morgan, N. and Piercy, N. (1988). 'Marketing organisation in the financial services sector', *International Journal of Bank Marketing*, vol. 6(4).

Mottura, P. and Munari, L. (1990). 'Competition and competitive strategies of Italian banks', *International Journal of Bank Marketing*. In press.

Mueller, D. C. (1988). 'The life cycle of firms', In *Internal Organisation, Efficiency and Profit*, (Thompson R. S. and Wright M. eds). Oxford: Philip Allan.

Newman, K. (1984). *Financial and Marketing Communications*. London: Holt Reinhardt and Winston.

Nicholas, T. (1985). 'Strategic management of technology in competition in world banking', *International Banking Summer School*. Institute of Bankers.

Nottingham Evening Post (1987). 'Banks and building societies – the role they play in Nottingham. *Nottingham Evening Post*, Market Research Department, February.

O'Brien, D. P., Howe, W. S., Wright, M., O'Brien, R. (1979). *Competition Policy, Profitability and Growth*. London: Macmillan.

Office of Fair Trading (1987). *Study of Insurance Intermediaries' Costs – Report of a Survey*. London: OFT.

O'Shaunghnessy, J. (1988). *Competitive Marketing: A Strategic Approach*. Boston: Unwin Hyman.

Piercy, N. and Peattie, K. J. (1988). 'Matching marketing strategies to corporate culture: the parcel and the wall', *Journal of General Management*, vol. 13(4), pp. 33–44.

Piercy, N. and Giles, W. (1989). 'Making SWOT analysis work', *Marketing Intelligence and Planning*, vol. 7, pp. 5–7.

Porter, M. E. (1980). *Competitive Strategy*. New York: Free Press.

Porter, M. E. (1985). *Competitive Advantage*. New York: Free Press.

Porter, L. W. and Steers, R. M. (1973). 'Organisational, work and personal factors in employee turnover and absenteeism', *Psychological Bulletin*, vol. 80, November, pp. 151–76.

Price Waterhouse (1989)

Richardson, B. A. and Robinson, C. G. (1986). 'The impact of internal marketing on consumer service in a retail bank', *International Journal of Bank Marketing*, vol. 4(5), pp. 3–30.

Roach, C. (1989). 'Segmentation of the small business market on the basis of banking requirements', *International Journal of Bank Marketing*, vol. 7(2), pp. 10–16.

Robbie, K. and Wright, M. (1988). *Personal Financial Services*, London: Euromonitor.

Robson, J. (1989). Unpublished research on Building Society marketing strategies, Plymouth Business School, Polytechnic of the South West.

Rothwell, M. and Jowett, P. (1988). *Rivalry in Retail Financial Services*. Basingstoke: Macmillan.

Sanderson, S. M. and Luffman, G. A. (1988). 'Strategic Planning and Environmental Analysis', *European Journal of Marketing*, vol. 22(2), pp. 14–30.

Saunders, J. (1989). 'Analysing the Competition'. In *Marketing Handbook* (Thomas, M. J. ed) Gower.

Scheuing, E. E. and Johnson, E. M. (1989). 'New product development and management in financial institutions', *International Journal of Bank Marketing*, vol. 7(2), pp. 17–22.

Shelton, T. (1989). 'The effect of the financial service act polarisation rules on independent intermediaries', *Managerial Finance*. In press.

Simmonds, D. (1988). 'Direct marketing – direct mail'. In *Insurance Marketing* (Dyer N. and Watkins T. eds). London: Kluwer.

Smith, A. M. (1989). 'Service quality: relationships between banks and their small business clients', *International Journal of Bank Marketing*, vol. 7(5), pp. 28–36.

Smith, A. M. and Lewis, B. (1989). 'Customer care in financial service organisations', *International Journal of Bank Marketing*, vol. 7(5), pp. 13–22.

Smith, D. and Harbisher, A. (1989). 'Building societies as retail banks: the importance of customer service and corporate image', *International Journal of Bank Marketing*, vol. 7(1), pp. 22–7.

Spicers Corporate Finance (1989). 'Building societies and financial services', *Spicer and Oppenheim Financial Services Update*, August.

Stanley, T. J., Moschis, G. P. and Danko, W. D. (1987). 'Financial service segments: the seven faces of the affluent market', *Journal of Advertising Research*, vol. 27(4), pp. 52–67.

Stevenson, B. D. (1989). 'Product management in corporate banking', *International Journal of Bank Marketing*, vol. 7(1), pp. 17–21.

Teas, R. K. (1981). 'An empirical test of models of salespersons job expectancy and instrumentality perceptions', *Journal of Marketing Research*, vol. 14, May, pp. 209–26.

Teas, R.K., Dorsch, M. J. and McAlexander, J. H. (1988). 'Measuring commercial bank customers attitudes towards the quality of the bank services marketing relationship', *Journal of Professional Services Marketing*, vol. 4(1), pp. 75–95.

Thompson, R. S. and Wright, M. (1988). *Internal Organisation, Efficiency and Profit*. Oxford: Philip Allan.

Thwaites, D. (1989). 'The impact of environmental change on the evolution of the UK building societies', *Service Industries Journal*, vol. 9(1), pp. 40–60.

Turnbull, P. W. and Gibbs, M. L. (1987). 'Marketing bank services to corporate customers: the importance of relationships', *International Journal of Bank Marketing*, vol. 5(1), pp. 19–26.

Tyagi, P. K. (1982). 'Perceived organisational climate and the process of salesperson motivation', *Journal of Marketing Research*, vol. 19, May, pp. 240–54.

Wilcox, R. and Rosen, D. (1988). 'Marketing financial services'. In *Financial Services*, (Coler, M. and Ratner, E. eds). New York Institute of Finance.

Walker, O. C., Churchill, G. A. and Ford, N. M. (1977). 'Motivation and performance in industrial selling: present knowledge and needed research', *Journal of Marketing Research*, vol. 14, May, pp. 156–68.

Watkins, T. and Wright, M. (1986). *Marketing Financial Services*, Guildford: Butterworths.

Watson, I. (1986). 'Managing the relationships with corporate clients', *International Journal of Bank Marketing*, vol. 4(1), pp. 19–34.

Whitmore, A. (1988). 'Market analysis'. In *Insurance Marketing* (Dyer N. and Watkins T. eds). London: Kluwer.

Winer, L. and Schiff, J. S. (1980). 'Industrial salespeoples views on motivation', *Industrial Marketing Management*, vol. 9, pp. 319–23.

Worthington, S. (1986). 'Retailer credit cards and direct marketing – a question of synergy', *Journal of Marketing Management*, vol. 2(2), pp. 125–31.

Worthington, S. (1988). 'Credit cards in the United Kingdom – where the power lies in the battle between the banks and the retailers', *Journal of Marketing Management*, vol. 4(1), pp. 61–70.

Wright, M. *et al.* (1986). 'The future of the building societies', *Economist Intelligence Unit Special Report 1057.*

Wright, M. and Diacon, S. R. (1988). 'The regulation of long-term insurance'. In *Insurance Marketing* (Dyer N. and Watkins T. eds). London: Kluwer.

Wright, M. and Ennew, C. T. (1990). 'Strategic bank marketing and the single European Market: an overview', *International Journal of Bank Marketing*, vol. 8. In press.

Index